The MINNESOTA *Table*

Recipes for Savoring Local Food throughout the Year

By Shelley N. C. Holl
with Recipes by B. J. Carpenter

Voyageur Press

First published in 2010 by Voyageur Press, an imprint of MBI Publishing Company, 400 First Avenue North, Suite 300, Minneapolis, MN 55401 USA

Voyageur Press titles are also available at discounts in bulk quantity for industrial or sales-promotional use. For details write to Special Sales Manager at MBI Publishing Company, 400 First Avenue North, Suite 300, Minneapolis, MN 55401 USA.

To find out more about our books, visit us online at www.voyageurpress.com.

ISBN-13: 978-0-7603-3626-7

Editor: Kari Cornell
Design Manager: Katie Sonmor
Designed by: Pauline Molinari
Printed in China

Photo Credits: All of the photographs and watercolors used in this book are by Shelley Holl, with the exceptions of the following images from Shutterstock: pages 11, 23, 28, 32, 33, 38, 41, 43, 54, 56, 59, 70, 83, 99, 125, 128, 139, and 162.

Library of Congress Cataloging-in-Publication Data

Holl, Shelley N. C.
The Minnesota table : recipes for savoring local food throughout the year / Shelley N.C. Holl with recipes by BJ Carpenter.
  p. cm.
ISBN 978-0-7603-3626-7 (plc)
1. Cookery, American. 2. Cookery—Minnesota. 3. Minnesota—Social life and customs. 4. Menus. I. Carpenter, B. J. II. Title.
TX715.H7324 2009
641.59776—dc22
                        2009028830

Contents

Introduction 7

April 8
  April Adventures
  Every Man a King 9
  Sidebar: Ogling Asparagus on the Side 11
  In Search of Local Lamb .12

May 19
  May Adventures
  Pickles and PhDs 20
  Shopping for Morels 22
  Sidebar: Spring Salad Greens Care 26

June 29
  June Adventures
  Pick Your Own 30
  Planning Ahead Sidebar: Freezing Basics 33
  Planning Ahead Sidebar: Freezing Berries 33
  Wine for the Winter Hardy 34
  Sidebar: The Perfect Pot of Tea 43

July 44
  July Adventures
  On the Seventh Day, a CSA (Common Ground, Simple Harvest) . . .45
  Nick's Eggs and More 47
  The Pickle and Pepper Guys 48
  Planning Ahead Sidebar: Frozen Beans and Other Vegetables . . .50
  Sidebar: Vegetable Blanching/Freezing Timetables 51

August 60
  August Adventures
  Asian Farmers: All in the Family 61
  Sidebar: Asian Greens Primer 63
  Raising the Bar 64
  Planning Ahead Sidebar: Oven-Roasted Tomatoes 65

September 72
  September Adventures
  Putting the Wild Back in Rice 73
  Askov: The Real Rutabaga Capital of the World 76
  Freezer Treasures at the U of Moo 78
  Sidebar: Storing and Cooking Wild Rice 81
  Planning Ahead Sidebar: Drying Herbs 84

Our calendar of culinary adventure begins in April, when Minnesota's first fresh produce appears.

October *88*
    October Adventures
    Minnesota's Own—from Haralson to Honeycrisp™ 89
    Sky Blue Waters: Great Blue Cheese 92
    The Yak Man 94
    Sidebar: Apples of Your Eyes 95
    Sidebar: Great Pumpkin Patches 95
    Sidebar: Apples from Heaven 100

November *102*
    November Adventures
    Bringing Home the Bacon 103
    The King of Kale 105
    Planning Ahead Sidebar: Make Space for a Modern Day Root Cellar 107

December *114*
    December Adventures
    The Last Lutefisk Supper 115
    Sidebar: The Communion Wafer Factory 117
    Seed Caps and Cowboy Hats—Thousand Hills Grass-Fed Beef 118
    Sidebar: Lorentz Meats 120
    Sidebar: The Art of Deglazing 122

January *130*
    January Adventures
    Finding Faith in Center City 131
    Sidebar: Smokin' the Waters 133
    Buffalo Gal 134
    Sidebar: Where the Buffalo Roam 136

February *144*
    February Adventures
    Love Tree Farms 145
    Sidebar: Farmstead *Fromage* 147
    Dry Weather Creek Farm 148

March *154*
    March Adventures
    Keeping it on the Farm 155
    Seeds of Change 157
    Planning Ahead Sidebar: Seed Catalogs 159
    Planning Ahead Sidebar: Taking Stock While Making Stock 163
    Sidebar: Sons of Italy on the Range 168

Contact Information 172
Index 174
About the Authors 176
Acknowledgements 176

Introduction

In the late 1990s, I was living in Louisiana making weekly forays into the back bayous to write and sketch for my illustrated travel column in New Orleans' *Times-Picayune* newspaper. Interviewing alligator wrestlers and plantation owners had its pleasures, but long drives home across the Atchafalaya Basin in the heat were mind numbing, so I began to stop and gather groceries at roadside stands and Cajun butcher shops as a diversion. Each week I brought home a cooler full of handmade chicken pies from Breaux Bridge, crawfish from St. John's Parish and okra, fresh crowder peas, greens, berries, or Creole tomatoes.

When my long-time chef-friend BJ Carpenter visited from Minneapolis, she came along and I had a chance to play culinary tour guide for the day. BJ, who had just closed her own restaurant and was now teaching cooking, was thrilled with old-fashioned Louisiana food ways and colorful cooking instructions that began: "Heat some oil and add what we Cajuns call the Holy Trinity—onion, peppers, and garlic." We had such fun, and by evening carried home the ingredients for a splendid, only-in-Louisiana meal.

That night, the idea for *The Minnesota Table* germinated over corn, crawfish, and potatoes at a newspaper-covered kitchen table, where we found ourselves comparing Minnesotan and Louisianian cuisine and ingredients. Though Minnesota's less-spicy cuisine paled a little in the presence of her more colorful southern cousin, it was healthier: less added fat and salt, leaner meats, and more concentration on serving vegetables fresh from the field. From the viewpoint of that steamy southern kitchen where greens are not greens unless they are stewed with ham or bacon, we recalled that Minnesota's sun-soaked, and sometimes frost-finished, fruits and vegetables burst with flavor. There is nothing on Earth to compare with the crisp freshness of Minnesota's apples.

Minnesotans were early adapters of the local foods movement: our friends joined co-ops back in the 1970s to find foods produced with fewer chemicals, and by the mid-1990s, the Minneapolis and St. Paul farmers' markets had been in full swing for years. In contrast New Orleans had just started a weekly farmers' market for city residents (the French Market had long devolved into a place for tourist souvenirs). Our day on the road foraging for

Authors Shelley Holl (left) and BJ Carpenter (right) on a culinary adventure.

local delicacies in Louisiana led us to believe that this delightful pastime could be enjoyed in other parts of the country. On the other end of the Mississippi, only BJ's friends in the restaurant trade were in the habit of following food from the market back to the farm. Hunting for fresh, local ingredients is both fun *and* educational; we thought the idea could take hold not only for food aficionados but for the increasing number of people who want to experience eating local foods in season for economic, environmental, and health reasons.

A mere fifty years ago, our grandmothers ate local foods in season out of necessity. They would be shocked to think something so fundamental is now considered a lost art. This book is designed to serve as a year-round companion for those who want to explore Minnesota-grown and -produced foods. Beginning with the asparagus sprouts in early spring and chronologically following throughout the year, we reflect on what we learned in our travels, show the food we made, photographed and ate on the family china, give suggestions for monthly menus, and present recipes and tips for foods of the season that you'll return to again and again. We include instructions for drying and freezing along with simple, wholesome ideas and recipes to see you through the northern winters when there is nothing local, fresh, or green.

It is not intended to provide a compendium of ingredients, recipes, or food sources, but rather to inspire your search for the best and freshest ingredients for your table by giving you an intimate, and sometimes artistic, look at the searches we made for our own. The watercolors are imbued with the pure jewel tones found in our gardens, from the chartreuse of spring sorrel to the autumn rainbow of swiss chard.

We hope that the lessons we learned, funny moments, occasional missteps, and illustrations—both visual and verbal— will ignite a spark and send you off on your own great adventure.

April

Asparagus · Bulgur · Maple Sugar · Lamb

If the weather has not made April fools out of us, we are outdoors in earnest now—wearing padded cotton jackets we have worn forever because, being too light for winter and too warm for any other time of year, they never wear out. Cold nights and warm days jump-start the maple sap, and we stare almost in disbelief when we stumble over the first asparagus stalks near the trilliums in the woods. We are still eating dried and frozen foods at this time in Minnesota, but on the first cold early-morning trip to market, we find asparagus, and our hearts turn cartwheels because we can finally add one local shade of green to Sunday supper.

Every Man a King

Louis XIV loved asparagus with such passion, he had greenhouses built so he could eat it whenever his kingly heart desired. These days, out-of-season asparagus is no longer the provenance of kings. With the aid of Congress, President George H. W. Bush turned the traditionally spring-only vegetable into everyday American fare when, in the early 1990s, the humble asparagus spear became his weapon of choice in the U.S. government's War on Drugs.

Trying to reduce the flow of South American cocaine by encouraging Peruvian farmers to grow asparagus instead of coca, U.S. government subsidies made Peruvian asparagus cheap and available year-round. As a result, the bottom fell out of the American market, and many domestic growers were forced out of business. Because Peruvian farmers continue to grow coca in the highlands while planting asparagus at sea level, critics claim the U.S. government's actions have done little to stem the flow of cocaine into America.

However, what was once the bane of large-scale domestic operations has proven a boon to its small growers: imported Peruvian asparagus is not as good or fresh as the locally grown spring product found in farmers' markets, and savvy buyers know the difference.

A small crowd was vying for asparagus at the St. Joseph Farmers' Market when BJ and I first saw Russ Willenbring of Produce Acres. He and his shy, well-behaved son stood perfectly erect behind a table lined with paper bags of beautiful, ready-to-cook asparagus. In contrast to the chatty university types that formed the market crowd, these two were quiet and stood a little apart, the way the Amish do when selling their wares to tourists. They wore no special uniforms, only an air of clean respectability.

The boy, who appeared to be attached to the father by an invisible leash, was having his turn at market day—a treat, since it meant he didn't have to stay home on the farm and pick asparagus. Several times a month, Willenbring makes the lengthy drive into the Twin Cities to sell at the Minneapolis Farmers' Market. He and one of the children leave the farm by 2 a.m. in order to set up their market stall by dawn. It makes for a long day, but when we asked the child if he enjoyed the trip, his face lit up as if he were going to Disneyland.

Willenbring's perfect asparagus and other-worldly ways intrigued us, so when the St. Joseph market was finished for the day, we drove through the picturesque hill country west of town to visit his farm.

In pioneering days, Produce Acres' long narrow drive and hilltop homestead might have been a stronghold from which inhabitants could see approaching intruders. The Willenbrings did indeed seem to know we were coming, because they were waiting. Russ Willenbring greeted us at our car, while a group of children lingered near the edge of the farmyard staring at us like curious kittens. Within minutes his wife, a compact dynamo of a woman, and another of their nine children emerged from the large, recently built house to visit with us for a while. The Willenbrings were religious people, with strong opinions about everything from water quality to the dormitory-style housing of their supersized family.

Unlike the many hobby farmers whose picturesque places dot the Avon hills near St. Joseph, Russ Willenbring came from local farming stock. An independent spirit and an aversion to middlemen made him a perfect candidate for direct selling at farmers' markets, where he was shrewd enough to notice that asparagus brought in more money than most crops. We sensed that organic farming and the hard work it entails seemed to go hand-in-hand with their religious ethic, making asparagus, a crop that requires relentless tending, an especially good fit. As we talked, the sun was setting rapidly and our chances of seeing more of Produce Acres was growing slim, so we traded further conversation for a tour.

Willenbring hauled us out to his fields on a low mechanized contraption designed for weeding with his two youngest children, a gap-toothed boy and tow-headed girl, running alongside. The kids were breathless by the time we reached the place where

As long as the farmers' markets have customers who insist on freshness . . . a little family business like Produce Acres will do just fine.

the strawberry, raspberry, and asparagus fields met, but eager to help their dad show us the crops.

We saw asparagus from twenty-two-year-old stock growing next to two-year-old plants. To the untrained eye, it was a bit hard to distinguish between the two because, unlike the even, antiseptically tidy crops seen on many Midwestern farms, Produce Acres' fields have plenty of weeds between the rows, which Willenbring considers a hallmark of organic farming without herbicides.

Keeping the weeds down on half a dozen acres of asparagus looked to be a daunting task. The machine we rode into the fields would be employed for some of it, and the rest would be hand-pulled when Willenbring, his wife, or their children worked the fields.

When ready, the crop is handpicked; it would be hard to do it any other way. Asparagus has a short, oddly punctuated growing season, which in Minnesota is pretty much finished by June. The spears spring from rootstock, called crowns, and at first are picked once every couple of days. As the season goes on, asparagus can grow as much as seven inches a day, making picking a daily, sometimes even twice daily, event. Unless there is a multigenerational labor source like the Willenbrings', the cost of handpicking becomes critical to the success of an asparagus grower's business.

Many of the large California farms that failed were also family businesses, but they had grown so large they had to rely on seasonal labor. This meant that such growers had to operate at a loss or plow crops under when competing with lower-priced imported asparagus.

Russ Willenbring sets up his asparagus stand at the St. Joseph Farmers' Market, which is open every Friday from May through September.

As long as the farmers' markets have customers who insist on freshness, a minimum of added chemicals, and a picture-perfect product, a little family business like Produce Acres will do just fine. As for imported asparagus, its year-round presence in the local grocery store only serves to dampen one's enthusiasm, especially when, come spring, Willenbring and a starry-eyed child will be selling asparagus fit for a king from a farmers' market stand.

Ogling Asparagus on the Side

If you search for "asparagus" on the Internet, a bewildering combination of vegetable trivia and romantic lore appears. The strangest fact about asparagus is that it can grow up to seven inches in one day; and you can almost see it grow (8mm per hour in some tropical climates); the oddest lore is its reputation as a romantic enhancement among the likes of Madame Pompadour.

Asparagus was revered in the *Tales of the Arabian Nights* as an aphrodisiac, and the Moors introduced it to the Spanish. Then the French, always precocious in matters of the heart, caught on and soon asparagus spread across the Channel. Even the English lay claim to its sensual properties. What was it about asparagus—the sensuous shape or the willowy fronds studded with luscious red seeds? Or, maybe, the rather strong, organic smell associated with its consumption?

Its aphrodisiac reputation didn't reach American soil with the British. Native Americans had identified asparagus as an edible plant early on in their history. And it's remained a part of our cuisine, though we approach it differently here than they do in Europe. Americans eat asparagus unpeeled, often opting for just the tips, while the Continentals peel the stalks, cook them whole, and eat them in the traditional, seductive manner: dipping the spears in a delectable sauce, followed by the licking of the fingers.

Cultivation and color seem to be matters of national preference too. Americans like their asparagus thick and green; Belgians, French, and Germans favor the more succulent white spears, grown in complete darkness until plump; and Italians like the deep purple–tipped variety.

Asparagus is low in calories and has high levels of vitamins A, B, and C, oxalic acid, and phosphorus. And, according to folklore, it has medicinal properties too: it restores eyesight, relieves toothaches, and works as both a laxative and a diuretic.

When buying asparagus, always look for firm spears with good color, closed, rounded tips, and a bit of white at the bottom. Limp spears with open, spread tips and ridged stalks will be tough and stringy and have poor flavor. To store, trim the bottoms and place the spears, cut end down, in a glass or tall-sided container with about an inch of warm water, and refrigerate. Use as soon as possible, storing no longer than three days if raw, two if cooked.

Peeled or unpeeled, asparagus breaks naturally at the toughest point on the stalk; just bend slightly and snap. Rinse under cold, running water to remove any sand that may be trapped in the tips. Asparagus lends itself well to piquant vinaigrettes and smooth, creamy sauces. Serve it hot or cold as a side or a salad, folded into omelets, or puréed for soups and soufflés.

Though it came later to France than to other places in Europe, the French proclaimed their method to be the classic preparation. Madame Pompadour, noted French naughty lady and courtesan of Louis XV, was a firm believer in the lust-producing properties of stimulating foods. Here is her recipe that allegedly brought all of France to its knees: "Dress the asparagus sticks in the normal way. Slice them obliquely toward the tips in pieces no longer than the little finger. Take only the choicest sections, and, keeping them cool, allow them to drain while the sauce is being prepared in the manner following:

"Mix 100 grammes of Bulgarian feta and light-green avocado together, a good pinch of powdered nutmeg and the yolks of two eggs diluted with four spoonfuls of lemon juice. After mixing this sauce, drop in the asparagus tips, and serve in a covered casserole."

> *When buying asparagus, always look for firm spears with good color, closed, rounded tips, and a bit of white at the bottom.*

In Search of Local Lamb

When face to face with the object of "Mary had a . . . ," most people melt, and shepherds Norm and Lori Pint at Prairie Haven Farm, from whom we chose to order lamb, were no exception. Raising lamb is rather like being in the nursery business: the Pints know everything about their stock, study their habits, note their individual qualities, and nurture and watch over their health, but it is very unlikely that they give them names—for the Pints eat lamb, as do BJ and I.

The atmosphere was tense among those of us in the lambing barn, and when Lori Pint's cell phone rang with the bleat of a lamb, everyone started at the sound. One of their ewes was having trouble, and Lori had been standing by the fence wringing her hands while her husband, and finally her pregnant daughter-in-law, a former ob-gyn nurse, assisted in the pen. When the lamb wasn't breathing, the daughter-in-law swung it gently by its hind legs until it did, toweled it off, and set it on its feet. Lori breathed a sigh of relief, then turned to the phone, where her daughter, a student in a food and agricultural school, waited, holding her breath as well.

BJ and I watched for a while, then left the soft straw of the lambing pen behind, following long rays of light into the farmyard where a low afternoon sun and a cloudless sky conspired to make the Pints' Victorian farmhouse and red barn into a pretty hobby farm, instead of a fourth-generation family farm that had been homesteaded by Norm's great-grandfather. Actually, Prairie Haven had been a hobby farm during the years that Norm was in law enforcement and Lori worked as a medical transcriber, but since 2003 they've been raising lamb on pasture.

Though we'd long planned to order lamb, we didn't know where, and our connection to Prairie Haven had been a happy accident: a spur-of-the-moment call when we were on the road followed by an invitation to stop by as if we were old friends. Lori had just finished giving a horseback riding lesson to a neighbor girl, part of her 4-H requirement, when we arrived. We stood in the shade of a tree that had been planted when Norm's grandfather had been born, and she explained how ordering lamb worked. We would place our order, pay Prairie Haven farm when it came time the following fall, then she would give us a number and we would retrieve the meat from our choice of one of two processors the Pints used.

I tried hard not to think about the individual lambs over the months, wondering if when Lori contacted us in the fall, the memories of the spring would have dimmed. BJ, who is a hunter and a chef, had come to terms with the link between farm and table long before I had and promised to handle the details. I squeamishly stayed on the outskirts of the final negotiations, knowing I'd have to face the music when it came time to drive to the meat market. In November, instructions arrived from Lori, and I was told to drive to Schmidt's Meat Market in Nicollet, near New Ulm, and contact Larry about our lamb: number 007.

Oh dear. For all my efforts, the lamb had a name after all.

We went to fetch "James" on the deer hunting season opener, a gray, cheerless weekend; there was snow on the cold wind and so little sun that had I not been on a mission, I'd have felt quite dreary. The hour and a quarter's drive went quickly—a long progression of suburbs that finally finished just before Jordan—then started up again, until finally we were in the country speeding over rolling antler-velvet hills and through bunched hollows of spiky, leafless trees.

Nicollet was a cold-looking cluster of buildings at the intersection of a highway and a county road where cars slowed as little as possible in their hurry to get somewhere else. I paused at the crossroads, scanned the horizon in front and in the rearview mirror, and counted a total of five cars. Around the corner, a complex of white stucco buildings with a faux Bavarian face that said "Wilkommen" and "Schmidt's Meat Market" spanned the length of an entire city block. It was cold outside the car, and my feet were dragging with thoughts of oncoming winter, the demise of James, and the apparent emptiness of town. But when I tried to pull open the door to the market, the wind grabbed it, it flew open with a loud bang, and no fewer than fifty people paused and turned toward the sound. Where on Earth had they all come from?

It was Christmas, or at least deer season, inside Schmidt's Meat Market. The employees—and there were as many of them as there were customers—scurried about behind the meat counter sporting jaunty red and blue uniforms and pleasant, patient smiles. The customers, many of them large, beefy men, some with their wives—all with delight in their eyes—scanned

Though we'd long planned to order lamb, we didn't know where, and our connection to Prairie Haven had been a happy accident: a spur-of-the-moment call when we were on the road followed by an invitation to stop by as if we were old friends.

deli cases that stretched the length of the store, choosing first this, then that variety of summer sausage, beef sticks, or jerky. The walls were lined with awards for garlic sausage and bacon. Some people, like us, carried coolers and were either dropping off deer meat or picking up deer sausage, the making of which was the main reason the owners of this meat market work fourteen-hour days between now and Christmas.

After I told her about 007 and the reason for my call, a woman at the counter sent me to one of the owners—who just happened to be her brother-in-law—and showed me how to get around behind the counter to find him. It was a little like wading into a river, with rolling racks of sausages and carts loaded with meat for the smoker moving as if on a current from one part of the crowded workroom to another. I ducked beneath a tray of fat summer sausages one young man was hoisting overhead like a waiter in a beer hall and ran straight into Bruce Schmidt, who despite the sense of urgency back there stopped everything—as if he'd been waiting all day for me to make contact and was willing to tell me everything he knew.

"We're the Summer Sausage Kings," said Schmidt about the product that originated with his father and now has devotees from as far away as Texas. From one variety, they had expanded to fifty, all of which could be sampled from trays on the shoulder-high counters that lined the front of the store. Now they are making over a half a million pounds of sausage a year, plus jerky, snack sticks, salads, and, of course, deer sausage—180,000 pounds of it between now and the end of the year.

To prove the point, he had me follow him out into the alley, up a set of metal stairs, through heavy plastic flaps, and into a refrigerated semitrailer truck where boxes of sausage were piled floor to ceiling from the front to the end of the truck—so far that I could not see through the clouds of frost. People sent deer from far away places (Montana, Canada, Louisiana) and I got the impression that hunters—not just of deer, but elk, turkey, caribou, and geese—were just plain crazy about the flavor found at Schmidt's.

Gary told me the tangy flavor I found so appealing in their summer sausage is from natural fermentation that takes place over two days in the smokehouse where the temperature is raised slowly to eighty degrees—the perfect temperature to attain the correct pH. Men were loading carts stacked with screens spread with slices of beef that would be rolled into the smoker and come out as beef jerky. We took a claustrophobic trip down a set of cement stairs where the fires that smoldered beneath the smoking chambers were fed into the night from a huge pile of basswood. Schmidt did all the firing himself and would spend every evening between now and Christmas stoking fires every few hours: at 4:00 p.m., 6:00, 7:30, and then 11:30 with a cooldown overnight.

We talked for a long time, following a set of channeled tracks that snaked across the ceiling from the meat locker to workstations across the room. Finally, I asked him about 007. He located our lamb, and one of the ladies packed it into our coolers and took our fifty-dollar processing fee—and I breathed a sigh of relief. At this point buying lamb had no more emotional tug than a trip to the meat counter at the neighborhood grocery store, though I must say Schmidt's Meat Market was one impressive store.

Gary Schmidt recommended lunch in New Ulm to put a thoroughly Teutonic spin on the day, so we drove there, stopping at the Kaiserhof—just as the town's glockenspiel rang—and dined on ribs and dark, harvest-style beer in a plump leatherette booth beneath the warm glow of beer signs.

Once home, we divided up the white meat-market packages between our freezers and didn't think much more about it . . . until we needed to make a really good dinner for a really tough customer: someone who knows the difference and will say so, good or bad, loudly and totally without charm. That's when we both looked at each other and said, "James" in one voice—knowing without a doubt that this would be the best lamb any of us had ever served. And it was.

April Menu

Asparagus Vinaigrette

♦

Minted Crown Roast of Lamb

♦

Bulgur Pilaf

♦

Maple Sugar Crème Brulée

Asparagus Vinaigrette

Serves
4 to 6

Prepared in this fast, simple way, asparagus is sure to satisfy; especially when eaten in the French manner—with the fingers, of course.

1 lb. (approximately 2 bunches)
  fresh asparagus
Kosher salt, for steaming
2 small shallots, minced
Juice and zest from 1 lemon
  (approximately 2–3 tbsp. juice)
2–3 tbsp. white wine or
  champagne vinegar
½ tsp. coarse sea salt
Freshly ground black pepper,
  to taste
½ c. high-quality extra-virgin
  olive oil

1. Rinse the asparagus under cold running water to remove any sand trapped in the tips. Bend spears until they break at their tender spot. Spears the diameter of your little finger or larger benefit from peeling before cooking.

2. Place in a steamer basket over boiling, lightly salted water. Cover and cook until spears are less rigid, no less than 1 minute and no more than 4 minutes, depending on spear size. They should have a slight snap or crunch.

3. Remove asparagus to an ice-water bath to cool completely; this preserves texture and heightens color. Drain and roll in a cotton cloth or paper toweling to absorb excess water. Set aside.

4. Prepare vinaigrette: combine minced shallots, lemon zest, 2 tsp. lemon juice, 2 tsp. vinegar, sea salt, and pepper in a medium-sized bowl. Whisk olive oil into the mixture, in a steady stream. Taste and adjust seasonings.

5. To serve: Lay dried asparagus on a platter, whisk vinaigrette to emulsify, and pour over asparagus. Serve with chilled dry white wine or champagne.

Minted Crown Roast of Lamb

Serves
4 to 6

If you want to impress people, this is the dish for you. It will look like you've spent days in preparation, when it's actually simple to do. The racks of ribs will easily bend into two half circles when they are split and the chine, or backbone, has been removed.

2 racks of spring lamb, about
 8 lbs. total; ribs split and
 backbone removed
1 tbsp. fresh rosemary needles, or
 1½ tsp., dried and crushed
5 garlic cloves, peeled and finely
 minced
1 tbsp. kosher or coarse sea salt
3 tbsp. crushed peppercorns,
 equal amounts of white, black,
 and green
½ c. fresh mint leaves, torn, or
 1½ tsp., dried
2 tbsp. prepared Dijon-style
 mustard
2 c. finely crushed, unseasoned
 bread crumbs, sourdough, or
 other dense white bread

1. Dry all surfaces of lamb with paper towels.

2. Mince the rosemary and garlic with coarse salt. Add 1 tbsp. crushed peppercorns and mint. Firmly press the mixture onto the surface of the lamb.

3. Brush exterior surfaces with Dijon-style mustard. Mix remaining crushed peppercorns with bread crumbs and press into mustard-covered sides of the lamb. Cover with parchment or waxed paper, then food film, and refrigerate for at least 8 hours.

4. An hour before roasting, take lamb from refrigerator, remove food film, leave parchment in place, and bring to room temperature. Preheat oven to 450°F. Place oven rack in the lower third of oven.

5. Roast the lamb for 20–25 minutes, remove from oven, and fill center cavity with warm Bulgar Pilaf; the bulgur will absorb the flavorful lamb juices. Return to the oven to roast for another 10–15 minutes for rare or 20 minutes for medium rare.

6. Let the roast sit for 10–12 minutes before removing the string. Separate the individual chops with the tip of a sharp boning knife or nonflexible slicer. For presentation, mound pilaf in the center of a serving platter and fan the chops around the edge.

Tip

Create each crown by bending each rack in an arc, so the bones are on the interior edge. Place the racks end-to-end, tightly wrapping 2 to 3 lengths of kitchen string around the racks and tying to secure the crown shape. Alternately, thread a larding needle with kitchen string, bend the racks in semicircles, and join with 2 or 3 tight stitches at each side. This keeps the crown upright while roasting and makes the perfect place for Bulgur Pilaf.

Bulgur Pilaf

This recipe is easily increased, with very happy results, so make more than you will immediately need. After the main attraction, this quiet side dish can stand on its own as a cold salad with the addition of tomatoes, pitted cured olives, lemon zest, salty feta, and a dash of vinegar and oil—oh, and leftover lamb, if there is any. Add caramelized onions, celery, lamb, and some stock to extra pilaf, and it can do double duty as a dinner hotdish.

1 tbsp. canola oil

3 tbsp. unsalted butter

½ c. yellow onion, diced

1 large carrot, peeled and
shredded, about 1 cup

½ c. currants or golden raisins

3 c. #3 coarse bulgur, presoaked
in cold water for 15 to 20
minutes and drained

2–3 c. chicken stock, preferably
homemade; if using commercial,
taste for salt and adjust

Salt, to taste

¼ tsp. freshly ground pepper

½ tsp. dried tarragon

1. Place canola oil in 3 qt. saucepan, add butter, and place over medium heat. Add diced onions and cook until golden.

2. In the same saucepan, add carrots and currants, and stir gently for about 30 seconds; add presoaked bulgur, chicken stock, salt, pepper, and tarragon. Cook over medium-high heat about 5 minutes, stirring occasionally. Lower heat, cover, and continue to cook for 15–20 minutes, until grains are tender and stock is absorbed. Taste and adjust seasoning.

3. Fill the center of the lamb crown with pilaf for the final 10–15 minutes of roasting; place remaining pilaf in an ovenproof dish and heat in oven for the final 15 minutes of roasting.

4. To serve, turn pilaf from ovenproof dish onto a warmed serving platter, top with pilaf from center of crown, and fan chops around the edge.

Maple sugar is a concentration of pure maple syrup that has been cooked down to a point where it will crystallize once cooled. This stage is marked by a temperature 25°F above the boiling point of water, or 237°F (114°C). Because boiling syrup rises very fast, make sure you have a pan large enough to accommodate the expansion. Vigilance and an accurate candy thermometer are two key tools. Though it may seem to take forever for the syrup to come to a boil, taking your eyes off the thermometer at the wrong moment can prove disastrous. It takes mere seconds for the temperature to climb higher once it reaches the traditional boiling point of 212°F.

For 4 oz. of maple sugar, pour 2 c. of pure maple syrup into a large, heavy-bottomed saucepan, securely attach a candy thermometer to the inside, and place the pan on a burner over medium-high heat. Watch the pan carefully, and bring the syrup to a rolling boil. Once it begins boiling, let the syrup reduce, cooking at full heat, without stirring. Constantly monitor the thermometer. The instant the temperature reaches 237°F, remove the pan from the burner and set it away from the heat in a place where it won't be disturbed, and allow to cool to room temperature. Cover with a loose piece of parchment. Be patient. The speed at which syrup cools determines the sugar's texture. Don't attempt to accelerate the cooling by refrigerating or placing in an ice-water bath. The coarse, large-grained crystals desired for maple sugar are achieved by slowly cooling the syrup, with only occasional stirring. Remove the maple sugar from the pan by carefully scraping with a wooden or metal spoon, or spatula. If the sugar comes out in large or uneven-sized pieces, break down to desired size by pulsing briefly in a food processor, crushing with a rolling pin, or breaking apart using a large mortar and pestle. Store in a tightly closed container in a dark, dry, cool place.

Maple Sugar Crème Brulée

Makes 6 individual or 1 9-inch square custard

Maple sugar gives this classic French dessert a northern plains twist. Older folks will remember maple sugar as glistening maple leaf–shaped candies, and a less decorative version can still be found in co-ops and natural foods grocery stores. You can also make it from scratch. The instructions for making maple sugar are to the left of the Crème Brulée recipe. The results of this fun, easy Saturday project will satisfy the sweet tooth of kids large and small, and can add a personal touch to Easter baskets.

⅓ c. heavy cream
⅔ c. whole milk
¼ c. maple syrup
3 large eggs, whole,
    room temperature
3 large egg yolks,
    room temperature
½ tsp. pure vanilla extract
Pinch of fine-grained sea salt
Hot water
¾ c. maple sugar

1. Preheat oven to 300°F. Place rack in bottom third of oven. If using individual custard cups, evenly space them in an ovenproof pan, and set it aside.

2. Gently heat the cream, milk, and maple syrup in a heavy-bottomed saucepan; do not boil. For extra insurance, a double boiler may be used.

3. Beat eggs and yolks together in a medium-sized bowl. Whisk about 1 c. of the heated cream mixture into the beaten eggs, and immediately stir back into the cream in the saucepan.

4. Cook over medium heat while stirring constantly with a wooden spoon. Remove from heat once the custard coats the back of the spoon. Stir in vanilla and a pinch of salt. Ladle custard into the cups and place the entire pan in the bottom third of oven. Fill the outer pan with hot water up to the same level as the custard. Bake for 30–35 minutes for individual custards or 35–45 minutes for one large custard, or until the center is set. Remove from outer pan, cover, and chill.

5. Several hours before serving, remove the custards from the refrigerator and evenly sprinkle with the maple sugar. Preheat the broiler and place the custards under the broiler element, or flame with a small torch, until the tops are evenly browned. Remove and refrigerate, or serve at room temperature, as desired.

Morels · Eggs · Spinach · Baby Salad Greens · Rhubarb

Outside at night in May, the Earth has a pungent, breathtaking scent and you can actually hear the sounds of growing things: dried brown leaves pop and splinter, casualties of tiny earthquakes as big, fast-growing shoots push the garden soil aside. Spinach, rhubarb, and morels muscle up through moist, dark soil with great bursts of energy, looking bewildered in their new surroundings and, as if surprised at their nakedness, attempt to hide behind the skirts of last year's leaves. Mother Earth won't offer shelter for long; an early morning raid on the henhouse, some lucky-find morels, a handful of the garden's first leafy greens, plus a few blushing pink stalks, and you'll have the makings of an elegant dinner to honor spring.

Pickles and PhDs

Compared to the bustle of a big city market, St. Joseph's fledgling farm market has the relaxed atmosphere of a British country fair. Perhaps it's the bike riders, helmets in hand, who wander in from the Woe-be-gone Trail less than a block away, or the preponderance of retired St. John's and St. Benedict's professors who exchange cheery greetings over lettuce and eggs, or maybe it's just that the market is on Fridays and the freedom of the weekend is in the wind.

It was early for most farm produce when we visited; fewer than two dozen vendors faced one another in a tidy rectangle on the grass next to the parking lot of Resurrection Lutheran Church. Despite their small numbers, they offered a charming diversity reflecting the eclectic tastes of a university town. Their products ranged from yak meat to mushrooms, with maple syrup and just-picked asparagus in between.

For its size, the market had more than its share of artisan bakers. Among them was Fred's Bread, a St. Cloud hearty favorite, and at the other end of the spectrum was a specialty baker whose exquisite brioche rivals any from the Twin Cities' fanciest bakeries. There were even those who tried their hands at grinding grain and baking rhubarb cake in the farmhouse kitchen.

On one end of the rectangle, a spinner turning out long, wavy ropes of wool from the fleece of Icelandic sheep that, from their pictures, looked like little woolly mammoths. The other end was completely closed off by a semi trailer whose billboard-sized side panel advertised Forest Mushrooms, a unique market attraction that drew customers as soon as the vehicle jockeyed into position.

One of St. Joseph's small business success stories, Forest Mushrooms runs a high-tech production facility for growing oyster and shiitake mushrooms on a nearby farm. In addition they distribute dried mushrooms, from chanterelles to morels, throughout the Midwest.

Like most of the sellers at the St. Joseph Farmers' Market, Forest Mushrooms' owner, Kevin Doyle, was enlisted because of his special relationship with one of the market founders, Angeline Dufner: long before visions of mushrooms filled his head, she was his college biology professor.

The market was the brainchild of Angeline Dufner and her friend Sister Phyllis, two retired professors from St. Ben's who took the college's mission of community service to heart. They had taught in different disciplines, Sister Phyllis in biology and Dufner in English, but they spoke the same language when it came to community service and global responsibilities. Sister Phyllis had already started a CSA—Community Supported Agriculture, a system in which consumers support a local farm through advance subscriptions for agricultural products. In addition, she thought the whole community could benefit from a farmers' market. After an exhaustive feasibility study, the two friends threw their energy into organizing St. Joseph's Farmers' Market, which opened in 2000.

"Besides, there's always a bit of friction between town and gown, and I figure anything you can do to pull them together helps create a community," said Dufner.

If you're lucky enough to see them at the market, they'll charm you with their warmth and humor, but beneath their engaging public faces, a sober philosophy operates. With lightening speed, Dufner gave us an education in agri-business, rattling off statements that later sent us scurrying to the library for confirmation.

"I'm not a farmer, but I have empathies. And you can't have empathy for someone unless you understand what they do. America has an unjust food system. I grew up on a farm and everybody knows that the farmers don't get much and the middlemen get everything," Angeline Dufner stated.

How much does the farmer earn? Only about twenty cents on the dollar, and most of the rest goes for labor, packaging, transportation, and retail expenses. The costs to the American consumer are high in part because foods travel an average of 1,500 miles before appearing on our tables.

"These days, many farmers work an eight-hour job and have to go home and farm. That is an unjust food system which does not link the food eater with the food producer."

So who's watching the family farm? Hardly anyone. It is a little-known fact that fewer Americans are farming than are incarcerated in our prisons.

"Studies have shown that if you can keep money generated in a community within that community, it is worth three times as much," she intoned.

Farm fresh eggs from the St. Joseph Farmers' Market.

"The farmers that work for the big poultry processors don't own their own chickens. They are even told what to feed them by headquarters, so basically they become serfs. We wouldn't have a commodity farmer in our market, not that they would ask—they're too busy doing what they're told."

Dufner's scathing description of the commodity farmer painted a clearer picture of the creativity, ingenuity, and wisdom that goes into farming.

"If a farmer can't even decide what feed to give the animals in his care, he's simply not using the wealth of his experience."

Since large corporations produce 98 percent of all the poultry we consume, and only four firms handle more than 80 percent of beef that is slaughtered, there are a lot of farmers raising the poultry and beef who are towing the company line.

Dufner showed us around the market, introducing us to former students and fellow faculty members. Her presence might have triggered the topics we heard discussed that day. From regulatory measures for organic farming to the economics of home canning, it began to look as if there was as much educational value in the St. Joseph market as nutritional.

Dufner told us that she and Sister Phyllis worked with a team of students to conduct the feasibility study prior to opening the market. On paper, the results indicated that the market could work, but whether the town and university people would support it was still a matter of speculation. What it took to get the project going was the ignorance of youth, which to an educator, is an irresistible catalyst.

It was the otherwise bright graduate student who, on first seeing a dill plant said, "But where are the pickles?" that finally convinced Dufner the market was needed.

She chuckled as she recalled, "I told her that if you just barely scratched the earth around the plant, and looked really closely, you'd see very tiny ones."

Shopping for Morels

If you're a novice morel tracker like me, and you're really counting on morel sauce for Mother's Day, it's best to have a trick or two up your sleeve. Trick number one: cheat. Begin your mushroom hunt online where websites like the Minnesota Mycological Society post dates and locations of last year's mushroom finds; check your calendar and reserve all the mornings between the end of April and the end of May for hunting; then sacrifice a goat or two to the Gods of Fungus for good luck—you'll need it.

Trick number two: befriend a bona fide mushroom hunter. Mine comes from Poland, where I'm told people spend much of their free time combing the countryside for mushrooms. And since he's had so much experience finding Polish mushrooms, he's confident about Minnesota mushrooms too. Don't know a master mushroom hunter? Consider a fifteen-dollar membership to the Minnesota Mycological Society (www.minnesotamushrooms.org) so you can learn about morels, then tag along on an organized collecting trip. When it comes to mushrooms, it's really not a good idea to go it alone. We've all heard the stories.

It would be hard to confuse mushroom hunting with an Olympic sport, but you can get some decent exercise following someone who is experienced and energetically pursues the prey. My friend takes long strides, moving quickly along hedgerows and across pastures, pausing briefly to check beneath low-hanging branches and alongside fallen trees. My function is to follow behind with the basket.

We go in the spring for morels and in the fall for other varieties. The following-behind-thing is a bit humbling, but I should not be the one identifying mushrooms, because to me, the ones that are left behind (and there are many) look just like the ones that go into the basket.

My role is a bit more functional when it comes to hunting the morel with its distinctive swiss cheese holes and fairy tale shape. An extra set of eyes is helpful because, like fairies, morels are elusive and well camouflaged. No matter how long and hard the search, some people, who we meet returning from the forest with empty baskets and hangdog expressions, never even find one. They may be the unbelievers, those skunked hunters, but I can't criticize them since I don't believe either, until I see the first morel.

Unfortunately, I'm never the first to spot a morel. Like I said, they're elusive, changing color and assuming slightly different shapes in each locale. Generally speaking, morels are yellow (also called white) and black (which are often sort of gray), and though mushroom hunters include them among "the Foolproof Five," there's a brownish false morel, too, that is close enough in looks to fool an overexcited beginner like me. Usually I have to wait for my fellow hunter's "halloo," and, when I reach him, stare and stare to see if I can spot a morel before it's shown to me. Once I've seen one and retrained my eye for the disguise of the day, I can begin to hunt in earnest.

Even though I know they are in the neighborhood, when I finally do spot one by myself, I freeze in place and rub my eyes in disbelief. I don't move—not that I think they'll see me and run away. I've learned if there's one morel, there are others, and I almost stepped on this one.

It takes a soaking rain sometime in the previous week, temperatures over seventy degrees, and warm soil for morels to appear. Expert mushroom hunters seem to think they know where morels grow, but as far as I can tell they are as surprised and pleased as the next guy when it comes to a big find. Morels sprout near dead wood, under trees (elm, oak, ash, beech, aspen, and cottonwood, among others), atop open sunny hills, on burned-over areas, on south-facing slopes, in sandy river

bottoms, and then, when it's getting too hot, on north-facing slopes, in shady hollows and . . . . If you add up all the likely habitats, they're everywhere. And nowhere.

Last season my friend and I made several trips to the same swampy area. The first time we were late for the opera, and since it was Mozart, we gave the hunt short shrift. It was too hot and dry anyway.

On our way back to the car, we met some hunters who'd found morels there in previous years. They didn't look nearly as happy as their dog, who grinned from ear to ear because he'd been walked for hours and allowed to stop and sniff almost every tree. I would have thought their experience was proof positive that the place was mushroomless, but apparently this is not the way a real mushroom hunter thinks. Trading on the previous successes of the other hunters, and the preponderance of likely habitat, my friend thought we should try another day.

Conditions were perfect when we returned, but after an hour of poking around charred trees, it looked like we'd struck out again. On our way back I was thinking grumpily that the darn things were so perverse, they'd probably show up three feet from the car. Just then we came upon a lake where a romantic couple shared one side of a picnic table. The ground was pretty well trampled, so I didn't even bother to look, but my friend, who I swear can smell mushrooms, took another look, then suddenly hollered over to me. There among a perfect camouflage of sweet woodruff, old oak leaves, and hamburger bun wrappers were three or four. Then he found three or four more—and more after that too. Feeling awfully lucky, we took nearly two dozen of them home and prepared half the next day.

There was another week to go before Mother's Day, so I figured I'd have to relinquish my vision of hors' d oeuvres garnished with fresh morels and violets and settle for dried morels instead.

But my friend kept going back—and always to the same spot. Not only did he save my Mother's Day treat, he gave mushrooms to everyone else and dried a couple of pounds just for himself. Surprised, I asked if he wasn't wearing out that picnic spot.

"No, Shelley, that's how it is with mushrooms," he replied in his charming Polish accent. "When you find them, you go there; as if you were going to the store."

Sautéed Morels on
Buttered Toast Points

♦

Spring Green Salad with
Tarragon Vinaigrette

♦

Eggs Lorene

♦

Ready Set Rhubarb

Sautéed Morels on Buttered Toast Points

Serves
4 to 6

It's been said morels are the one American fungus whose aroma comes close to the intensity of truffles. But truffles need to be imported from the south of France or northern Italy, are only available in the fall, and come at a very dear cost: $200 to $400 per pound. Morels herald spring in Minnesota and can be found April through May in metropolitan co-ops and at farmers' markets for $30 to $40 per pound, a real deal compared to its continental cousin. Available off-season, dried morels are sold statewide in retail grocery stores and co-ops year-round. Still, $30 to $40 per pound can be pretty pricey. To cut costs and cure cabin fever, you could try hunting them on your own.

Weather, location, and patience permitting, morels are often found in abundance under stands of oaks. And, except for the cost of gas to get to them, they're free. But then, can we really put a price on rustic adventure and elegance?

4–6 tbsp. unsalted butter

4 oz. fresh morels, or 1 oz. dried

½ tsp. kosher salt

Freshly ground black pepper,
   to taste

4 tbsp. fresh parsley leaves, dried
   and minced

5 –6 slices of dense white bread,
   trimmed, buttered, and toasted;
   method follows recipe

5–6 slices Pullman-style
   sourdough or other dense bread

1 stick, 4 oz. or 8 tbsp., unsalted
   butter, softened

1. Gently rinse fresh morels to remove any sand; dry with paper towels. Cut the biggest morels in halves or quarters from tops through the stems, and leave the smaller ones whole. If using dried morels, reconstitute in ½ c. hot water for 10 minutes. Use a slotted spoon to lift morels from water, and drain on paper towels. Strain the liquid through cheesecloth to remove any sand or sediment. Use the liquid in the sauce, or save and freeze for another use.

2. Melt 4 tbsp. unsalted butter in a sauté pan over medium heat. Increase the heat to high, add the morels, and toss. Add 1–2 tbsp. of the remaining butter, as needed. Keep the morels from sticking to the pan by frequent shaking, but allow them to brown slightly.

3. Season with salt and pepper to taste. Serve over buttered toast points, garnished with chopped parsley.

4. Preheat oven to 400°F. Trim the crusts from bread. Quarter each piece on the bias, spread both sides with a thin layer of softened butter, and place on a cookie sheet; leave space between pieces to ensure even browning. Place in the middle of the preheated oven and toast until golden brown, about 5 minutes. Serve 2 toast points per person.

Spring Green Salad with Tarragon Vinaigrette

Serves 4

A recipe is only as good as the ingredients that go into it. Nowhere is this truer than in dishes that don't require cooking. Vinaigrettes are a classic example. They can be made with as few as four ingredients: an acid, an oil, salt, and pepper. The acid, usually vinegar, needs to be of good quality, the oil fresh, the pepper newly ground, and the salt pure and clean. The same holds true of any additions—recently dried herbs, quality condiments, ripe fruits, etc. The ratio of liquids is usually the same: 1 part acid to 2 parts oil. If the acid component is too sharp, it can be amended with a little cold water, and if the oil too heavy or pronounced, a little more of the acid will cut it. Dijon-style mustard, dry tarragon, and fresh garlic give voice to this basic vinaigrette.

Vinaigrette

1 tbsp. Dijon-style mustard

2 tsp. dried tarragon, crumbled
   or rubbed

1 clove garlic

1–2 tsp. coarse salt

Freshly ground black pepper,
   to taste

⅓ c. good-quality red wine vinegar

⅔ c. good-quality extra-virgin
   olive oil

While this may not make a lot, it's quick, easy, and fresh, which is always best when it comes to green salads!

1. Place mustard in a glass, ceramic, or stainless-steel bowl large enough to accommodate a whisk, or small jar with a tight-fitting lid. If using a bowl, place damp cloth or paper towels beneath the bowl to anchor it in place; this keeps the bowl from "walking" while you pour with one hand and whisk with the other.

2. Hand-crumble or rub the tarragon between your fingers, into the bowl; this releases essential oils, adding flavor. Mix into the mustard.

3. Flatten the garlic clove to remove the skin. If the clove has begun to sprout, slice in half and remove the green and white core; it can be bitter. Flatten garlic with the side of a knife, place in a mini-processor, sprinkle with salt, and process to a paste; or hand-macerate on a cutting surface by sprinkling salt over flattened garlic and mash/scrape with the knife blade. Add to mustard and tarragon, along with a few grinds of pepper.

4. Add vinegar and whisk until ingredients are incorporated.

5. Slowly drizzle the oil into the vinegar/mustard while whisking constantly. Taste to check salt, pepper, vinegar, and oil levels and adjust.

Spring Salad Greens Care

Baby salad greens are among the first seeds to push their little heads up through the soil each spring. The cool night temperatures and gentle, warming sun make for sweet or tangy, tender leaves that take little more than a drizzle of the simplest vinaigrette to dress them up. And, just like all newborns, they must be handled with care.

Gentle but thorough washing is needed to remove any dirt, compost materials, and critters that may be hanging on. The best method is to fill a clean sink or large bowl with cold, not icy, water, add the greens, and gently agitate with your hands. If you have whole heads of baby lettuces, gently plunge in the cold water several times to loosen any dirt around the core leaves.

Carefully remove from the water to a colander or drainer rack; don't squeeze or bunch them to remove excess water. Check the whole heads for any dirt remaining around the inside near the root end; some greens may require a second washing.

Careful drying of new lettuces is important too. Tender greens break down easier when wet, and dressings tend to slip off. Using a salad spinner can be too harsh for delicate leaves, and tearing may bruise them. Instead, lay the washed, whole leaves flat on all-cotton toweling or several connected sheets of paper towel and gently roll up; the toweling will absorb excess moisture. To crisp, slip the wrapped lettuce into a plastic bag and refrigerate for several hours or overnight. When handled in this way, many greens will keep for up to a week when carefully placed and sealed in a zip-top bag.

Place salad-sized plates in the refrigerator to chill; cover with toweling to keep clean. Do this well in advance so they will cool completely. Chilling salad plates in the freezer is to be avoided, since it causes greens to wilt.

To prepare salad for service, remove stems from washed greens, and separate large leaves from small. Place the whole bite-sized ones in a large, dry bowl. Carefully tear individual large leaves and add to the bowl with smaller ones; toss to mix and set aside. In a second large mixing bowl, place 1½ oz., or 3⅓ tbsp., of vinaigrette for each salad. Just before serving, add one large handful of cleaned mixed greens per person to the vinaigrette; gently toss. Taste and adjust greens or vinaigrette amounts as needed. Put equal-sized portions of dressed greens on the well-chilled salad plates. Individually garnish with nothing heavier than a few edible flower blossoms such as nasturtiums, violets, or pansies; minced delicate herbs like chives, chervil, or parsley; paper-thin radish or mushroom slices; finely grated baby carrots; or toasted sesame seeds. Heavier fruits, vegetables, and nuts will weigh down the salad or sink to the bottom of the pile, plus they are difficult to keep on a fork with dressed greens.

Eggs Lorene

Lorene Holl, with adaptation by BJ Carpenter

Serves 4

One Easter I asked Shelley's 86-year-old mother, Lorene, about an egg, spinach, and white-sauce dish Shelley remembered fondly from childhood. She shared the recipe and several charming anecdotes related to this do-ahead Sunday brunch dish from the 1960s. I decided to update the dish a bit by substituting a dilled soubise for the white sauce with the eggs, and I added Bar 5's Hungarian Pepper Bacon as the meat accompaniment. I served it to Lorene on Mother's Day, and she gave it her hearty approval.

8 eggs, extra-large or large

1½ c. fresh sourdough bread, torn
　　into large crumbs

1 lb. fresh spinach, washed
　　and dried

1 stick, 4 oz., unsalted butter, at
　　room temperature

1 small yellow onion, minced

3 tsp. dried dill weed

1½ c. whole milk,
　　or half & half, heated

4 tbsp. all-purpose flour

Kosher salt, to taste

Freshly ground white pepper, or
　　pinch of cayenne, to taste

Coarse salt for garnish

Paprika for garnish

1. Preheat oven to 350°F. Place 8 large eggs in a medium-sized saucepan, and fill with cold water to cover. Bring just to a boil, remove from the burner, cover, and let the eggs sit in their cooking water for 8 to 10 minutes; set a timer. Prepare an ice-water bath in a bowl large enough to submerge the eggs. Drain the eggs, place in the ice-water bath and chill for 5 minutes. Roll the eggs individually to crack the shells, and peel under cold running water; rinse well to remove any bits of shell. Cut in half lengthwise, place cut side up on a plate, cover with paper towel, and set aside. The yolks should be bright yellow, firm, and not hard, and the whites tender, not runny.

2. While the eggs are cooking, tear the sourdough loaf into 1-inch pieces, place in a big bowl, and set aside. Wash the spinach in several changes of cold water and dry in a salad spinner; set aside.

3. Melt the stick of butter in a medium-sized saucepan, remove half (4 tbsp.) and set aside. Add the minced onion to the remaining butter in the saucepan and cook over medium heat until soft but not colored. Add 2 tsp. of the dried dill weed to the onion and mix in. At the same time, heat the milk or half & half in the microwave, or on the stove, until just warm.

4. Stir the flour into the sautéed onions, and cook over low to medium heat for 1–2 minutes. Add warmed milk to the onion/flour mixture, stirring until slightly thickened. Remove from the heat, season to taste with salt and pepper, loosely cover, and set aside in a warm place.

Cont.

Bacon Made Ahead

Preheat oven to 350°F, and position a rack in the middle.

1. A day ahead: place a cooling rack inside or over a jellyroll pan. Lay the bacon strips over the rack; place in the preheated oven and cook until just underdone. The rack serves as a drain, keeping the bacon up out of the fat.

2. Remove pan from oven, roll par-cooked bacon in paper towels, wrap in food film, and refrigerate overnight.

3. Reheating for service: Place the cooling rack over the jellyroll pan as you did when par-cooking the bacon. Remove bacon from paper toweling and lay out on the rack. Place in the oven on a shelf below the casserole, and finish in the last 5 minutes the eggs are baking.

Tip

To get out of the kitchen and spend more time with Mom, all the elements can be made and assembled ahead of time, then finished in the oven just before serving—even the bacon.

5. Add half of the reserved melted butter to the torn bread, toss to coat, and spread evenly on a jelly roll pan. Toast in the middle of the preheated oven until lightly browned, about 10 minutes.

6. Place the remaining melted butter in a sauté pan, return to medium heat, and add the washed spinach; sauté until wilted. Remove from the heat, lightly season with salt and white pepper, and set aside. Place 1 tsp. dill weed in a small dish with 1 tsp. coarse salt and set aside.

7. Butter an ovenproof 1 qt. casserole dish that can be used on a buffet or breakfast table, and place on a table or other low surface. To assemble, place all prepared ingredients behind the casserole in order of assembly:
   - Sautéed spinach
   - Cooked eggs
   - Soubise sauce
   - Toasted croutons
   - Dill and salt mixture

8. Place sautéed spinach in the bottom of the prepared casserole; evenly nestle the cooked egg halves into the bed of spinach, cut side up. Garnish each with a pinch of coarse salt and dried dill weed. Evenly ladle the soubise sauce over the eggs and spinach and top with the lightly toasted, buttered croutons. Wrap tightly with heavy-duty food film, place an oversized sheet of aluminum foil over to completely cover the film, and refrigerate.

9. The next day, while the oven is preheating to 350°F., remove the casserole from the refrigerator and bring to room temperature. Place in the oven, still covered with the plastic wrap and aluminum foil, for 10–15 minutes. The film will keep a skin from forming on the soubise sauce and the eggs from overcooking. (As long as the plastic wrap is completely covered with aluminum foil, it will not melt onto your food. It works and has been done in restaurants for generations.) Remove wrappings, sprinkle lightly with paprika, and return to oven until bread is golden brown, about 10 minutes.

Ready Set Rhubarb

Serves
4 to 6

Rhubarb isn't a spring-only offering. Cut and freeze it when it's available in abundance following freezing directions in the "Frozen Beans and Other Vegetables" sidebar on page 50; then, when unexpected company stops by, or you find yourself deep in winter's shadows, you can throw together a warm dessert in no time flat.

3 c. day-old sourdough or similar style white bread, cut into 1-inch cubes
½ c. unsalted butter, melted
3 c. rhubarb, sliced into 1-inch pieces
¾–1 c. granulated sugar

1. Preheat oven to 350°F.

2. Mix all the ingredients together in a large bowl.

3. Lightly grease a 9-inch square, or 8x10-inch baking pan, and add the batter.

4. Bake in the center of the preheated oven for 1 hour or until an inserted toothpick comes out clean.

5. Serve warm or at room temperature with crème fraiche or heavy cream and coffee.

June

produce · produce Trout · Sugar Snap Peas · New Potatoes · Mint · Strawberries · Wine

Lilacs, strawberries, new wine, and boats, a Midsummer's Eve warm enough to sleep outdoors, lake cabins, and lawn mowing—everything seems *so* permanent in June. This is the month when the well-honed Minnesota practice of denial about those other, less-colorful months is operating in earnest. Why live anywhere else? After an evening dip in the St Croix, I can't possibly remember. Can you?

Pick Your Own

At harvest time, farmers, who are the very souls of invention, come up with the darnedest contraptions to make picking easier.

The Asparagus Assister we once saw near Lorence's u-pick strawberries was a perilously low picking perch that was hauled along the rows by tractor. The picker, whose rear end is hovering just above the asparagus crowns, can snap off asparagus spears with ease.

Another attempt to save the back was devised by a Norwegian strawberry farmer, who took an old massage bed, added a wheelbase that straddled the berry plants, and strung a rope from one end of the row to the other. With his face positioned over the hole in the bed, the picker could pick any strawberries within reach, then grab the rope and pull himself along the row. Eureka! A massage bed that puts itself out of work.

But the best labor-saving invention of all came to us from Tom Sawyer, who, instead of hoisting a brush, got his friends to whitewash his Aunt Polly's fence by telling them it was so much fun.

Tom had it right: work that's fun doesn't feel like work at all. U-pickers, who are out for a day in the sun and a bucket of berries, have no need for inventions to lighten their load.

A day in the fields picking your own is a chance to sample the skill and rhythm of picking, wonder over the beauty of the plants, and take the best home to eat. For toddlers, this is an especially delicious, squishy experience, full of eye-level color and mystery. Parents teach children, friends halve the work and split the take, and everyone goes home with memories: sand under knees, arms freckling in the sun, a hard spit of rain, the drum roll of a slowly filling pail, and the satisfying pop when a perfectly ripe berry, tomato, or pepper parts from the stem.

Back home in the kitchen, cleaning and sorting echoes the rhythm of picking. Ice cream, pickles, and jam are always more work than anyone imagines, and at this point the extra hands that would be helpful for hulling and slicing tend to vanish. But don't worry, they'll be back for a taste.

Whether it's strawberries, asparagus, or beans, pick-your-own farms have a special etiquette to be observed by guests; it could be where you park or how you pick, but most pick-your-own farms establish guidelines before entrusting their carefully tended plants to people whose horticultural experience is limited to the lawns in front of their houses.

With strawberries, for example, picking begins at a point marked by a flag that is replanted when you are finished to show the next person where to start; strawberries won't ripen off the vine, so only red, ripe ones are fair game; and though the grass always appears greener, and the strawberries redder, on the other side of the patch, courtesy dictates that you stay in your own row.

Pick-your-own asparagus, by contrast, is more like searching for morels: you pick 'em when and where you see 'em. There are few places that offer pick-your-own asparagus, and the window of opportunity is small, but the experience is, well, educational. We'd been trying to find a place to pick asparagus for a couple of years and had all but given up, when on our way back to the Twin Cities at the end of a long day of driving, we chanced upon a box of freshly picked asparagus next to the cash register at a smart-looking garden center in Aitkin. The price was right so we bought some; then learned we could pick it ourselves for less at their farm just north of Lake Mille Lacs on Highway 169. Oh well, you can never get enough asparagus; up the highway to Great River Gardens we went.

A large, colorful sign marked the farm. From the highway we followed a long, tree-lined drive that curved around a modest farmhouse, past an orchard in bloom, and ended in a surprisingly large complex of greenhouses and machine sheds. We parked next to a fleet of trucks bearing the Great River Gardens logo outside a series of high-tunnel greenhouses where half a dozen workers were tending colorful annuals. Beyond the buildings we saw fruit trees spreading across an expanse so wide and flat, it could have been a cotton plantation in the Mississippi Delta.

Wiping the grease from his hands, owner Joe Riehle emerged from beneath a tractor just long enough for a brief hello, then gave us a bag and cursory instructions for picking. We drove in the direction he'd pointed but almost missed the field. From a distance, the asparagus bed looked like bare, plowed-over ground with a stalk sticking up here and there like a cowlick on a kid's head. He'd said it had been picked over the day before, and maybe those leggy stalks were all that was left.

We started down the rows of asparagus crowns, unsure of what to look for, but when we found an asparagus ripe for picking, there was no mistaking it: it was big and muscular, like a nuclear warhead pushing up through the sandy soil. Testing it for the breaking point I snapped off that spear, then found another ten feet down the row and got that one too.

Looking back across the fields, the nursery compound appeared to waver in the oppressive heat, while the blue sky above was pale with haze, and a towering storm cloud gathered strength in the distance. Now it not only looked like the Mississippi Delta, where field workers could look forward to short, but violent, rainstorms most afternoons, but it felt like it too. The picking was slow, and with the next asparagus spear seemingly miles away, we wondered whether we would get to it before the storm would get to us.

Eventually we filled one small bag and drove back to the compound where Joe Riehle weighed our meager pickings, then took a few minutes to talk. He was tired and covered with dirt from a long, taxing day, but had the relaxed easiness of someone who spends most of his time outdoors. He began Great River Gardens on this plot of land in 1986, and it had grown large enough to supply two garden centers and seven farmers' markets—all the while maintaining pick-your-own green beans, berries, tomatoes, and asparagus on the farm. Obviously, the man has a green thumb, but his double major in agronomy and horticulture hasn't hurt either, because if it could be grown in Minnesota, we saw it at Great River Gardens. BJ had been looking for sources of black currant bushes and wisteria without success for years and found them both there. Later we learned that anyone in search of solutions for a garden or lakeshore can get help from a sophisticated, but user-friendly, plant-search function on Riehle's website at www.greatrivergardens.biz.

Picking asparagus was hunting and pecking with an unpredictable rhythm that made our backs ache. But this was a good ache—triumphant, like the soreness that comes from lifting weights at the gym. Our newly gained picking skill was unlikely to break any speed records, but by the end we were beginning to feel a solidarity with asparagus pickers worldwide.

On our way back to the Twin Cities at the end of a long day of driving, we chanced upon a box of freshly picked asparagus next to the cash register at a smart-looking garden center in Aitkin. The price was right so we bought some; then learned we could pick it ourselves for less at their farm just north of Lake Mille Lacs on Highway 169. Oh well, never enough asparagus; up the highway to Great River Gardens we went.

Pick your own, pay by the pound. Great River Gardens owner Joe Riehle weighs our hand-picked asparagus.

From asparagus to pumpkins, Minnesota offers many opportunities to get down with the foods you love to eat; there are pick-your-own places in every direction and in every season except winter—so many it's hard to list them individually. Here are a few we've tried:

Aitkin County

Great River Gardens—in-season pick-your-own and pre-picked asparagus, strawberries, raspberries, and blueberries. 43507 U.S. Highway 169, Aitkin, MN; (218) 927-2521 or (877) 286-3408. Asparagus pops up early—May through mid-June; strawberries are usually available from late June through July; raspberries start in mid-July and run through early fall; and blueberries begin in late July. Call for hours and prices.

Anoka County

Berry Hill Farm—pick-your-own and call-ahead-pre-picked strawberries and summer and fall-bearing raspberries and pumpkins are just some of the fun. Located ten miles north of Anoka and seven miles east of Elk River; (763) 753-5891. Call to arrange weekday school, scouting, or church picnic groups, and other farm-tour and child-care appointments. Open the last weekend of September and all weekends of October for family fun with u-pick pumpkins, wagon rides, farm animals, squash, gourds, ornamental corn, corn bundles, hay bales, and much more. Don't get lost in their large field maze!

Dakota County

Lorence's Berry Farm—strawberries and raspberries for pick-your-own and pre-picking and asparagus, which is always pre-picked. Open May through mid-October in Northfield, Minnesota; (507) 645-9749. Their hours can vary, so call ahead for pick-your-own strawberry and raspberry times; pre-picked berries and asparagus can be ordered up to twenty-four hours in advance. Children are welcome with family supervision, and containers are provided. If none of the Lorences are available, pre-pick orders are left at the roadside stand, with payment by cash or check on the honor system.

Itasca County

Uncle Joe's Berry Patch—six varieties of pick-your-own blueberries in the piney woods south of Grand Rapids, west of Highway 65. Weather dependent, they're generally open weekends mid-July through Labor Day at 34469 Eight Mile Road, Grand Rapids, Minnesota; (218) 327-8056; www.unclejoesberrypatch.com; e-mail: jblauer10@msn.com

Bailey's Raspberries—just across Highway 65, also on Eight Mile Road, east of Uncle Joe's, deep in the woods, you'll find an idyllic setting with three large pick-your-own raspberry patches. These hardy cultivars from the University of Minnesota bear fruit from mid-July through early fall. Be sure and call ahead for hours, (218) 326-5103. This long-established berry patch helped the three Bailey daughters pick their way to college.

Washington County

The Berry Patch—pick-your-own and pre-picked strawberries in June, raspberries and blueberries in July, and orders for tree-ripened Michigan peaches and sweet cherries are also taken in season. Open daily June through September, weather and crop permitting, and located five miles east of Forest Lake, Minnesota, on Hwy 97. Call for hours and complete directions; (651) 433-3448. Supervised children are welcome, and containers are provided.

Natura Farms (formerly North Star Gardens)—you-pick, pre-pick, and wholesale strawberries, raspberries, blueberries, apples, currants, grapes, melons, tomatoes, sweet corn, peppers, other vegetables, herbs, and flowers, all grown by natural, sustainable, environmentally safe practices. Clean, indoor restrooms are available, and children are welcome! Open June–September, Tuesday–Saturday; 10 a.m.–7 p.m., and by appointment. Call to see what's in season. 19060 Manning Trail North, Marine on the St. Croix, Minnesota; (651) 433-5850; e-mail: pmo@chof.net.

Planning Ahead

Freezing Berries

Freezing berries is a good way to preserve fruit. It's fast, simple, and not nearly as messy or time consuming as canning. Except for raspberries, all berries should be rinsed after sorting. If rinsed before freezing, raspberries will turn to mush once they are thawed. The one thing you will need is freezer space. If you can, move frozen foods to another location or an ice chest temporarily to free up room.

Before you begin see "Freezing Basics" on this page.

Equipment you will need:
· Large bowl for washing
· Paper towels for blotting
· Several sided sheet pans lined with parchment or wax paper

Here are a few tips to keep in mind and help you get organized.

1. Sort berries, removing stems and any bruised, spoiled, or overripe fruit. Cover lightly with paper towels and refrigerate until chilled; this chilling is important, as chilled berries are easier to wash and less subject to bruising when handled than those at room temperature.

2. Place several layers of paper towels on the counter next to the sink to use as a draining station.

3. Place a large bowl in the sink and fill it with cold water.

4. Quickly pass berries through the water by hand and remove to the covered counter or board to drain and dry; don't crowd. When the toweling is filled with a single layer of berries, place several sheets of paper toweling on top and gently blot dry.

5. Once they are dried, spread the berries on parchment-lined sided sheet pans in single layers. Don't crowd.

6. Place in freezer, stacking pans in a crisscross fashion, taking care not to rest upper pans directly on top of the berries. Once berries have frozen solid, remove to gallon-sized freezer bags, and stack flat in freezer, one on top of the other. Berries can be frozen up to 9 months.

7. To quick thaw, place sealed bag of berries in a large bowl of cold water for ten minutes, or place the bag (or amount needed) in a bowl and thaw in the refrigerator. Turn berries into sieve- or colander-lined bowl; the juices will collect in the bottom of the bowl. The berries will not be as firm as fresh, but their flavor will be extraordinary. Use the juice for sauces or in reductions for baked goods and syrups.

Wine for the Winter Hardy

For those who have never gone wine tasting in Minnesota or who tried some years ago and were discouraged by unfavorable comparisons to California's Napa Valley, it may come as a surprise that there are now more than twenty farm wineries with tasting rooms where one can linger on a rainy day—even a Sunday—and among those, several where one can leave carrying a case of very creditable wine.

Alexis Bailly Vineyard and Cannon River Winery are two we think stand out from the rest for quality of wine, enjoyable tasting experiences, and the fun of helping with the harvest or becoming a friend of the winery. Both are founding members of the Three Rivers Wine Trail, a tour route in the St. Croix, Cannon, and Mississippi river valleys of six wineries that co-host events, such as Cheese and Chocolate Sunday. Though they are our current personal favorites, there will surely be others thanks to the world-class enology department at the University of Minnesota, where grape varieties like Frontenac, La Crescent, and Marquette have been developed specifically to withstand the rigors of our climate.

One of the nicest aspects of wine tasting in Minnesota is the relative absence of wine snobbery. Despite possessing a skill that would make anyone proud, our vintners see themselves as part of the greater community of local food producers and still have their "we try harder" winning smiles.

Cannon River Winery

Maureen Maloney put aside her natural aversion to walking in deep grass and followed her husband into a cornfield. Had she not, Cannon River Winery might not exist. John Maloney had been searching for a place to plant a vineyard for some time, when the owners of some property where he'd hunted wild turkeys offered him a parcel and he jumped at the chance. The well-drained, south-facing slopes were perfect, but it was hard for Maureen to envision grapevines in place of the corn, which was almost taller than she was.

"I thought he was crazy, but he knew how to grow things. Still, if I'd known what it entailed . . . ."

The Maloneys had owned an environmental restoration business, and John had been planting prairie grasses along highways, restoring wetlands, and controlling erosion for years,

so he could easily envision the major agricultural project they were about to take on. Maureen, however, had economic rather than agricultural expertise, and all she could see was that they were flirting with disaster every step of the way.

It would take thousands of steel stakes, an investment in root stock, and careful tending for three years before the Maloneys would harvest grapes and begin making their own wine. After the stakes were driven into the ground, Maureen's presentiments of disaster returned. "If the venture failed," she thought, "how could anyone else ever farm this land?

Today Maureen sees the chance to buy that cornfield in the rolling Sogn Valley southwest of Cannon Falls as the first in a string of divine interventions. A second was the coincidence that led them to a uniquely qualified vintner, Vincent Negret, who had contacted the enology department at the University of Minnesota looking for a position with a winery at the same time the Maloneys had called looking for a vintner. They struck gold with Negret, a third-generation winemaker from Columbia whose family business had become impossible to continue because of interference from the drug cartels.

A third act of providence, according to Maloney, was the chance to reuse the old Lee Chevrolet building in the historic district of Cannon Falls. The showroom was roomy, yet warm and comfortable, with enough space for wine tanks in the back and a tasting bar, a sales counter, and tables and chairs for visitors in the front.

A beautiful old stone wall that was discovered behind outmoded paneling inspired the decorator in Maureen Maloney. The area that had been the dealership's parts department became a private dining room and has been used for everything from Vincent Negret's Wine 101 class to bridal showers. "If you'd asked me if I'd ever be in the wedding planning business, I would certainly have said no, but the winery quickly became a popular spot for parties, and it's turned out to be fun," said Maloney.

One gloomy Saturday morning, we left town early thinking a wine-tasting trip to Cannon Falls might be the perfect way to shake off the creeping chill from unseasonable weather. Though the tasting room had just opened, a dozen like-minded people were already inside, some clustered around the tasting bar, others in quiet conversation at tables. Toward the back of the room, separated from the cheery warmth by no more than low lighting, were shiny new thousand-gallon tanks, waiting to replace smaller ones the winery had outgrown.

The winery was about to harvest for the fourth time and expected thirty tons of grapes from their twenty acres of land, making them Minnesota's most self-sufficient winery. Vintners often import grapes they cannot grow; Cannon River Winery does too, but only about 30 percent. They're able to grow enough and need only bring in grapes like Chardonnay or Zinfandel that cannot be grown in our climate.

For a three-dollar tasting fee, visitors could taste the winery's fifteen releases. We turned our backs to the weather, edged into a spot along the tasting room bar and began with West 7th White, one of two wines developed for Mancini's Restaurant in St. Paul. The icy rain that pelted the old showroom's windows became ever less important as we worked our way through Cannon River's list. We favored their whites, found some reds worthy of note, and

Wine tasting at Alexis Bailly Vineyard on the Three Rivers Wine Trail.

lingered over the winery's blush (rosé) wines to hear the story of their award-winning label designs. Each rosé carried a picture of one of the owners' grandmothers—all strong personalities that the Maloneys thought matched the distinctive character of their intense fruity blush wines. One was named for Rosella, a mother of fourteen; another for Lorraine, who played piano in St. Paul's Criterion Restaurant; and one for Irene, a schoolteacher. There was even a sweet red wine called Go-Go, for a grandmother so dynamic that a racehorse had been named for her as well.

By the time we finished tasting, the happy specter of the winery's potential cornfield disaster realigning as divine providence was irresistible; so we left Cannon Falls and drove into the Sogn Valley to the vineyard. There among the rolling hills and postcard-pretty farmsteads we found the sign for the vineyard and, because no one was working, a locked gate. But that didn't stop us from visualizing the historic barn the Maloneys had just moved into the vineyard. The iron stakes, née stalks of corn, which haunted Maureen Maloney would be barely visible beneath newly greening vines, and the spiky threat of failure completely overshadowed by the promise of barn dances, weddings, and harvest luncheons. Readers who want to see for themselves rather than trust our imaginations can check the website and donate half a day at harvest time. And while they are gathering the grapes and indulging in the fruits of the harvest, look for signs of cornstalks in between the vines.

Alexis Bailly Vineyard

On our last visit to Alexis Bailly Vineyard—a trip we've taken for fifteen years now—we saw that the front line of Hastings's suburban homes had narrowed the distance between the city and the vineyard—like an army that moved silently in the night, leaving only the faint memory of its heavy trudge. The city's edge has advanced, but not close enough to ruin the wind-in-your-hair feeling that settles over us as we pass beneath the entrance arch and fall in sync with the rows of passing grapevines that propel us toward the grassy forecourt and open door of the winery's tasting room.

We've often gone for festive events, annual open houses, vintage releases, or harvest parties, when the tasting room is filled to overflowing and small groups of visitors have spilled

A day in the country. At the Alexis Bailly Vineyard in Hastings, BJ samples a spring release during the annual June open house. Winter-hardy vines developed at the University of Minnesota have enabled a healthy winemaking industry to flourish in Minnesota.

outside to camp beneath the pines or under the vine-covered pergola. They taste and talk, cradling glasses in their hands or wander off to inspect the vines.

Sometimes there are so many people we don't see master winemaker Nan Bailly right away. It's never long though, before her deep voice and warm infectious laugh welcomes us, and we bask in the notion that we are part of the winery's extended family. We certainly don't know everyone, but there is a thread of familiarity that runs through the crowd that, if we could see the family tree, would connect us all back to Nan or her husband, Sam. They have a way of making us feel so much at home, that if anything's new or different, like the bocce ball court or another bench out back, we take pride and imagine these improvements were added purely for our comfort and enjoyment.

At harvest time we are invited to help, kind of an age-old Tom Sawyer thing that vineyards do, when—with a minimum of instruction—they entrust us with snips and send us to pick between flags in the vines. Wagon loads of grapes are moved from the fields to the winery's cellar during the picking, but the result of our efforts is a small pile—a mere token of goodwill for which we are amply rewarded with wine and treats and allowed to revel in the thought that without us the harvest would not have come in . . . or so the vineyard's employees are kind enough to let us believe. We can leave, but their work is dictated by the elements, their hours at times endlessly long. One harvest it was well after dusk before we set down our glasses and headed for home. The last tractor had just trundled down the cellar ramp, and in the bright spear of light coming from between the still-open doors we could see Nan, bicep high in grape juice and skins, turning and checking the fermentation in huge vats of wine.

Alexis Bailly Vineyard was one of the first to make a real go of winemaking in Minnesota; the vineyard motto, "where the grapes can suffer," tells it all. Founder David Bailly, Nan's father, started the vineyard in 1978, importing the first vines from France. Though he passed away in 1990, his passion for winemaking lives on; we hear about him and Nan's brother, who ran the operation before she did, from growers they befriended across the state.

Their early vines were far from winter hardy, so every fall the vineyard workers were faced with the task of laying the vines in trenches, then covering them with straw, only to unearth them again in spring. Those that have survived are still babied in this way, but with the advent of new winter-hardy grapes, the original ranks of vines have been reinforced with made-for-Minnesota varieties. The awards and rewards have been beyond everyone's expectations. Our current favorite is Voyageur, a blend of grapes from the vineyards newest and oldest vines, which is winning medals, further filling a display wall in the tasting room that is already crowded with ribbons.

The wall of medals makes it look so easy: just blend it like last year's and you win more ribbons—right? Well, maybe. Except that those long-suffering grapes never turn out the same way twice, and the process requires constant adjusting—sometimes at the most inconvenient of times: "I can't tell you the number of times Sam and I have been making wine in our pajamas," Nan once told us.

Come midwinter, we could be thinking of David Bailly's suffering vines or Nan and Sam, who with their pajamas and freezing feet are tinkering with silently sleeping vats of next year's wine. But we, who so eagerly take possession of the winery in summer, are back in the city, well behind the lines of advancing suburban homes, tucked safely in our houses and oblivious to all but the romantic visions of wind in our hair and summer picnics at "our" winery dancing in our heads.

Minnesota Ice:
a Sorbet of Bailly Vineyard's Ratafia

Serves 6

The following ice is nice served as a summer starter, an intermezzo—a between-course summer palate cleanser—or in autumn with crisp ginger snaps after a rich cassoulet.

2 tbsp. Ratafia, Alexis Bailly
   Vineyard's fortified dessert wine
1 c. ginger tea
1 c. apple juice
2 tbsp. granulated sugar
6 sprigs of mint for garnish

Combine all ingredients, stirring so the sugar dissolves, and freeze in a shallow metal or glass dish for one hour. After one hour stir with a whisk, making sure you scrape the sides. Freeze for another half hour then whisk again. Continue freezing for half-hour intervals, scraping with a fork until large fluffy ice crystals are formed. This will take between two and three hours, depending on how full your freezer is. Serve in iced dessert dishes, garnished with sprigs of mint.

June Menu

Minnesota Ice

♦

Grilled Rainbow Trout with
Lemon Pepper Butter

♦

New Potatoes with
Chive Butter

♦

Minted Sugar Snap Peas

♦

Strawberry-Rhubarb
Sunburst Pie

♦

Muddled Mint Tea

Grilled Rainbow Trout with Lemon Pepper Butter

Serves 4

Lake Trout—the big boys lurking in the deep waters—are a freshwater staple in these parts, but the pretty little rainbows flitting through the icy streams that feed the largest of the Great Lakes are the real trophies. Imagine the classic shore lunch: freshly caught fish grilled and basted with butter, a spritz of lemon and a dash of pepper eaten on Lake Superior's shoreline as the sun sets and the loons call; or, consider visiting one of the Minnesota trout farms, then go home, inflate the kiddie pool, make the Lemon Pepper butter, and fire up the grill. Just think of it as a dress rehearsal for next year's big lake vacation.

4 8–10 oz. whole rainbow trout

4 tbsp. fresh chervil or parsley,
  finely minced

Kosher salt and freshly ground
  black pepper

Light oil, canola or soy, for grilling

Lemon Pepper Butter,
  recipe follows

1. Preheat grill or broiler. Rinse each fish in cool running water; gently dry outsides and cavities with paper toweling.

2. Season outside and inside of fish with chervil, salt, and pepper. Brush outsides lightly with oil, and lightly oil grill grate or broiler pan.

3. Evenly space trout on grill grate or broiler pan. Grill or broil 1 minute; carefully flip fish by rolling on its backbone. Tuck 1 tbsp. of chilled Lemon Pepper butter in each cavity, cook 1 minute longer. Serve trout topped with additional butter.

Lemon Pepper Butter

A compound butter can give ordinary dishes a little touch of elegance. It's especially useful when cooking for a crowd; try it for grilling, broiling, or sautéing fish, poultry, and meats. Compound butter can be made ahead, refrigerated for several days, or tightly sealed and frozen up to 4 months. The combinations are endless: tomato and basil, lemon and caper, orange and red onion, thyme and sautéed mushrooms—your choice. All can be made at season's peak and brought out to brighten up a midwinter meal.

½ lb. unsalted butter, softened at
  room temperature

2–3 tbsp. fresh parsley, minced

Zest of 1 lemon, blanched
  and minced (see Tip)

Freshly ground black pepper,
  3–4 turns

Juice of ½ lemon

Place the softened unsalted butter in a mixing bowl. Beat with electric mixer on high until light and fluffy. Add the minced parsley, blanched, minced lemon zest, and ground black pepper, and beat again. Scrape down the sides of the bowl. Add the lemon juice, and beat on high until fluffy. Cover and refrigerate until ready to use.

Tip

Blanch citrus zest with the same method as blanched vegetables described in "Frozen Beans and Other Vegetables" on page 50: Bring a small saucepan of water to a boil; set up an ice-water bath; with a vegetable peeler remove lemon skin in thin strips, avoid cutting into the white layer under the skin (pith) as this is bitter. Drop the citrus peels into the boiling water for no more than a minute, and remove to the ice-water bath. Dry on paper toweling, and mince to the desired size with a sharp knife.

New Potatoes with Chive Butter

Serves 4

With most foods, the first and smallest are often the best and the easiest. Nowhere is this maxim truer than with the first crop of waxy, new potatoes. There's no need for elaborate preparations with these babies. Wipe their shiny red coats clean of dirt, cook in boiling, salted water until tender, toss with butter and salt, garnish with snipped chives—that's it.

1 lb. small, new potatoes

4 tbsp. unsalted butter

Coarse sea or kosher salt, to taste

4 tsp. fresh chives,
    minced (see Tip)

Freshly ground pepper,
    to taste, optional

Fill a quart-sized saucepan ¾ full with water, cover, place over high heat, and bring to a boil. While the water is coming to a boil, clean the potatoes by wiping with damp paper toweling. Add a pinch of salt and the cleaned potatoes to the boiling water, and cook uncovered until tender when pierced with a fork, about 20 minutes. While the potatoes are cooking, mince the chives with a sharp knife or snip with scissors. Drain the potatoes and return to the saucepan. Place the pan over high heat for approximately 30 seconds, shaking it to dry the potatoes. Remove from heat, add butter to the pan, and toss to coat potatoes. Add salt and pepper to taste, add minced chives, and toss to coat. Serve on individual plates or in a casserole.

Tip

Other tender herbs may be substituted for chives. New potatoes dressed with finely minced basil, parsley, garlic chive, or fresh dill can be served with chicken, pork, beef, and fish, respectively.

Minted Sugar Snap Peas

Serves 4

Another easy side dish that says summer's on its way.

1 lb. sugar snap peas

1 bunch fresh mint leaves,
  spearmint if possible,
  stems removed

2 tsp. unsalted butter, softened

2 tbsp. water; mineral or charged
  will add a little zip

Coarse sea salt

1. Top and tail sugar snap peas by pulling off stems and threadlike strings. Slice peas on the diagonal into ½-inch pieces. Remove mint stems, layer leaves on top of each other, and finely mince.

2. Place peas, mint, butter, 2 tbsp. water, and a sprinkle of salt in a medium sauté pan; bring to a boil. Reduce heat to medium, and cook about 3 minutes. The peas should be bright green, tender, and coated with emulsified butter and water.

Strawberry-Rhubarb Sunburst Pie

Serves
4 to 6

This rich, cream-filled pie gets its name from the pretty concentric circles of halved strawberries on the top. A layer of toasted almonds beneath the cream filling keeps the crust from getting soggy and adds an unexpected crunch with a burst of rich flavor to the strawberries and cream.

1 9-inch ready-made pie crust,
    baked (see recipe on page 113)
¾ c. sliced almonds,
    toasted evenly
1–2 c. small to medium halved
    strawberries, enough to cover
    the top of the pie

Cream Filling
¼ c. cold water
1 envelope unflavored gelatin
2 tbsp. strawberry-rhubarb
    jam, warmed
1 c. whole milk, scalded
½ c. granulated sugar
¼ tsp. salt
4 large egg yolks, slightly beaten
½–¾ c. heavy cream, whipped
½ tsp. almond extract

Glaze
4 tbsp. strawberry-rhubarb
    jam, warmed
1 tsp. hot water

Crust
1. Preheat oven to 400°F. If using a premade crust, thaw in the refrigerator; for an easy homemade crust, see recipe on page 113.

2. Line pie crust with parchment or aluminum foil and fill with dried beans or pie weights. Place in the center of the oven, and bake for 10 minutes. Remove paper and beans/weights, and continue baking for 5 minutes, or until light golden brown. Remove from oven, and set aside to cool; turn off oven.

Cream Filling
1. Soak the gelatin in the ¼ c. cold water to soften; stir into warm jam and set aside.

2. Scald the milk in a heavy-bottomed saucepan over low heat, stirring occasionally, bringing it just below the boiling point. When bubbles form around the inside edges of the pot and steam is beginning to come off the milk, remove from the heat. Let the milk cool to room temperature so it doesn't cook or heat any of the ingredients to which it is being added. While milk is scalding, fill the bottom of a double boiler ⅓ full of water and bring to a simmer.

3. Mix sugar, salt, and beaten egg yolks in the top of the double boiler; gradually stir in several tablespoons of scalded milk until mixture is smooth and sugar begins to dissolve. Gradually stir in the remaining scalded milk.

Tip
Poking the crust with a fork, a technique called docking, releases the air from the pastry to keep it from puffing up while baking.

Cont.

4. Place pan over, not in, simmering water in the bottom of the double boiler. Increase heat to high, bringing the water in the bottom to a boil, while constantly stirring the egg/milk mixture. When the mixture begins to thicken, stir in softened gelatin and jam mixture until dissolved, reduce the heat and continue stirring until the mixture is thick enough to heavily coat the back of a spoon. Loosely cover with parchment or wax paper, refrigerate until cool or partially set, about 30–45 minutes.

5. Whip heavy cream until stiff, adding almond extract at the end; set aside. Remove pastry cream from refrigerator, stir vigorously with a spoon to smooth and quickly fold in the whipped cream. Cover and refrigerate until almost set, 1–2 hours.

Assembly

Sprinkle toasted almonds over the bottom of the cooled crust. Fill crust with chilled, but not fully set, cream filling. Smooth the surface with the back of a large spoon that has been dipped in cold water. Carefully arrange halved strawberries in concentric circles on top of cream filling, cut side up as shown below.

Glaze

Place the strawberry rhubarb jam in a glass measuring cup with a lip, gradually stir in hot water, and stir until smooth. Slowly pour over the top of the strawberries, spreading evenly with a pastry brush. Keep refrigerated until serving time.

The Perfect Pot of Tea

Tea must be the most universal of beverages; thousands of years and millions of cups tell us so. Brewed for purposes of pleasure, as well as for its restorative powers, by generations of alchemists and grandmothers, tea can be made from almost any dried, nonpoisonous plant, and mint is the most common of these.

The greatest concentration of essential oils and the fullest flavor is achieved when all of the tea ingredients are thoroughly dried in a cool, airy, dark environment. With few differences, every pot is brewed the same way:

Fill a teakettle with freshly drawn cold water and bring it to a boil. In the meantime, warm the teapot with very hot water. Once the water comes to a boil, remove the kettle from the heat; drain the teapot, and add 1 rounded tsp. of dried tea for each cup, plus 1 for the pot. Pour the boiled water into the teapot, cover, and let steep for 3–5 minutes.

The type of tea dictates the amount needed for brewing a proper cup:
- Black and whole leaf teas: 1 heaping tsp. per cup
- Processed or bagged teas: 1 scant tsp., or one bag per cup
- Herbal teas: as much as 1 tbsp. dried leaves per cup
- Iced teas: brew double strength; chill and serve over ice

For instant iced tea, make it triple strength. To keep the glass from cracking, place a metal tablespoon in the glass before adding the hot tea. Pour over ice, leaving room so you can add more ice if needed.

Muddled Mint Tea
Serves 4 to 6

Muddled Mint Tea is a Mint Julep without the whiskey.

8–10 fresh mint leaves

4 tsp. dried mint

1 tbsp. granulated sugar

4 fresh mint springs and 4 lemon
  slices for garnish

Rinse fresh mint leaves and place them in the bottom of a 1 qt. pitcher or a 1 qt. glass measuring cup. Add dried mint and sugar and bruise, or "muddle," with the back of a spoon or a pestle. Add boiling water and let steep 3–5 minutes. Taste for sweetness, and adjust while the tea is still hot. Cover and refrigerate or strain over ice if serving immediately. Serve in tall glasses garnished with fresh mint leaves and a slice of lemon.

July

Honey · Farm Fresh Eggs · Pickling Cucumbers · Hungarian Pepper-Bacon · Potatoes
· Beets · Blueberries · Raspberries

July. The word lies languid on the tongue. Come midsummer evenings, even busy Minnesotans linger at the picnic table to listen as nature pulses all around. Hummingbirds and bees skirmish over the phlox until sunset, the garden grows wild when no one's looking, and the scent of dill from cucumbers turning into pickles on the kitchen counter fills the house at night. Before dawn, trucks fairly bursting with plenty—flowers, squash, and curly greens—jockey for position at our farmers' market stalls, the colors of summer spilling out as vendors hurriedly spread their wares. Now is the time to take a long-neglected friend berry picking, because the bushes are loaded and conversations come easy when there's a field ahead to be journeyed one berry at a time.

On the Seventh Day, a CSA

Whether in acronym or in full lackluster form, the term CSA, or Community Supported Agriculture, is maddeningly ambiguous. Whoever came up with it should pay penance by renouncing further affiliation with nouns, because, grammatically speaking, how can a garden or a farm be an agriculture?

Simply put, a CSA is a cooperatively run agricultural enterprise funded by shareholders who, in return for buying shares, get weekly boxes of vegetables, a turkey for Thanksgiving, or a constant supply of fresh flowers. There are CSAs for everything—cheese, wine, honey, chicken, eggs, or butter. The permutations of this good idea are endless. Shares can be purchased with cash, labor, or both, but some startup seed money is necessary, almost always paid in advance. The goods can be picked up on the farm, at a convenient distribution spot, such as a farmers' market, or, more rarely, delivered directly to your door.

The first time I saw home-delivered CSA produce it came in a dog food bag, still covered with dirt; but now that CSAs come in all sorts of shapes and sizes, some growers have made product presentation a high art form. At the farmers' market in Stillwater, we saw boxes of colorful, carefully washed, and artfully arranged produce from Blue Roof Organics. For sale alongside them, as if to underscore the idea of shopping for beautiful edibles, were color photos of the boxes that had been made into picture postcards.

BJ and I liked the idea of Mother Nature making the grocery list, so we decided to do a little CSA shopping to untangle the options. Here are two we found particularly interesting.

Common Ground Garden

"When I taste the summer's first tomato it's just like tasting the wine of God," said the quiet but sure voice on the other end of the phone when I'd called to ask about the benefits of buying a share in Common Ground Garden, a CSA located in St. Joseph, Minnesota.

If those words had been uttered by any other tomato lover, I might have glossed over them. Instead, I adjusted the telephone, sat up straight, and took note of Sister Phyllis' musings. Sister Phyllis, after all, was not only a nun and an octogenarian, but thirty-five years as a professor of biology at the College of St. Benedict underscored her authority on the subject of physical sustenance. Her garden sounded like it was divinely inspired, but from all reports, its role as a sustainable food resource for St. Joseph, Minnesota, is rooted firmly in the Earth.

Retirement was just a comma rather than a full stop in a list of lifetime accomplishments for the sprightly sounding Benedictine. Freed from the school year's schedule, Sister Phyllis' interest in the natural world took wing. At the time, the ideas she adopted were revolutionary for St. Joseph, but Sister Phyllis was determined to put what she'd gleaned about sustainable agriculture around the world into practice. The first American CSA was established in New Jersey in the 1980s. When ground was broken on St. Ben's campus in 1993, Sister Phyllis knew of no other CSAs in the state. And so, not long after the first American CSA was established in New Jersey in the 1980s, ground was broken on the St. Benedict's campus for Common Ground Garden, the region's first CSA. Once the garden was up and running, Sister Phyllis saw a further need and cofounded the St. Joseph Farmers' Market.

"My aim is to teach people not to eat cherries in December. Eat local and eat in season," she said, inviting us to the monastery for a tour of Common Ground Garden. She didn't have to ask twice.

As a Norwegian-Lutheran who spent seven years in the heavily Catholic city of New Orleans writing about St. Joseph's Day altars, Blessings of the Fleet, and All Saints Day, I am irresistibly drawn to the decidedly un-Lutheran mysteries of the mother church. Among my Gulf Coast friends are those who bury statues of St. Joseph upside down in the lawn to improve chances of a quick home sale; others are otherwise unflappable urbanites who hastily utter prayers to St. Anthony when their house keys go missing or uptown socialites who display ashes with their hangovers on the Wednesday after Mardi Gras. So when Sister Phyllis invited us to join her at the monastery for dinner, I pictured us among sackcloth-robed men whose life work was sliding bread in and out of big cavernous ovens at St. John's University.

Though we did go to the monastery, BJ and I met no monks, nor did we see a single loaf of the famous St. John's handmade bread. It turned out that ever since Vatican II, "monastery" is the gender-neutral name for both monasteries and convents, and we were in what was formerly a convent: only sisters, no brothers, and the woman who met us at the market was hardly the wimpled nun I'd imagined on the other end of the telephone.

Slight and wiry, with fine gray hair cut in a bang that swept her brow, Sister Phyllis motioned for us to follow as she jumped into an anonymous and scrupulously clean Buick with the number forty-six pasted to the dash.

It was part of the convent fleet, she confided as she drove purposefully across town, "but there aren't forty-five others."

Presided over by the dark, iron-colored dome of St. Benedict's chapel, St. Joseph resembles a Grant Wood Midwestern landscape with velvety green lawns and towering elms. There was no clear demarcation at the edge of the town, and we'd been on church grounds for several blocks before we realized we were at the monastery. All the institutional buildings, some with matronly brick edifices, others of practical 1950s construction, were golden and glowing, painted by a setting sun that sank smartly toward the horizon beneath a mushrooming bank of purplish blue clouds. At one vantage point the buildings petered out, leaving a long unbroken view of fields and woods.

When the first Benedictine nuns came to St. Joseph, the monastery was required to be self-sufficient, and nearly 300 acres were devoted to producing their own food. Today the sisters are more likely to get their fare from a food wholesaler, but the land and some of the farm buildings remained, and Sister Phyllis had worked to rededicate a small area to something closer to its original use—a sustainable food source, this time for those outside the monastery.

As we drove onto the monastery grounds, we passed sturdy vegetables planted in charmingly crooked rows, a handsomely constructed high-tunnel greenhouse, and a children's garden—planted by local grade-schoolers.

College-aged student workers whose after-school work is to plant, harvest, and painstakingly remove potato bugs under the tutelage of Common Ground's only full-time, paid gardener were just packing up their tools for the day and waved at Sister Phyllis as we passed. The workers grow for sixty-five families, each of which buys a $375 annual share that can feed four throughout the entire growing season. The garden operates as an outreach mission as well, welcoming children and parents for garden blessings, taste tests, and ice cream socials.

The Common Ground office was a whimsy of engineering located in an old milk house next to the barn that once housed the convent's dairy herd, and Sister Phyllis had patched solar panels, golf cart batteries, and car parts together to provide light and electricity. In keeping with the CSA's "no waste" philosophy, a compost system of impressive proportions was cooking away not far from the barn. Everywhere we saw that normally discarded objects had found new life through recycling—even the straw mulch around the grapevines was an agricultural byproduct from one of the St. Joseph Farmers' Market vendors, Forest Mushrooms, who'd exhausted its function as a medium for growing fungus.

While we were admiring the vineyard, an elderly sister with a wimple peddled slowly past us on a three-wheeled bicycle whose rear basket was loaded with packages. Sister Phyllis giggled, "That's the preferred means of transportation around here."

Once there had been more traffic on the monastery grounds. When Sister Phyllis joined the order in 1949 there were 1,200 nuns, but at St. Ben's today there are only 260, many in their eighties and nineties.

"Our diminishing numbers doesn't mean we're going to die. We're just being culled I think. Oh, that's not the best word, is it?"

Despite diminishing numbers, they were a cheerful group, welcoming BJ, her service dog, Grace, and me to the evening meal. You would have thought Grace had dropped straight out of heaven just to make them smile. It's not politic to pet a service dog, but it seemed even less politic to say no to a circle of elderly nuns, all with outstretched arms.

The meal was barely finished when a tornado siren sent us all scurrying for cover. Alice in Wonderland would have felt right at home in the tunnel beneath the St. Benedict's chapel. The report of a funnel cloud spotted one mile west of town passed from nun to nun, but no one seemed the least bit concerned.

"If only we brought our cards," said one as she passed beneath the arch that proclaimed *Ora et Labora* (Work and Pray). "We could have played poker."

Nick's Eggs and More

"A full stomach is the best fence," opined Kathy Zeman regarding the animals roaming all over Simple Harvest Farm, her budding CSA next to Nerstrand Big Woods near Northfield.

Sheep, cattle, goats, pigs, ducks, and chickens graze freely or in large penned areas on this work-in-progress farm, and though the free-range animals might stray across the road, they're usually home for dinner. Besides, someone's home keeping an eye on everything, because Kathy Zeman loves her farm home and seldom leaves it, making contact with this CSA easy and entertaining. People stop by for eggs, to order a goose, or just to hang out and chat, which is ok, until visiting time cuts into Kathy or Nick Zeman's chores.

When we visited, Kathy did her best to keep things rolling while telling us how her present farming methods marry state-of-the-art agricultural practices with what she learned growing up on a farm. As we talked, Kathy checked on piglets, watered her goats, and recorded the temperature of the incubators temporarily housed in her farmhouse living room.

The fourth of twelve children raised on a dairy farm, this former Princess Kay of the Milky Way is happier on a farm than any place else on Earth. Half of her brothers and sisters are farmers too and, like Kathy, are the modern version: college educated, environmentally savvy, and articulate. Two of them became her partners when she bought the small sixty-acre farm with its rolling hills and highly eroded soil. Abused by years of row cropping, the land was only good for grazing, but free-range animals were exactly what Kathy, her sister Theresa, and brother Nick had in mind when they took on the place the year before. Nick and Kathy live on the premises and run the CSA full-time, with marketing help from Theresa, a registered nurse who has converted a nearby farm into a long-term care facility.

Before they began farming in earnest, the siblings had to spend most of their time hauling garbage out of the grove of trees near their farmhouse and repairing buildings. It took the greater part of a year to remove old farm equipment, baby carriages, and cars left by several generations of the farm's former owners; a lesson that became a small crusade for Kathy, who now lectures every old farmer she can find about dumping on the land. Now the small wooded area is home to a romping herd of pigs, a gaggle of geese, ducks, and a flock of Icelandic sheep, whose wool Kathy spins into yarn during long winter evenings.

So far, of all the farm's products Nick's eggs are the most profitable. They are a source of pride for the entire family.

The yarn and forty kinds of homemade goat's milk soap are fruits of the farm's winter activities, while in summer, there's a cornucopia of offerings available at the farm or for purchase at the Northfield Farmers' Market. In addition to traditional weekly garden produce, chicken, lamb, pork, ducks, geese, and turkeys can be ordered ahead through the CSA. Even though the business is just getting off the ground, it's already been established as a farm tour destination for area elementary schools.

So far, of all the farm's products, Nick's eggs are the most profitable: They lure people back time and time again and are a source of pride for the entire family. Nick was born with Down's syndrome, and his parents obtained a solemn promise from the other eleven children to teach and guide him. Now in his thirties, Nick carries many farm responsibilities, including the raising and care of poultry and the egg sales.

Nick came home while we were walking the farm with Kathy. He showed us the charming hen house made from the old farm granary and, as we chatted, deftly gathered eggs from beneath chickens who clucked contentedly in their sunlit cubicles. He sells his pale blue, brown, and speckled golden eggs to customers who stop by the farm, at the co-op, and in gift baskets that also feature bounty from a number of local farmers. Nick also holds a part-time job at the co-op in Northfield.

Even the pigs at Simple Harvest Farm benefit from Nick's endeavors—produce department and deli leftovers become part of their feed. At the end of our visit, when we were sitting at the kitchen table, Nick went outside and rummaged around in the refrigerator on the porch. He returned carrying a bag, which he presented to BJ with a proud smile. To BJ's delight, Nick launched into a sales pitch for the homemade dog biscuits he makes in his spare time. Since Grace automatically assumed the biscuits were hers, BJ could not get away without buying them. She would have anyway, because Nick and his sales pitch were so completely irresistible.

The Pickle and Pepper Guys

I used to think that vegetable preserves were a lost art, the province of nostalgic, easy-going middle-agers like BJ and me or the long, dear habit of our most elderly relatives, until two friends of mine, both male, casually referred to their home canning projects in the same week. They are middle-aged too, and very likely nostalgic, but they just don't fit the mold. These two, each in their own way, are the two edgiest men I know.

One of them makes pickles and the other pickles peppers. If you put them together, and believe me you wouldn't want that much testosterone in the same kitchen, you'd get the Pickle and Pepper Guys from Poland and her naughty neighbor to the south, Serbia.

Despite the fact that both emigrated from Eastern Europe in their youth, they are dissimilar as the dill pickles and sweet hot peppers that come out of their kitchens. One is a scientist, creative in an elegant theoretical way but, dogged by the goose step of a highly competitive job, he's inclined to use a slab of duct tape to solve real-world problems. The other is an artist, who's managed to live in the outskirts of the working world most of his life. Half Serbian and half Austrian, he builds everything with the precision of a Swiss watch; his tasty, slightly wacky designs put a Euro-modern spin on an array of whimsies from bird houses to bathroom mirrors.

The scientist makes pickles, crock pickles, the kind that sit on the kitchen counter under a gray froth of bacteria for a few weeks, filling the house with the delicious scent of dill and garlic. During the brining process you can grab them at will, rinse, and eat them out of hand. If the bacteria have gone a little too far, they start to go soft, and the pickles migrate to the fridge, where they last longer.

In Poland the pickles are called sour cucumbers, and the source of my friend's yen for them was a crock filled in autumn by the family cook in the Warsaw walk-up flat where he lived as a child. When the yen reaches the pickle-making point he begins with a few calls to the now-aged cook, a peek into a dog-eared Polish

> *The scientist makes pickles, crock pickles, the kind that sit on the kitchen counter under a gray froth of bacteria for a few weeks, filling the house with the delicious scent of dill and garlic.*

cookbook and a search for spices whose names simply wouldn't translate into English.

Next is a trip to the farmers' market where, in his Eastern European way, he looks over every bushel of cucumbers in the whole market before parking himself in front of the best and starting to bargain. The Midwestern farmer who grew the cukes is usually so stunned by the audacity of this dickering foreigner that negotiations come to an abrupt conclusion, and our scientist begins again, this time setting his sights on fresh dill.

Once home, he gathers a jewel-like assortment of Polish glass vases, assesses their collective volume, and boils enough salt water to cover the cucumbers. Then he turns to washing the future pickles. I've watched the pickle-making process several times, and the spices may vary from year to year—once he even added bread—but the homily that is delivered while he stands before a sink full of bobbing cucumbers is always the same: "The Wonder of Bacteria" and how much of the useful stuff might be washing down the drain.

The final step is to layer the washed cucumbers in the containers with sprigs of dill, garlic cloves, and spices; add the salt water and float little saucers on the top to keep the cucumbers from popping up. *Nosdrovia!* Within the week there are pickles, of which he eats mountains, gifting the rest to a privileged few during the month or so that he has them.

His pickles have a texture and a flavor so much fresher than anything found in a store that I've started to think of them as soured—or dilled—cucumbers too. When you bite into one, the skin resists a bit then gives way with a snap, filling your mouth with flavor and juice. Since they are not hot-water-bath canned like conventional pickles, the sour cucumber season is pretty short, and I've come to crave them in late summer and early fall. Now every time I smell fresh dill I think of fall, and the whole pleasant process comes to mind again.

And now for the Austrian/Serb and his Hungarian peppers. He came to this country as a child and brought a lifelong craving for strudel and sweet brined peppers along with him. At home, a coffee klatch is usually in progress and his front door admits a steady flow of visitors, most with offbeat jobs like his, who come to admire his latest project or kvetch a little about the world. Unlike my friend the pickle man, the pepper guy is into presentation and out to produce an impressive batch of uniformly perfect pepper jars.

He begins the same way, buying the prettiest banana peppers he can find at the farmers' market—some sweet and some hot—then he boils a syrup of vinegar, sugar, salt, dill seed, peppercorns, and cumin for twenty minutes and strains it into a small army of canning jars filled with pepper slices, adding a garlic clove and a slice of jalapeno pepper before closing the jars. Now comes the best part: he rigs a black background and photographs himself under a key light studying a pepper as if it held the mystery of the universe, then he makes a label for the top of the jar.

At the end of his endeavors, the kitchen counter is full of uniform glass jars, each with a handsome black label, just waiting for the next friend to stop by. The pickled peppers are stored in the refrigerator and, just like the sour cucumbers, they are part of the ephemera of the season, lasting only as long as it takes for us to eat them all.

Frozen Beans and Other Vegetables

Freezing vegetables is a great way to preserve the garden's bounty. Essentially, the technique is the same used for berries and other fruits, but the preparation takes more time. Once washed, cut the vegetables, other than peas and corn, into same-sized pieces; this ensures they will freeze and cook evenly. Most vegetables will need to be blanched and shocked prior to freezing. Blanching partly cooks the vegetables so their flavor will be sealed, and shocking stops the cooking, preserving texture and color. Below are general tips and a timetable on blanching, shocking, and freezing individual vegetables.

Before you begin, refer to Freezing Basics on page 33.
You will need:
Large pots for blanching
Large bowls for ice-water bath
Strainers and colanders
Slotted spoons and spatulas
Long tongs
Paper and/or terry towels to wipe spills and containers
Several sets of hot pads; it's important to keep them dry

1. Lay out all equipment and utensils needed, in the area and in the order you will be using them.

2. Wash and cut vegetables to desired size.

3. Bring 4 quarts of unsalted water to a boil.

4. While water comes to a boil, set up ice-water bath. Set colander in sink near ice-water bath.

5. Blanch vegetables by plunging briefly into the boiling water; timing starts the second the vegetables hit the water. Do no more than 1 pound of vegetables at a time.

6. Blanch vegetables for the time specified on the table.

7. Remove with a strainer to the ice bath for shocking. This step is very important because it instantly lowers the core temperature of the vegetable, halts the cooking, and results in a par-cooked rather than an over-cooked product.

8. Once blanched and shocked, drain in colander and shake off excess water.

9. Spread in single layers on cookie sheets and freeze.

10. Once frozen, transfer to gallon-sized freezer bags, shake to flatten, and freeze in stacks.

11. Use frozen vegetables within 8–10 months. For best color and texture, do not thaw before cooking.

Vegetable Blanching/Freezing Timetables

Amounts given are equivalent to 1 pint in volume, or 2 cups. Blanching time is calculated according to the sizes of the individual vegetable pieces.

Vegetable	Size	Quantity	Time (minutes)
Asparagus	1 inch or spears	1–1½ lbs.	2–4
Beans	¼ inch or whole	2–4 lbs.	2–4
Beets	peeled, sliced ½ inch	1¼–1½ lbs.	3–5
Broccoli	1–2-inch florets	1½–2 lbs.	3–5
Brussels Sprouts	¾–1 inch	1–1½ lbs.	3–5
Cabbage	quartered and cored	1–1½ lbs	3–4
Carrots	peeled, 1 inch or whole	1–1½ lbs.	cut: 2/whole: 5
Cauliflower	1–2-inch florets	1¼–1 ½ lbs.	2–4
Celery	½–¾ inch	¾–1 lb.	3
Corn	kernels	2–2½ lbs.	3
Eggplant	peeled, ½-inch slices, salted and blotted dry	2–3 lbs.	1 ½
Greens	see individual names in Greens, page 63.		
Kohlrabi	peeled; ½-inch dice	1¼–1½ lbs.	½
Parsnips	¾-inch slices	1¼–1½ lbs.	2
Peas	shelled and pods	2–3 lbs.	1½
Peppers			
Bell	roasted, peeled, halved, seeded	1–3 lbs. no need to blanch	
Jalapeño	roasted, whole/halved, seeded	1–3 lbs. no need to blanch	
Banana	halved, seeded	1–3 lbs.	no need to blanch
Rhubarb	½–1-inch dice	⅔–1 lb.	1
Rutabaga	peeled; ½–1-inch dice	1¼–1½ lbs.	1
Squash			
Summer: zucchini, yellow, patty pan	trimmed; ½-inch dice	½ lb.	2–3
Winter: acorn, Hubbard, turban	peeled, seeded, cut until soft—best roasted	1½–2 lbs.	

July Menu

Not Your "Big Box" Lunch

Honey Lemonade

♦

Nick's Devilish Eggs

♦

Crock Pickles

♦

Minnesota BLTs

♦

Pickled Pink Potato Salad

♦

Blueberry-Raspberry

Honey Lemonade: A State Fair Favorite

Of the many offerings at the Great Minnesota Get-Together every August, nothing is as satisfying as the sweet-and-sour honey lemonade found in the bee and honey exhibition. Escape from the heat of a hot Fair afternoon into the distinctively shaped Agriculture-Horticulture building, grab a glass of this ice-cold sweet-sour elixir, and chill out in the exhibit. Minnesota is one of the largest honey producers in the United States, and, as a stroll along the glass-fronted display cases crammed with live hives, candles, and baked goods reveals, the state's many hobby beekeepers have been as busy as the insects they tend. Don't forget to grab a seat for one of the hourly honey extraction demonstrations.

Honey is high in sucrose, so a lesser amount is required when using it in place of granulated sugar. The ratio is: 1 liquid-measure c. of honey for every 1½ dry-measure c. of granulated sugar when using it as a substitute sweetener in cold and hot liquids. The key to combining honey effectively with other liquids is to warm it. This is done easily by immersing the whole jar or container of honey in warm water for a few minutes.

Honey Lemonade Syrup

Makes
3 c. syrup

Make this syrup in quantity and store it in the refrigerator for lemonade on the spot.

¾ c. light honey
1 c. water
⅛ tsp. salt
Rind of 2 lemons, cut into strips
Juice of 6 lemons

1. Combine the honey, water, salt, and lemon rind in a heavy-bottomed saucepan and bring to a boil for 5 minutes.

2. Cool and add the freshly squeezed lemon juice.

3. Strain and refrigerate in a tightly covered glass jar.

Honey Lemonade

To make the honey lemonade, fill an 8 oz. glass with ice; add tap, spring, or carbonated water and 2 tbsp. of the lemonade syrup, and stir. Garnish with a bruised sprig of fresh mint and lemon zest if desired.

Nick's Devilish Eggs

Serves 6

While searching southeastern Minnesota for Laura Ingalls Wilder's Big Woods, we found a young, smiling, multitasking man named Nick gathering eggs from his dozens of chickens, geese, and ducks. Nick has, according to his older sister, a rather impish demeanor that he comes by quite naturally.

1 dozen large chicken eggs

½ c. prepared mayonnaise

½ c. full-fat sour cream

½ tsp. dried mustard

¼ tsp. cayenne pepper for seasoning, plus a sprinkle for garnish

Kosher or coarse sea salt, to taste

¼ lb. bacon, crisp-cooked and crumbled

¼ c. parsley leaves, finely minced

1. Fill a large saucepan with enough cold water to cover the dozen eggs. Add a pinch of salt, place the uncovered pan over high heat, and bring to a boil. Once the water begins to boil, remove the pan from the heat, cover, and let sit for 12–15 minutes.

2. While the water is coming to a boil and the eggs are resting, mix mayonnaise, sour cream, mustard, cayenne, and salt in a medium-sized bowl. Add crumbled bacon and minced parsley; set aside. Prepare an ice-water bath in a large bowl.

3. Drain the hard-boiled eggs, and immediately place in the ice-water bath for 5–10 minutes. Once cooled drain again. Refrigerate unshelled eggs in a tightly covered container for up to 3 days. If using right away, roll the eggs in a kitchen towel to crack the shells; the shell should peel off easily and cleanly. Cut the eggs in half lengthwise, scoop the yolks into a bowl, and arrange the whites on the kitchen towel, cut side up.

4. Mash the egg yolks in a large bowl with the back of a fork or push through a ricer. Fold in the prepared dressing, taste for seasoning, and adjust. Place egg yolk mixture in a pastry bag fitted with a large star tip or in a gallon-sized zip-top bag and snip one corner off after filling; pipe into the cooked egg whites.

5. Line a platter or shallow bowl with chopped lettuce or cabbage leaves, arrange the egg halves on the top, garnish with cayenne, and serve.

You Can Teach an Old Chef New Tricks—A Recipe for Crock Pickles

Serves
4 to 6

I came from a long, long line of prestige pickle makers and always dreamed of getting my recipe on the Gedney Pickle Jar. But when I tasted these wonderful old-world crock pickles I knew I had some serious competition. Far easier than canning pickles, this quick method of pickle making is a short-term science project the whole family can enjoy.

½ bushel or 30–40 cucumbers: 3–4 inches long and 1 inch in diameter

2 qt. water

4 tbsp. rock salt

2 bunches of mature stalks of dill (the woody stalks are the important part; the seed heads are just window dressing)

2 tbsp. white vinegar

4 bay leaves

Small piece of dried pepper, or ⅛ tsp. dried red pepper flakes

1 tsp. mustard seed

4 black peppercorns

2 whole cloves

1 tsp. coriander seed

4 garlic cloves

2–3 whole allspice

1 slice of sourdough rye bread

A 2-gallon straight-sided pickle crock, or several large glass containers

A ceramic dinner plate or saucers to fit inside crock/containers

1. Make the brine by boiling 2 qt. water; add the salt and cool.

2. While the brine is cooling, wash the cucumbers, but don't scrub too hard. The bacteria in the cucumber skin are key to the pickling process.

3. Layer the cucumbers with the dill stalks and other spices in the pickle crock or glass jars—if you are using glass jars, this can be done in a decorative way.

4. Mix vinegar with the brine and pour enough into the container(s) so the cucumbers will be fully submerged when topped with a weighted plate.

5. Add the bread and place a sealed jar of water on the plate heavy enough to submerge the pickles. Keep in a place that isn't too cool.

6. After 3 or 4 days a scum will start to form on top of the container and the smell of dill will fill your house. Good, the process is working! Be sure to keep the pickles fully submerged, out of contact with the scum.

7. The length of time it takes for the pickles to mature depends on the warmth in your kitchen: 7–10 days is a good guess. Test after a week by pulling one out of the brine, rinsing off the foam, and tasting it.

8. If you like the firmness (we think they're best when the outside is crisp and the inside is full of juice), remove the bread, pull a few out, rinse, and serve. You can now eat them a few at a time for several weeks. If they are getting soft, you'll want to remove them from the brine altogether and rinse to stop the pickling process. Store them in the refrigerator; it is not necessary to keep them in liquid.

If It Ain't Broke . . . Minnesota BLTs

Makes 4
sandwiches

What can we do to improve a BLT? Nuthin'. It's the all-American sandwich. Period. But new twists on old ingredients can raise it to new heights. We used spicy Hungarian pepper bacon and the best tomatoes we could find. This is not the place to scrimp on anything, and that goes for the mayo and the napkins too.

8 slices white sourdough toast

8 pieces of leaf lettuce, washed and dried

1 large vine-ripened beefsteak tomato, top and bottom trimmed, cut into four equal slices

6–8 slices Hungarian pepper bacon, crisply cooked

½ c. mayonnaise, homemade if possible

1. Lay 4 slices of toasted bread on a clean cutting surface and spread each slice with a generous amount of mayonnaise.

2. Top each toast slice with 1–2 dried lettuce leaves, followed by one slice of tomato and 1½ crisp slices bacon.

3. Place a dollop of mayonnaise on each slice of bacon; this will secure the top piece of toast. Top with remaining toast slices, pressing down on each.

4. Cut sandwiches on the bias and serve with some of those crock pickles you made last week.

Pickled Pink Potato Salad

Serves
4 to 6

This dish came into the world backwards. Shelley came up with a catchy name for pairing two of Minnesota's favorite vegetables, then I wrestled the roots into a recipe. Its color may shock you at first, but one bite and you'll be saying, "Why didn't I think of that?"

4 c. small red potatoes, with skins
2 c. pickled beets, homemade or the best commercial brand you can get
¾ c. good-quality commercial mayonnaise
¾ c. sour cream
4 tbsp. fresh tarragon leaves minced, or 2 tbsp. dried
3 tbsp. chopped chives
White pepper and salt, to taste
3 hard-boiled eggs, quartered
A nice, full sprig of fresh tarragon, for garnish
Course salt for garnish

1. Wash potatoes and cook whole in boiling, salted water, uncovered, until they are easily pierced with a fork.

2. While potatoes are cooking, drain and cut the beets the same size as the potatoes.

3. Mix mayonnaise, sour cream, tarragon, 1 tbsp. chopped chives, and freshly ground white pepper together.

4. Quarter potatoes while still warm, and taste the skin. If it seems bitter, peel the cooked potatoes before dressing.

5. Carefully mix cooked potatoes with beets; fold in mayonnaise mixture, taste for salt and pepper, and adjust.

6. Garnish the top of the salad with quartered hard-boiled eggs, and sprinkle them with remaining chopped chives, whole tarragon, and coarse salt. This salad is stable and can be served at room temperature inside or out. If you're eating outside, be sure to cover the salad with a napkin or paper towel to keep the uninvited guests, i.e., flies and hornets, away.

A Classic Gets a Dusting and an Update: Raspberry-Blueberry Cream Cheese Shortcakes

Serves
4 to 6

You've heard the expression, "Best leave well enough alone," but that's not always true. Here's an update on the classic all-American dessert, strawberry shortcake: substitute raspberries and blueberries, throw in some cream cheese, and dust with fancy, new-age turbinado sugar.

2 c. sifted all-purpose flour

3 tsp. baking powder

¾ tsp. salt

A pinch of granulated sugar

1 3-oz. package of cream cheese (original, not light), chilled and cut into small pieces

4 tbsp. unsalted butter, chilled and cut into small pieces

1 large egg, beaten

½ c. 2% or whole milk

2 tbsp. unsalted butter, melted

¾ c. turbinado sugar, available in co-ops, natural food stores, and most mainstream grocers

1 pint each fresh raspberries and blueberries

1 c. whipped or sour cream

1. Preheat oven to 450°F. Sift flour, baking powder, salt, and pinch of sugar together. Add chilled cream cheese and butter, cutting in with a pastry blender or two knives until mixture resembles coarse cornmeal.

2. Pour beaten egg into a measuring cup, and add enough milk to make ¾ c.; quickly and carefully stir into the flour mixture. Swiftly knead the dough in the bowl just long enough for the dough to hold together, about 20 seconds. Remember, DO NOT OVERMIX; that's why they call it "shortcake."

3. Pat half the dough into a greased, round 8-inch cake pan. Brush with melted butter and sprinkle with ¼ c. turbinado sugar. Pat the remaining dough on top of first layer, and sprinkle with another ¼ c. turbinado sugar.

4. Bake in center of the preheated oven for 20 minutes, or until golden brown.

5. Rinse the berries, add the remaining ¼ c. turbinado sugar, and let stand.

6. When the shortcake is done, remove it from the oven to a cooling rack. When cool, split the layers apart, spread ½ c. whipped or sour cream on the bottom layer, and top with half of the berry mixture. Cover the berries with the top layer of shortcake, pressing down gently. Top with remaining ½ c. whipped or sour cream and the remaining sugared berries.

7. Cut into wedges, and serve in low dessert, salad, or soup bowls.

August

Long Beans · Sweet Corn · Onions · Tomatoes · Peppers · Eggplant · Smoked Chicken · Jicama · Grape Juice · Rosemary

In August the market tables are piled high with produce, and beneath them baskets and boxes overflow with more: long beans, sweet corn, onions, tomatoes, peppers, and eggplant—the list could be five times as long, and every bit of it can be Minnesota grown. Nevertheless, it's always a good idea to look past the piles of vegetables to the boxes in which they were packed, just to make sure they don't say California or Michigan. Minnesotans can afford to be choosy in the season of abundance and ask not only where, but when, the corn—and everything else—was picked. Each hour farther from the field exacts its toll on flavor. We've been fooled too often, so now we seldom stop at the generic farmers' market stands that appear like a mirage in the parking lot next to our shopping mall.

Asian Farmers: All in the Family

Everyone loves to be part of a success story; that, in part, is why immigrants from Thailand, Laos, and Vietnam were so enthusiastically received when they appeared with their large families and low prices at the farmers' markets in the 1970s. At first, their market stands were overflowing with vegetables that most native Minnesotans couldn't recognize, much less prepare; and when asked, they struggled to give cooking instructions that left the customers baffled. Finally, the newcomers grew weary and answered every question the same way: stir-fry—the one Asian cooking technique everyone seemed to have mastered. Eventually the Asian vendors adapted to the marketplace, adding corn, squash, and tomatoes to more traditional Asian produce such as bok choy and lemongrass, and then the tables were turned.

"We sold the vegetables then asked the customers, 'What do you use this for?'" a high-school-aged Hmong girl told us, interpreting for her mother who gestured at the carrots on her sales table with disdain. It was a hot late-summer morning when we first met Ying Her and two of her pretty daughters behind a table of perfectly ripened tomatoes at the White Bear Lake Farmers' Market. At first she spoke with us through the girls because she was reluctant to display her English, but before long we were laughing so hard at her disgust with Minnesota's weather, that language hardly mattered.

"Either it's too hot or there's no business—and right now, it's too hot. I'm going to leave them behind," she said jerking her thumb over her shoulder at the girls, "and go back to Thailand where there are only two hot days a year."

The girls smiled knowingly at the familiar harangue, and the three of them began to pack up the booth with the sure and efficient movements of people who had done it a hundred times before. White Bear was only one of several markets where Her sold, and she told us that of all of them, Bloomington—the market where she sold on Saturdays—was the one with the most Asian vendors. "We sell everything there except the bread and that's only because we don't know how to bake it—besides, baking bread is even hotter than working in the field," and she let out an effervescent laugh.

Lining up a time to visit Ying Her wasn't easy. She had exactly one hour free on a Sunday morning—two weeks later. When the day came and we stood waiting at the front door of her suburban home in Roseville, I worried that we'd fallen through the only tiny crack in her schedule. Her's college-aged son and his little brother came to the door, called their mother on her cell to remind her of the appointment, and invited us inside where we waited, talking to the older boy while staring at a pyramid of pictures that climbed the height of the living room wall.

"My dad was in the Vietnam War," he said of the picture of a handsome uniformed man at the top. The boy, and later his sisters, spoke of their father with respect and affection, saying he had been a leader in their home country, and here he was the head of a counsel that governed the local Hmong community. But we did not see him that day, and it appeared that he had little involvement with the market business; in fact, given the size of the family, relatively few members worked in the field or sold at the market.

Of the family's six children, there were four still at home; all but one had been born in Thailand, where Her, originally from Laos, lived in a refugee camp until moving to the United States in 1987. One older daughter was married, the other was studying overseas, and the oldest boy who waited with us at the house was in game design and development at Brown College; the younger brother was only seven, and that left the two girls we'd seen at the market. During summer the two high-school-aged girls work three to four hours a day in the garden and at the sales stands, while their mother seemed to be working around the clock.

Ying Her sells in Osseo on Tuesdays, Champlain on Wednesdays, White Bear Lake on Fridays, and Bloomington on Saturdays; on Mondays and Thursdays she spends the day gardening and picking produce for Tuesday and Friday. She also tends to the garden on market days, which begin at 5 a.m. and end around noon, resting for only an hour or so before heading back to the field to get more produce, for she is intent on having nothing less than the freshest produce and flowers for the following day. She commutes to her

> *Ying Her sells in Osseo on Tuesdays, Champlain on Wednesdays, White Bear Lake on Fridays, and Bloomington on Saturdays; on Mondays and Thursdays she spends the day gardening and picking produce for Tuesday and Friday.*

gardens—three rented plots of land in Lake Elmo, Ham Lake, and Hastings—eats her meals behind the wheel of her car, and drives home when it's too dark to garden so that she can work into the night arranging floral bouquets.

When Ying drove into the yard, her two daughters were already on board for the day. Their tightly packed late-model van was a complete market stall on wheels: plastic bins for produce, buckets for flowers, tables, and tents squeezed together with the sales staff. Her idled the van just long enough to say hello, then, motioning for us to follow, took off for Lake Elmo where her favorite garden plot was the endpoint of a route so long and circuitous it caused us to marvel at both. The last half-mile, a dust cloud obscured her van as it bounced and dodged potholes along a maze of dirt roads that snaked around an old gravel pit and climbed to a plateau where, after a quick swing to the left near a clump of trees, we arrived at her one-acre plot.

Grace bounded out of the car followed closely by Her's younger girl, who frolicked with the dog while we talked and walked the length of the field. With the older daughter interpreting, Her talked about customs in the Hmong community and the life that had been left behind in Laos, punctuating her remarks with swift stabs at picking and pruning. I don't need to recall the horror stories of the Laotian conflict, which rendered life in Laos hardly a life at all; suffice it to say that life in America means that marriage, dowries, and education have supplanted rape, torture, and mutilation in the minds of the two girls who wandered with us in the field.

Ying Her started the business when she came in 1987, growing vegetables in a plot the size of her market van behind the family's apartment house. The first American vegetables she brought to market—potatoes and radishes—gave Her almost nothing in return for the labor, but she kept going, stopping for only four years when her children were small.

The Lake Elmo plot, the favorite of Her's three gardens, was the most recently acquired and is the one with the best soil. The tomato plants that grew in the field around us had been grown without chemicals, looked like they could do push-ups, and yielded fruit that was plump and without spots. Surrounding the tomatoes, flowers fanned out around us in a rich tapestry of color. Ying Her grows other produce: spinach, kohlrabi, kale, lettuce, and cilantro—but in smaller quantities—for, after fifteen years in business, she has learned that tomatoes and flowers are the most profitable items.

A few rows away, with Grace in tow, the youngest girl sauntered through the flowers sucking on a stalk that looked like a slender version of sugar cane. I had seen it before at the Minneapolis Farmers' Market, where the vendor surprised me by saying he'd grown it in Rosemount. He called it sugar cane, but it was a smaller version of the cane I'd seen growing throughout the Mississippi River Delta.

"We don't know the name of that plant but its sweet. You can try it and see," said Her heading off toward a stand of what looked like ornamental grass. She cut a few stalks then walked back, stripping the husk off the cane with her teeth; as she did, I could not help noticing that Ying Her's walk looked carefree, and her face had the smooth, untroubled look of a teenager. "Sometimes late at night when I still have work to do I have some and it helps" she grinned and lifted her hands as if she was boosting a child.

When the growing season is over, the Hmong celebrate the New Year, a multifamily event for which there are weeks of preparation; two pigs, a cow, and chickens are butchered, everyone has new clothes, and the houses are ritually cleaned. The exact date for the Hmong New Year in America seems to be a matter of consensus rather than calendar. In Laos it would be celebrated when the rice was harvested, but here no one would want to skip it altogether since it is considered necessary for good luck in the coming year.

"One year I didn't, and later I cut off the end of my thumb," said Her.

Festivals, weddings, and family celebrations are the focus of the tightly knit Hmong community. The girls could look forward to large, elaborate weddings, with a sizable dowry (paid to the girls' family) that is regulated by clan decree not to exceed five thousand dollars. But that would come later; for now, the fifteen-year-old is concentrating on her studies. She already speaks six languages—French, Chinese, English, Spanish, Japanese, and Hmong—and she is learning her sixth by watching Korean movies.

"I watch movies too," said Her when we asked about her off-season activities. "I just watch Hmong movies and laugh all winter long."

Asian Greens Primer

In the late twentieth century, there was a large Southeast Asian cultural addition to the melting pot that is the United States, and Minnesota was the beneficiary of some of the larger groups. In summer if you visit farmers' markets, drive along roads at the city's edge, or peek into the backyards in any Southeast Asian neighborhood, you're sure to see greens, vegetables, and fruits not native to our climate. So what are these beautiful and beguiling mysteries, and how do you prepare them? To sort out this cornucopia, we've put together a primer of ten typical Asian greens and vegetables, along with a few herbs and flavorings, that can be grown here and are found in most Minnesota grocery stores, farmers' markets, and roadside stands.

The Top Ten List: Asian Greens and Vegetables

Bok Choy—familiar since the 1960s when Chinese food swept the nation, this Asian vegetable is now readily available in a small version, with a much sweeter taste.

Broccoli rabe [watercolor illustration]—tasty and nutritious, there's no waste with this easy-to-prepare green. It is at its best when stir-fried with garlic, spritzed with lemon, then added to sautéed shrimp, chicken, or pork; mixed into soup; or just eaten as a solo vegetable.

Chinese/napa cabbage—one of the more versatile of the Top Ten, finely shred for inclusion in soups, egg rolls, and dumplings. Torn leaves can be stir-fried or added to salads, and whole leaves make easy-to-handle wrappers for Asian-style cabbage rolls.

Daikon—this giant white radish doesn't have the fiery bite of the small, round red ones, and that's a good thing. Whole or in pieces, a little goes a long way. Wrapped in paper toweling and stored in a tightly closed plastic bag, it keeps well for long periods of time; just trim the cut edge to get back to the heart of this economical tuber. This long, white radish is always used raw and is great in salads, in slaws, and as a crudité. We cut them into coin shapes and used them with the Edamame Dip on page 160.

Jicama—this vegetable keeps well and has a high yield, much like daikon. Used in similar ways, its flavor and texture are much like that of water chestnuts, and they make great crunchy snacks.

Long beans—these extra-long green beans can be treated much like their short cousins; or try the classic Southeast Asian preparation of frying with sesame oil and serving with a salty tamari–hot pepper sauce.

Mizuna—this delicate, spiky leafed green is best raw in salads, but adds great color and flavor to stir-fries and soups. Store loosely wrapped in paper toweling slipped into a plastic bag; use within a few days.

Mustard greens—a common thread between Asian and African cuisine, these leaves are best steamed with a little vinegar to cut their peppery bite.

Oriental eggplant—a small, white, round sibling to the long purple varieties, with a similar texture and more pleasing taste; use in stir-fry dishes and vegetable soups and stews.

Tatsoi—a flat cabbage with small, round, deep green leaves; store and use in the same way as mizuna.

Five Flavorings

These distinct flavors are often used individually as the primary seasoning in many Asian dishes.

1. Cilantro—often called Chinese parsley, this flat-leafed herb has the flavor most often associated with Thai and Vietnamese cooking. When let go to seed, the plant produces the more familiar coriander, a staple in Spanish and Mexican cuisine.

2. Garlic chives—a flat, flavorful cousin to onion chives, use as a substitute or in combination with its round relative. The pretty white flowers make a great garnish for summer soups and salads and serve as effective aphid deterrents when planted at the base of rose bushes and fruit trees. If you do plant them, make sure to remove all flowers before they produce their thousands of tiny, easily airborne seeds, or you, and all your neighbors, will be seeing garlic chives for years to come.

3. Lemongrass—from stir-fries to teas, facial steams to herbal infusions, this distinctive, edible grass ranks right up there with all the great seasonings.

4. Shiso—as one of the more important Japanese spices, shiso has been giving foods a distinctive sharp anise and licorice-like flavor for more than three hundred years. Also known as red or green perilla, this calcium- and iron-rich leaf is used in its entirety. Fresh or dried, whole, cut into strips, crumbled, flower buds, and seeds, use shiso to season tofu, tempura, pickled plums and ginger, soups, sushi, red meats, and rice.

5. Thai peppers—these tiny red peppers pack a punch. So small they're difficult to seed, one included in a dish is usually sufficient. They add great seasoning to pickles, and they dry nicely when still on the vine.

Raising the Bar

As the slogan "From Wings to Feet" implies, the Wemeier family of Bar 5 sells everything but the quack and the oink to their customers at the Minneapolis Farmers' Market. It's tricky to arrive at the market with just the right selection when the products range from chicken wings to pepper bacon, and more than once we've waited hopefully while Laura Wemeier searches hastily through the mounds of white freezer paper packages in her truck. Most often she has what we're looking for, but if not, there's usually some new product to ease the disappointment of sold-out smoked chickens or bacon burgers. One Easter Bar 5 was even the source for table decorations because the family's children had added colored chicken eggs and hand-blown goose eggs to their wares.

We visited the Wemeiers on the day before Easter, just as they were packing up after market. Suddenly an icy spring-defying wind sent the feather-light goose eggs careening over the parking lot, which, in turn sent the giggling Wemeier daughters scrambling to get the precious eggs before they cracked or rolled out of reach. Their mother Laura smiled as she watched from the warmth of a nearby car where she'd taken refuge from the unseasonably cold wind-chill. Some people might not have taken Mother Nature's rebuff with such good humor, but this family can take an occasional setback in stride.

Much trial and error is needed to develop unique and memorable products for the competitive, big-city farmers' market; but in less than ten years this resilient young family has developed a distinctive line that ranges from smoked duck to chicken blueberry sausage. Anyone who's tried Bar 5's Hungarian smoked pepper bacon or their maple-cured smoked chicken might think these are closely kept, generations-old family recipes, but that's only partially true.

John and Laura Wemeier's marriage brought two fourth-generation farm families together: his raised chicken, and hers, beef and pork, both in the area around Arlington, Minnesota, a two-hour drive west from the Twin Cities. The young couple settled on John's grandfather's place, unsure of the direction their own farming would take. Because times had changed and traditional meats and poultry weren't enough to meet market demands, they realized they needed to spread their

> *"Would you like to buy this? I don't know what it's called, but it sure is good."*

wings and make a statement all their own; and, by chance, they learned of an elderly couple hoping to retire from their chicken processing business.

Matt and Betty Polemeier were delightful old-school farmers who sold chickens from the back of their truck at eleven Twin Cities area farmers' markets. The Wemeiers bought the couples' customer list and equipment, sent a letter of introduction, put on their best smiles, and set out to do the same thing. It wasn't long before John and Laura realized that Matt and Betty's way of charming customers from the tailgate of a pickup day after day just wasn't their style; so they decided to cut back on the markets, began smoking chickens with hickory, green ash, and maple, and developed a line of ready-to-serve products. When Minneapolis Farmers' Market Manager Larry Cermak tasted their smoked chicken, he called them immediately to offer them a place at the market. Five years later, the Wemeiers and all four of their children sell at both Minneapolis' and St. Paul's Farmers' Markets, driving two fully loaded trucks into the Cities every Saturday and Sunday.

Laura says she likes to meet the people she feeds, and she has noticed a few things in her market customers over the years: older folks look for the foods they grew up eating and young people are more food conscious; many customers aren't cooks and want things to be easy; others come asking for cooking instructions; while still others arrive with suggestions—a little more pepper here, less garlic there, or a lighter touch with the smoke—ideas that have shaped Bar 5's recipes. When a product doesn't make the grade, the Wemeiers change or drop it quickly and move on.

Instead of selling whole ducks, they sell single breasts for entrées and save the dark meat for confit, a popular dish among more sophisticated cooks. When the turducken rage reached Bar 5, Laura added her own sausage, cornbread, and apple/celery dressing to the turkey. In the end, there were few takers, probably because it's a dish designed to feed a large family like the Wemeiers, who number forty-seven for holiday dinners, instead of the smaller portions more common among city dwellers. Products come and go, but the family's business continues to grow.

Bar 5 produces ten thousand chickens a year, which, along with beef, pork, and waterfowl, are all raised and processed by John, Laura, their four children, and two neighboring farm retirees. The kids live and breathe farm life, much as their parents do, linking sausages, plucking chickens, and adding their sparkle to the family's presence at the farmers' markets.

All the children have participated in 4-H and are no strangers to competitive events. Eldest daughter Lizzy went to the Poultry Knowledge Bowl four times, even taking third place in the nationals. Knowing the name of every feather, she had gone as far she could in poultry husbandry; so, to give her a new challenge, the Wemeiers began raising sheep, and Bar 5 added lamb to their products. And the Wemeiers were trying something new yet again.

Laura Wemeier, the youngest of nine children, grew up twisting sausage links in her parents' basement and is proud that her children are continuing the tradition.

There are plenty of people selling meat in the Twin Cities markets, but this family doesn't mind, claiming competition keeps them on their toes. It simply sends them back into the kitchen, where they'll cook up something other vendors won't have. The latest? Bacon burgers that incorporate bacon ends into the ground beef, and chicken/blueberry link sausage made with Minnesota dried blueberries.

Jacob, their youngest, was only five when he became top salesman for Chicken in the Middle, a pork tenderloin rolled in a basil/herb mixture with a smoked chicken link in the middle. His father simply set him on a stool at the St. Paul Farmers' Market with a plate, where he attracted customers by waving his fork around and saying, "Would you like to buy this? I don't know what it's called, but it sure is good."

Planning Ahead

Oven-Roasted Tomatoes

By August, you may be up to your eyeballs in zucchini, green beans, and tomatoes and about ready to give something up; but come midwinter you'll thank yourself for saving your tomatoes from the compost pile. Oven-roasted tomatoes are the perfect solution.

1. Preheat oven to 250°F.

2. Select tomatoes that are ripe but still firm; Italian plum tomatoes are generally best. Cut off the stems and bottom ends of the tomatoes, and cut in half lengthwise.

3. Lay the tomatoes on a cookie sheet, cut side up, without crowding. Place in the preheated oven to dry; this should take up to 4 hours or longer. If your oven has a convection mode, use it to shorten the drying time; this will also result in more uniformly dried fruit. The tomatoes are dry when they are flexible and leathery without pockets of moisture. Place them inside a tightly sealed glass container, then store in a cool, dark spot; they will last up to 6 months, or even 1 year.

Spicy Vietnamese
Long Beans

♦

Grilled Corn with Lemon
and Pepper

♦

Smoked Chicken Salad
with Jicama

♦

Pears Poached in Isis Wine
with Raspberry Coulis

East Meets West:
Spicy Vietnamese Long Beans

Serves
4 to 6

First impressions can be quite deceiving. It appeared that most of the Southeast Asian population seeking refuge in the United States in the 1970s arrived with little more than the clothes on their backs. What couldn't be seen at first was the wealth of extraordinary gardening skills, varieties of fruits, vegetables, and cooking techniques previously unknown to Midwestern palates. Today, these once-foreign foods can be found as seasonal stock items in produce departments everywhere.

1 lb. long beans, bundled together with string and tied at the cut end, leaving the tips loose.

4 c. canola or soy oil

1 c. raw shelled peanuts

2 tsp. minced, fresh ginger

2 garlic cloves, minced

2 scallions, green and white parts minced

2 tsp. chili paste (or more, to taste)

1 c. unsalted or low-sodium chicken stock

2 tbsp. cornstarch, mixed with 4 tbsp. cold water

Paper towels

1. Leave long beans tied and wash well under cold running water. Trim and discard loose ends of beans. Hold at the tied end and cut into 2-inch pieces. Dry well on paper towels; this is important because they need to be dry before they are put into the hot oil.

2. Heat oil in a wok or deep-sided pan to 400°F. Quickly pass the raw peanuts through the heated oil until just golden, 30 seconds to 1 minute. Remove and drain on paper towels. Carefully add the dry long beans to the hot oil and deep fry until they blister, about 3–4 minutes; a splatter screen is helpful here. Remove beans with a slotted spoon and drain on paper towels.

3. Carefully remove all but 2 tsp. hot oil to a heatproof container, and place out of harm's way.

4. Return wok with 2 remaining tsp. hot oil to the heat; add the ginger, garlic, and scallion, and stir-fry about 30 seconds. Add the chili paste and stock, stir to blend; add the cornstarch mixture, bring to a boil, and cook 1 minute until sauce thickens. Return beans to the wok, toss until warm and coated with sauce. Mix peanuts in and serve.

Grilled Corn with Lemon and Pepper

Serves
4 to 6

Back in the early part of the last century there were little rake-like forks called corn scrapers, designed to help the eater extract the most flavor out of an ear of corn. The proper technique was to grasp a hot ear of corn in one hand and, with the scraper in the other, rake down the length of the cob, piercing the kernels with the points of the tines. After scraping the kernels from the cob, the corn is dressed with salt, pepper, and butter, giving the eater an amazing burst of seasoned, sweet corn milk. As far as I know, these corn scrapers aren't made anymore, and, in my opinion, an ear of corn is not the thing to serve at elegant indoor sit-downs. So, take it outside, tuck a napkin under your chin, generously butter, salt and pepper the ear, and go for it. And, if you find some things that look like short forks with little, bent pointy tines at a yard sale, or in your grandmother's silver chest, grab them.

If you don't like to get your hands too greasy, there are those little corn-shaped skewers you can push in at either end; plus, they allow you to crook your little fingers for a more formal, dainty effect. Speaking of dainty, if you want to cut the fat, here's any easy, lo-cal version.

2 ears of sweet corn per person,
   plus a few extra for good
   measure
½ lemon per person
Freshly cracked pepper, to taste
Coarse sea or kosher salt

1. Heat the charcoal grill. While the grill is heating, remove outer leaves and silk from corn, retaining tight, inner layer of leaves. Submerge the corn in cold, salted water for 20–30 minutes, or until the coals are ready.

2. Place ears of corn on the hot grill and cook 5–10 minutes, turning several times.

3. Serve with lemon wedges, freshly cracked pepper, and coarse salt.

Smoked Chicken Salad with Jicama

Serves 4

With nods to culture and convenience, Shelley came up with this tasty, healthy, no-cook salad for the hotter days of summer. Everything, including the mayo, should be available at your local co-op or farmers' market, and beyond buying the ingredients, the only labor involved is a bit of peeling, chopping, mixing, and eating.

½ smoked chicken, about 3 lbs., skinned, boned, and cut into ½-inch pieces

⅔ c. jicama, peeled and cut in matchstick-sized pieces

1 large tart, red unpeeled apple, quartered, and cut into matchstick-sized pieces

4 large red radishes, thinly sliced

¼ c. commercial mayonnaise

¼ c. plain low-fat yogurt

1 tbsp. fresh tarragon leaves, chopped

Salt and pepper, to taste*

Lettuce leaves to serve

1. Cut chicken into ½-inch bite-sized pieces. Place in a large bowl. Add jicama, apple, and radish to chicken.

2. In separate small bowl, mix mayonnaise, yogurt, and tarragon. Add to chicken and other ingredients and toss to coat. Taste for salt and pepper, adjusting if needed.

   *Remember: smoked chicken and mayonnaise are already seasoned and salted.

3. Serve as individual salads, or family-style in a bowl lined with salad greens.

Pears Poached in Isis Wine with Raspberry Coulis

Serves 6

Poached pears are, in two words, elegant and easy. Made a day ahead in warm weather, this refreshing, calorie-friendly August after-course is equally good in the cold weather months served warm with a glass of brandy or cognac. Just make sure to freeze some raspberries in season for a cold-weather coulis

6 firm pears (Asian, Bartlett, Anjou), peeled with stem still on
Juice of ½ lemon
2 c. Alexis Bailly Isis Wine
1 2-inch strip of lemon zest
6 whole black peppercorns
1 1-inch slice of ginger root, peeled and split in half
1 pint fresh, ripe raspberries
Fresh mint leaves, for garnish

1. Slice a bit off the bottom of each pear so it will stand on its own. Use the tip of the vegetable peeler or paring knife to remove a 1-inch piece of the core from the bottom. Submerge pears in a cold water bath with the lemon juice to keep from browning.

2. In a separate pan or the microwave, warm the Isis wine until it begins to simmer.

3. Lift pears out of the lemon-water and place in a saucepan that is just big enough to hold them tightly, stems up, and deep enough to keep them submerged; the pears shouldn't float or they will poach unevenly. The pan should have a tight-fitting lid.

4. Pour the heated Isis wine over the pears, adding water to cover if needed. Add lemon zest, peppercorns, and ginger root, cover, and place over low heat to simmer until tender. The amount of time needed is dependent on the size of the pears. A thin skewer or toothpick should easily pierce the fruit at the thickest part. Remove from heat, cover, and chill in poaching liquid. Chill the serving dishes at this time as well.

5. To make the coulis, remove the chilled pears from the poaching liquid to a cooling rack placed over a sided sheet pan to drain. Place the saucepan over high heat, and reduce the poaching liquid by half. Remove to a separate bowl and chill until ready to use.

6. Puree raspberries in a processor or food mill, and remove the seeds by pressing the mixture through a sieve. Add enough reduced Isis wine to the puree to make a sauce that will cling to the fruit without separating.

7. To serve: place pears upright in chilled shallow bowls or plates; ladle a small amount of the raspberry coulis over the top of each pear; there should be enough so it pools around the bottom of the fruit. Garnish with a sprig of fresh mint; pass remaining coulis in a sauce boat.

September

Wild Rice · Beef · Garlic · Potatoes · Peppers · Butternut Squash · Romanesco Broccoli · Rutabagas

September's march, as orderly and predictable as the reappearance of plaid apparel, football, and shorter days, hustles us in the front door and out the back with only the most cursory of stops in the kitchen. Sated by the glut of summer's-end produce, our bodies begin to hunger for easy-cooking foods with elongated shelf lives—squashes, tubers, and nut-flavored wild rice. If there's a little extra time, we squirrel and stash some garden jewel in the freezer, or grieve the end of summer herbs by ceremonially drying sage or hanging mint top down in the garage as proudly as hard-hunted game.

Putting the Wild Back in Rice

During the steamy Minnesota summer, when city dwellers long for an opportunity to shed their working attire, don carefree attitudes, shorts, and sandals, and go in search of cool lakes and dark piney woods, BJ and I headed north toward the Canadian border in hopes of finding the source of the Mississippi and the quintessential Minnesota ingredient—wild rice.

While searching for the headwaters, we took what we thought would be a short detour to visit Native Harvest on the White Earth Reservation where Native Americans hand-harvest wild rice and tap maples for syrup.

We'd called the day before, but thought we'd dialed the wrong number when a businesslike voice answered, "Land Recovery Project." After some confusion, she told us they were Native Harvest too, and it was okay to stop by.

On the map Native Harvest appeared to be two thumbnails away from Lake Itasca and the Mississippi Headwaters. However, after driving around and seeing a good deal of the White Earth Reservation, it was clear we were lost. We'd passed many non–Native American resorts and farms checkering the edges of the reservation and desert-like expanses of government-issue housing. There were marshes brimming with wild grasses and waterfowl and a Catholic grotto deep in a pine forest, but there was no sign of Native Harvest. No cars. No people.

Eventually we spotted a spaceship-like building emblazoned with animal symbols and earth-toned patterns—an architectural style typical of contemporary, government-built tribal headquarters and schools.

The only people around were tanned and tattooed construction workers, who appeared a bit unfriendly as we approached with our lost expressions and dog-eared map. They silenced their jackhammers long enough to hear us out, conferred at length, and finally broke into boyish grins, each vying to give the best directions underscored by grimaces and flailing arms and perplexing instructions: "Look for ice-crackin', then stop and ask again."

"Ice-crackin'" turned out to be a lake and a lodge named for the thunderous sound of ice buckling throughout the winter.

"Hot spring down there," the lodge owner explained, gesturing to the lake as she pumped our gas. She gave us further directions to Native Harvest, then invited us to try one of her famous Thunder Burgers.

Instead, we continued driving for miles on soft-shouldered dirt roads marked by signs warning "Children Riding Horses." Our stomachs rumbled regretfully, sending up signals that sounded like: *Thun*-der Bur-gers. *Thun*-der Bur-gers.

Finally, we passed beneath a birch archway, entering an unimposing compound of trailers, sheds, and split-rail-fenced corrals. No sign announcing "Native Harvest." No one was around. Were we in the right place? A peek through the nearest screened door revealed dusty desks and copying machines buried under papers, a stack of realtor's multiple listing books, wall-mounted reservation maps, and what looked like campaign posters. Was this the alternative food supply depot we were seeking, a tribal office, or a campaign headquarters?

It took a moment to spot the product samples lined up on a display shelf and a long table filled with cellophane-wrapped gift packs: birch bark baskets of jam, maple butter, and hazelnut candy alongside miniature birch bark canoes filled with soup, hominy, and wild rice.

Then we saw the framed photograph and headline: "*Time* Magazine Names Winona LaDuke One of America's Fifty Most Promising Young Americans."

Remember the Nader/LaDuke 1996 and 2000 presidential campaigns? We'd stumbled onto LaDuke's Land Recovery Project foundation headquarters, a project much publicized during the campaign and still thriving ten years later.

LaDuke is Anishinaabekwe (Ojibwe), Harvard-educated, and a virtual powerhouse of progressive thinking. In 1989 she formed the White Earth Land Recovery Project, a nonprofit with a mission to buy back land given in treaty to the Anishinaabeg, the original name of the Ojibwe. The tribe's initial land grant included 836,000 acres, but only 56,000 remain in their control. Native Harvest raises money for the White Earth Land Recovery Project (WELRP) by marketing alternative foods to the general public.

Educating the tribe about the importance of a healthy diet is high on LaDuke's agenda, and her goals include addressing the issue of nutrition among the elders and reducing the soaring rate of diabetes within the tribe. One plan to reach this end is through returning tribal eating habits to their healthier origins, with wild and organic, locally grown foods. This approach addresses multiple issues of income-generation, sustainability, and respect for the environment.

Native Harvest produces all the jam and jelly, hominy, maple syrup, and candies we'd spied on the shelves. Most of the ingredients come from the reservation and are gathered and processed using traditional methods. Sap from local maple trees is processed in the reservation's sugarhouse, and some of it is made into maple butter; wild rice is harvested into flat-bottomed boats, then sun-dried, parched in drums over an open fire, and hand-winnowed in traditional Ojibwe birch bark baskets. Many fruits and nuts, among them wild plums and hazelnuts, are gathered from the extensive reservation forest.

When it's time to pick the fruit for jams and jellies, Native Harvest calculates the best wage it can pay according to market pricing; it anticipates sales volumes, passes the word on the reservation, and then hires pickers at the going rate. Not only does this provide a direct infusion of capital to the tribal economy, it also passes traditional wild food gathering methods from one generation to the next.

Since our first visit, Native Harvest has opened a café serving their own Muskrat brand of reservation-roasted coffee and a store offering a variety of gifts. Because small business loans help tribal members establish start-up businesses that produce crafts that Native Harvest buys outright and then sells, the café and shop are additional direct sources of income for reservation residents, selling craft items such as grass dancer earrings, bead and quill purses, unusual varieties of wild rice soup, and tepee-shaped birch bark birdhouses.

All Native Harvest gifts and foodstuffs—such as maple-hazelnut candy, wild rice asparagus soup, and hominy bison chili—can be purchased through a well-designed website, so you don't have to go to the headwaters of the Mississippi to get their products. This site is also a good place to catch up on LaDuke's and WELRP's ongoing efforts, whether wind-power generation, the reintroduction of sturgeon to area lakes, or bison burgers.

WELRP also sponsors education programs within the Ojibwe community, such as native culture and language development, women's leadership, the Circle Loan Program—which grants low-interest loans to entrepreneurs for native crafts—and a horseback riding program that teaches Native American children about their heritage and develops responsibility and good communication skills.

We drove away from Native Harvest pondering the White Earth Reservation map checkered with non-native in-holdings. The striking views surrounding us—soaring hawks, bulrushes mixed with water lilies, and crystalline lakes ringed with virgin pines—were overshadowed by the contrast between rundown trailer homes and prosperous-looking resorts. For all Native Harvest's successes, one sad fact remains: the average income on the reservation is startlingly low, less than $7,000 a year, and the restoration of tribal lands is a process that will take years to complete.

Naturally, we purchased an assortment of Native Harvest's foods before leaving. Once back on the road, the chant: *Thun*-der Bur-ger, *Thun*-der Bur-ger became: *Ma*-ple But-ter, *Ma*-ple But-ter.

Since neither of us had ever tasted maple butter we decided to give it a try. That butter never made it back to the Cities.

At What Price Wild Rice?

Plants aren't all that different from people. So many have come to American shores from other countries and cultures, it's unusual to find a true native in our midst. Wild rice, like the Native Americans who were the first to gather it, is one of those rarities.

Though it looks like long-grain white or brown rice, it isn't really rice, rather the seed of a marsh grass that was once found only in the lakes and rivers of northern Minnesota. Today "wild" rice is grown commercially in paddies, and a few firms dominate a $21 million industry, with California as the largest wild rice–producing state.

Paddy rice is parboiled so that it cooks at exactly the same pace as white rice, and it's found in most retail grocery stores, shelved alongside other varieties of rice, and served in restaurants across the country. But commercially grown wild rice is a far cry from the real thing, in appearance, flavor, and policy.

The distinctions between wild lake rice and cultivated paddy rice have to do with the differences in naturally grown species versus market demand for uniformity and convenience. Different habitats, from shallow muddy areas to deeper lake waters, determine the appearance and flavor of wild lake rice. Paddy rice such as the "wild" rice packaged by Uncle Ben's, Stouffer's, and other companies has been bred to produce uniform, large, black grains, and it costs half as much as traditionally hand-harvested, true wild rice. You'll know it's true wild lake rice if it takes fifty-plus minutes to cook.

Ricing is an integral piece of the Ojibwe culture, and this slow, thoughtful process is steeped in traditions generations old. Revered as a gift from the Creator, it feeds the spirit, mind, and soul; is a nutritious foodsource; and generates much-needed income for clothing, shelter, and transportation. Each fall in the month of August, the month of the wild rice moon, mature grass seeds—*Manoominike-Giizis*—are hand-harvested by two people in a canoe, the traditional Native American way. One stands toward the stern using a push pole to slowly propel the boat through the tall grasses, while the second kneels mid-canoe and gently poles (bends) the grass stalks over the bow and uses a rice knocker—*bawaîganaak*—to brush the ripe rice into the bottom of the boat. Each stalk bears multiple seeds that mature in different stages, allowing the same bed of rice to be harvested repeatedly in one season.

Primarily handled by the Ojibwe and, to a lesser degree, the Chippewa, the practice of ricing was traditionally reserved for tribal members nearest the rice beds. Each family riced in a specific area every season, tying bunches of stalks with ribbon or string of the same color to signify their spot, and all families used this system, respecting their neighbor's space.

Non-natives are now allowed to take rice from off-reservation lakes, but with restrictions. Permits, schedules, and lists of lakes must be obtained from the Department of Natural Resources (DNR). Lakes open at different times and for different hours, and some are reserved for exclusive use by the nearest tribe. Should a lake's border abut that of a reservation, the ricer will also need to get a tribal license. As a measure of protection for the rice beds, the type of boat, pole, and knocker are specified too. Contact the Minnesota DNR

Wild Rice: zizania palustris aquatica (Latin); mah-nooh-meen (Ojibwe) The ripe seeds of a grass native to North America; the official state grain of Minnesota since 1977.

at http://www.dnr.state.mn.us, (888) 646-6367, to obtain information about the wild rice harvest.

Processing is done in several exacting steps starting with the air-drying of freshly gathered rice, followed by parching in large metal barrels that are continuously rotated over a wood fire for two to four hours, depending on the dryness and ripeness of the rice, outside temperature, and humidity. The final step is winnowing in shallow, handmade birch bark baskets to remove the hulls loosened during parching.

For the Ojibwe of northern Minnesota, there is a fifth step known as "jigging," which involves dancing on the parched grains in soft moccasins to create a polished outer shell on the rice, giving it a near-white appearance similar to that seen on long-grain white rice.

Color, flavor, size, and texture of the grain differ with each location. It's extraordinarily nutritious, and far more flavorful than its commercial counterpart. According to the Ojibwe, wild rice tastes like the lakes: earthy and nutty. One cup of wild rice has about twice the protein as other rice and provides higher RDA (recommended daily allowance) levels of B-vitamins (20 percent of vitamin B6 for men, and 24 percent for women), folic acid (48 percent for men, and 53 percent for women), and niacin (35 percent for men and 45 percent for women).

A bit on the pricey side, a little goes a long way. It's easy to incorporate into your diet, blends well with other rice varieties, and lends flavor to hot soups, cold salads, casseroles, breads, muffins, pilafs, and even pancakes. So consider avenging the dam-building beavers, and help the struggling wild ricers: try cooking with the real thing.

Askov: The Real Rutabaga Capital of the World

Even the most experienced food foragers leave home with maps, snacks, and firm intentions but, failing to pack the spirit of serendipity, return with only empty gas tanks and grumpy children. Our first attempt to hunt the elusive rutabaga at an official festival turned out just that way.

After waiting for the parade of evening-gown attired princesses astride four-wheelers to make its ponderous way down the main street of Cumberland, Wisconsin, the alleged rutabaga capital of the world, we began to ask around about the rutabagas. The blank looks we received told the story. These days, rutabagas rank so low among dinner-plate offerings that most people have no idea what they are. There were none in the midway, which proffered only greasy French fries and cotton candy, or even among the offerings at a church bazaar. It seems the humble root left town long ago, leaving only the name behind to claim some kitschy fame; so, we settled for corn dogs and then left for home.

Later that summer, while hot on the trail of something completely different, we came face-to-face with rutabagas in the most unexpected disguise.

It was closing time on a windy, brisk Friday, when we followed the Kettle River into Askov, Minnesota, looking for the source of beef jerky we'd seen in North-woodsy display boxes on the countertops of area gas stations. At most we expected to find a closed jerky plant, but our eyes lit up with the sight of a tiny postcard-pretty town, with street signs in Danish and an old train depot. Next to the railroad tracks was a red-frame granary with the name *A. Henriksen* painted on the side, and below that, a slogan that caught our attention: Flour, Feed, Coal, Potatoes and Rutabagas.

The town appeared to be deserted. After driving around for a while, we pulled up next to a fanciful greenhouse with a sign to "Velkommen" us to Lena's Scandinavian Gifts, Coffee Bar, and Garden Center. Grace bounded out of the car and headed straight for the bushes by the greenhouse to relieve herself. BJ,

seeing that the bushes were lingonberries, a garden treasure she'd been seeking for some time, squealed with excitement and redirected Grace, just as a station wagon pulled up and a middle-aged woman in a long gathered skirt jumped out, introduced herself as Lena, and started talking.

Lena, whose real name was Linda, was handsome and imposing in an Earth mother sort of way, and after we had oohed and aahed over the lingonberries, she steered us through a gaily painted door in the long brick sidewall of an old, sober-looking building to her gift shop and coffee bar.

Lena wasn't the least bit Danish, but everything in her gaily jam-packed store appeared to be. On closer inspection, we saw the Danish flag was bracketed by Swedish Dalarna horses, Norwegian krumkake irons and lefse griddles. The food offerings at the front of the store—boxes of chocolates and salty licorice from all the Scandinavian countries, Germany, Poland, and Ireland—further expanded the theme.

From her rapid-fire conversation, Lena seemed to be in a terrible hurry to close up shop; however, half an hour later, when she was still talking, we realized we'd simply fallen into the whirlwind that is Lena.

In a torrent of town lore and self-promotion, she told us Askov, not Cumberland, was the longest-reigning rutabaga capital of the world. Though the subtle distinctions between the claims of Cumberland and Askov escaped us, one memorable fact remained: rutabagas are served at the Askov Rutabaga Festival. And the most famous rutabaga treat of all is Lena's own special culinary invention: the rutabaga malt.

Lena makes the malts year round at her coffee bar toward the back of the century-old store, and we now followed her across creaky wooden floors to the old-fashioned soda fountain and perched on stools beneath the high, stamped tin ceiling. The coffee bar serves thirty-two flavors of malteds, phosphates, cappuccinos, frappes, smoothies, cocoas, cokes, and Italian and ice cream sodas. One of Lena's sisters stood

A rutabaga, a rutabaga, my kingdom for a rutabaga. Cumberland, Wisconsin's Rutabaga Festival had royalty, marching bands, and cotton candy, but we had to go to Askov, Minnesota, to find an actual rutabaga.

behind the tall counter when we ordered our malt; as she prepared it, she kept up a running conversation with a third sister, the only other person in the store at that late hour. We settled in and sampled our first, and so far our only, rutabaga delicacy.

Made with a rich, vanilla ice cream, cooked puréed rutabaga, real malt, and maple syrup, Lena's malt could make anyone with a sweet tooth swoon; that is, if they like rutabagas. And, since hardly anyone knows how rutabagas taste, we recommend you travel to Askov to give it a try—you'll either like it or you'll hate it,

but Lena claims there's no in-between. One visitor who told Lena he loved rutabagas hated the malt, but it turned out he'd been confusing rutabagas with rhubarb.

We found a few other rutabaga recipes on the Askov city website, but none were as imaginative as Lena's malt. The recipes are worth checking out though, simply for the photos. When we first saw them we laughed out loud, thinking Lena's humor might be responsible because above each recipe is a photo of a table setting with a single rutabaga in place of a plate—just in case you don't know what one looks like.

Freezer Treasures at the U of Moo

When my dad recalled the 1940s and his college days at Moo U—the School of Agriculture at the University of Minnesota—he was fond of telling me about the all-you-can-eat ice cream with which his class was rewarded for completing Dairy Production Methods. He did like ice cream—enough so that we sometimes found the refrigerator packed with duplicate tubs of the stuff—but it's not the sweet flavor of his alma mater's ice cream that stayed with him for sixty years. But a trick was played on him and his classmates, the other skinny farm boys with their bottomless stomachs; the ice cream was so high in butterfat—24 percent, he claimed—that even those babes of the Great Depression could barely finish one bowl.

The University of Minnesota still makes high-octane ice cream, though not as high as Dad remembered, and the small store in a classroom building on the St. Paul campus through which it is sold—along with cheese, yogurt, and other dairy products—is one of the Twin Cities' better kept culinary secrets. When I learned about it, I was going to make a beeline for the place until I realized that the Dairy Store in Andrew Boss Laboratory and Meat Science Building on the St. Paul campus is open for only two hours a week—between 3 and 5 p.m. on Wednesdays. The University doesn't put much effort into extending its store hours or boosting what is already a terrific word-of-mouth reputation because the Dairy Store is simply considered an outreach arm of the school's teaching and research programs. In the University's Pilot Plant, students can observe or participate in the production of the ice cream and cheese, which are made primarily with milk from the University's own cows. The store itself is staffed by hairnet-wearing students who appear to be a little bemused by the frenzy of customers who vie for a chance to buy their products.

It took almost a year for my St. Paul errands to coincide with the store's hours, and when it did, it was over ninety degrees and I had no cooler. I arrived about forty-five minutes early, and wandered around the long, dimly-lit halls of the food science building until I found the store, a locked classroom door with paper covering the glass, where two other people were already waiting. Instead of hanging around by the door, I decided to go exploring and followed a sign next to the elevator to "Meat Lab Sales," another University-run store, located in the basement, which opened one hour earlier.

It was quiet, dark, and cool in the basement, but a light was coming from Room 26, inside which a tan young man who looked like he was dressed for golfing sat with his nose in a meat science textbook. He smiled and gave me little tour of the classroom-come-store, patiently explaining the differences between cottage, Canadian, and regular bacon that lay among the shrink-wrapped packages on the classroom tables. An unexpectedly large cross-cultural selection of sausages, plus lamb, pork, and beef cuts, were available in the freezer. The prices were far below my neighborhood grocers so I, thinking that frozen packages of meat would protect my ice cream as well as any block of ice, bought roasts, chops, and sausages, then borrowed a box from the kid to get them home. By the time I got back upstairs the two people waiting by the door of the Dairy Store had turned into ten, and when the rather harassed-looking dairy student finally unlocked the door, the line numbered twenty—many of them no taller than my shoulder.

To the irritation of the others in line, I and the two who had been there originally and saved a place for me joined the first wave of people who flooded the Dairy Store.

The room was just big enough for two students at a cashier's table, a refrigerator case of cheese, and two freezers of ice cream, pints in one and gallons in another. Some of the items were in short supply and sold out quickly, which explained the dirty looks I received when I'd gone to the front of the line. A dozen cartons of cottage cheese next to the cheese cooler disappeared in the first five minutes, so did the smoked gouda and some strawberry yogurt. There were a variety of other cheeses though—Blue Cheese, a white "blue" cheese they called Nuworld, Cheddar Creamy, and Dill Havarti—and I suppose that everyone went home with something, even if it wasn't exactly what they'd set out to get. I took the yogurt and some smoked Gouda, then froze in front of the ice cream and frozen yogurt, while the others in line reached around me to grab one favorite flavor or another.

There was a list on the wall of at least fifty kinds, more than their small test plant operation could stock at any one time; and many weren't available just then, but their names were nonetheless tempting. I chose a cross section—hoping my

The University of Minnesota still makes high-octane ice cream, though not as high as Dad remembered, and the small store in a classroom building on the St. Paul campus through which it is sold—along with cheese, yogurt, and other dairy products—is one of the Twin Cities' better kept culinary secrets.

ice cream–loving father would find something appealing among peach, chocolate peanut butter truffle, vanilla, coconut, and lemon yogurt—settled up and went out into the sweltering Minnesota summer rush hour.

Despite the insulation provided by the roasts and sausages, the ice cream was pretty close to soup by the time I made it home, but I took it as a good sign: lower quality commercial ice creams have so much gelatin that they melt into sticky, sugary goo; but the U of M ice cream was truly liquid, and when it was refrozen, the flavor was exactly the same though the texture had suffered a tiny bit from the mistreatment. Next time, I'd remember the cooler, though as it turned out it was so cold outside when I visited again that I needn't have bothered.

Dad had wanted the vanilla and ate it slowly . . . but the rest remained in my freezer, a little bit going a long way, though I shared it with every sweet tooth I knew. It was months later, and a kind of emergency, before I made it to the University's Dairy Store again. It would have had to be, or I would not have driven across town during rush hour on the day before Thanksgiving.

BJ, who is given to generous gestures, had promised pies to all her friends for Thanksgiving; and I, in turn, promised to take mine to someone else's house. When she got the flu, I decided to dress up a store-bought pie with the best possible topping since

my host—a contemporary of my father's—also loved ice cream above all other deserts.

It was just 3:00 when I arrived at the food science building on the St. Paul campus, but there were already people rushing away from the building cradling white cartons of ice cream. Inside, the line was stretching down the corridor again next to bulletin boards with signs about the special seasonal flavors offered that day: cinnamon, eggnog, pumpkin, and pumpkin pie. The difference between the latter two was graham-cracker crunch which had been added for the total pie experience.

My Thanksgiving host prepared a lovely feast, after which I took charge of the dessert, slipping store-bought apple pie beneath generous slabs of cinnamon ice cream. Being an ice cream aficionado first and foremost, my host pounced on my dessert offering, giving little or no notice to the store pie lurking beneath his creamy cinnamon reward.

The U's ice cream is only 12 percent butterfat now, which is a little less than Häagen Dazs and, at $2.50 a pint, about half the price. The store makes $25,000 a year; if half of that amount is the profits from ice cream, that's 5,000 pints, roughly 15,000 good-sized bowls. Even with its lower butterfat content, I—like my father and his classmates—have never managed to finish more than one bowl.

Students sunbathe with the cows in front of the University's Dairy building,

Wild Rice Dried Cranberry
Salad with Clementine
Vinaigrette

◆

Roasted Garlic Mashed
Potatoes

◆

Minnesota Meatloaf

◆

Butternut Squash with
Maple Syrup

◆

Romanesco Broccoli Sauté

◆

Lena's Rutabaga Malt

Wild Rice Dried Cranberry Salad with Clementine Vinaigrette

Serves 4 as an entrée salad, or 6 to 8 as a side dish

Most wild rice recipes seem to include cream of mushroom soup as an integral ingredient, so we felt it our duty to come up with a healthy alternative. Here's a recipe for a tasty wild rice salad with a modern twist. Economical in its use of otherwise costly ingredients, this salad can be made a day in advance. It is nutritious, travels well, and holds safely without refrigeration at moderate temperatures, making it ideal for summer camping and picnics. Both recipes can be easily increased for large gatherings.

1 c. raw (3–4 c. cooked) wild rice, washed and prepared according to basic cooking instructions described in "Storing and Cooking Wild Rice" on page 81.

1 c. long-grain white or brown rice (2 c. cooked)

¾ c. unsalted toasted, hulled hazelnuts, pecans, or hickory nuts

3–4 Clementines, peeled, sectioned, and seeded (tangerines, tangelos, or navel oranges can be substituted)

1 c. dried cranberries

2 bunches small scallions, cleaned and thinly sliced at an angle

Coarse salt, to taste

Pinch of dried red pepper flakes, or freshly ground black pepper

1. A day before, wash wild rice in cold water, and cook according to the directions on page 81.

2. Cook long-grain or brown rice in a separate pot. Use 2 c. lightly salted water for every 1 c. uncooked rice. Bring water to a boil and add salt and rice. Bring back to a boil, lower heat to simmer, and stir to loosen rice grains stuck on the bottom of the pan. Simmer, covered, until the rice has absorbed most of the water, about 15–20 minutes; the surface should be marked by little steam holes. Brown rice needs a bit more water and will take a little longer than white.

3. Remove rice from the heat and transfer to a large mixing bowl. Toss cooked rice with a little canola oil to keep the grains separate. Cover with plastic wrap, leaving a small opening to vent any steam, and refrigerate.

4. Preheat oven to 375°F, placing a rack in the center. Spread hazelnuts evenly over the surface of a sided sheet pan. Place in oven for a few minutes, or until the nuts begin to color. Shake pan to redistribute the hazelnuts, return to oven and continue browning. To remove husks, wrap hot, roasted nuts in a cotton dishtowel and rub. If not using immediately, let the hazelnuts cool to room temperature, store in a tightly covered dry container (tin or glass), and set aside. This step can be done a day ahead too. To keep their crunch, the nuts are the last ingredient incorporated into the salad.

5. Peel, section, and seed Clementines and place in large mixing bowl. Add cranberries, green onions, and chilled, cooked rice. Dress with Clementine vinaigrette, and toss several times to mix well.

Clementine Vinaigrette

Yields about 1½ c.

Fine zest of one Clementine
½ c. freshly squeezed
    Clementine juice
2–3 tbsp. white wine or
    champagne vinegar
Coarse salt, to taste
Pinch of dried red pepper flakes, or
    freshly ground black pepper
1 scant c. canola oil plus 1 tbsp.
    hazelnut oil if available

Combine zest, juice, vinegar, salt, and pepper flakes or pepper in a blender, a metal bowl with a whisk, or a glass jar that has a tight-fitting lid. Blend (or whisk or shake) until well mixed. Add oils in a steady stream. Blend or whisk again until thick. Taste and adjust seasonings. If it is too vinegary, add cold water to cut the acidity. If not using immediately, cover and refrigerate. Bring to room temperature before dressing the salad.

Storing and Cooking Wild Rice

Use wild rice in any recipes that call for long-grain white rice, especially those where the rice is cooked separately. Wild rice is prepared in much the same way as regular rice, except that it needs to be rinsed with cold water and takes much longer to cook.

Using a 4:1 ratio, i.e., 4 cups water for 1 cup rice, bring unsalted water to a boil. Add the wild rice, and cover with a tight-fitting lid. Lower heat to a simmer; continue to cook slowly until the rice is done. If it's a chewier texture you're after, reduce the cooking time. Cooking times will vary depending on the variety of rice, how it was processed, and how it will be used. All-black grains will take longer than variegated; true wild rice will take longer than cultivated, about 50–60 minutes.

For stuffings and salads, cook to desired texture; for soups, stews, and casseroles, undercook a bit before adding to the respective dish, and finish cooking. Taste for salt—none may be needed. If served alone, add unsalted butter or corn oil and some finely minced parsley for color contrast.

On its own, 1 cup of raw wild rice will yield 3–4 cups of cooked, easily enough for six servings. Once cooked, it will keep for a week in the refrigerator and up to 6 months in the freezer.

Take Your Lumps, and Enjoy Them: Roasted Garlic Mashed Potatoes

Serves 4 to 6

Mashed potatoes are one of the crowned heads of comfort foods. With the right potato and a few embellishments, you'll be eating a peasant's dish fit for a king. Just leave a few lumps to keep yourself humble.

2 large heads of firm, fresh garlic
3–4 lbs. unpeeled medium russet, Idaho, German, Yukon Gold, or yellow Finn potatoes
1–2 egg yolks
2–4 tbsp. unsalted butter
½–1 c. sour cream
Salt and freshly ground pepper, to taste

Preheat oven to 450°F.

1. Remove excess skin from garlic, cut in half laterally, and tightly wrap in aluminum foil, shiny side in.

2. Place on the lowest oven rack, and roast until the packet is soft and pliable, like a tube of toothpaste, depending on how large and how fresh/firm the garlic is. Remove from oven, peel foil back, and squeeze roasted garlic flesh out onto a plate.

3. While the garlic is roasting, bring a large covered pot of cold water to a boil. Salt the water once it begins to boil, allowing 2 tsp. for every 6 potatoes. Add the potatoes and cook, uncovered, until soft. Test with a skewer after about 20 minutes.

4. Drain the cooked potatoes well, return to the pan, and shake over the heated burner for a few minutes to allow them to dry. Peel, if desired.

5. Mash warm potatoes in their cooking pan. Mix in roasted garlic, egg yolks, butter, and sour cream. Add salt and butter to taste.

Some variations: Substitute creamed horseradish for roasted garlic; add finely minced fresh rosemary or snipped chives; mix in some crumbled, crisp bacon, a bit of freshly grated Parmesan, and freshly ground black pepper for an "Irish Carbonara." Or just use your imagination!

Minnesota Meatloaf

Yield:
2 standard
5x9-inch
loaf pans

Labor Day is supposed to be a holiday, and a day of rest, but how can it be with windows to wash, leaves to rake, and kids to get ready for school classes and sports? If your to-do list is the length of two football fields, try our fall menu. Everything but the salad can be made ahead and baked in the oven.

And the holiday table centerpiece? That old Midwestern time-saver: meatloaf. While some of the meats in our recipe may seem exotic and unfamiliar, they're delicious, low-fat, low-cholesterol, and readily available at most co-ops and natural and higher-end grocery stores, as well as any number of freestanding butcher shops statewide.

1 lb. ground bison

1 lb. ground yak or elk

1 lb. ground sirloin

2 pieces of bacon diced

1 tbsp. extra virgin olive oil

1 lb. sweet yellow onion,
    diced small

4 tsp. dried leaf thyme

1 tsp. freshly ground black pepper

3 large eggs

4½ c. dried whole- or multigrain
    bread crumbs

¾ c. whole milk

2 tbsp. yellow Dijon-style mustard

2 tbsp. tomato paste

2 tbsp. of ketchup

2 tbsp. Worcestershire sauce

Salt, to taste

Preheat oven to 375°F.

1. Place bison, yak, sirloin, and diced bacon in a large bowl. Mix well.

2. Sauté the onion in the olive oil over medium-high heat until slightly brown. Add the dried thyme and the freshly ground pepper and cook for 1 minute. Let cool before adding to the meat mixture.

3. In a small bowl, beat the 3 eggs with a fork; add bread crumbs and stir. Add the milk, and beat with a wooden spoon.

4. Combine mustard, tomato paste, ketchup, and Worcestershire sauce in a separate small bowl; add to bread/milk mixture along with sautéed onions.

5. Wash hands well. Combine the bread/milk/onion mixture with the meat. Mix well by hand; the mixture should be fairly loose. Test for seasoning by frying a small patty of the meat mixture; taste and adjust seasonings. Add salt if desired.

6. Divide mixture between the two loaf pans and place in the center of the preheated oven. Bake for 45 minutes, or until a thermometer inserted into the center of each loaf registers 180°F. Remove from the oven, let rest for 5–10 minutes. Turn meatloaf out on a cutting board that has been placed in a sided sheet pan to catch drippings. Slice and serve.

Freezing the Second Loaf

One meatloaf feeds four hungry people. If two meatloaves are too much, freeze one uncooked for up to three months. Line the loaf pan with two 12-inch pieces of plastic food wrap, fill with meat mixture, tightly fold the wrap around the loaf, and freeze. When frozen, remove from the loaf pan and store in a plastic bag. Before baking, unwrap loaf and place in a pan, tightly rewrap with new food film and thaw in the refrigerator. Cook as above.

Drying Herbs

Ahhhh, that sweet smell of summer's fresh herbs, so bountiful and cheap; and then comes winter when costs rise and flavors fall, and we seriously consider taking out second mortgages to satisfy our cravings. But is fresh really better than dried? When it comes to winter flavors and prices, no. The savory flavors of Midwestern winter dishes are often stronger and more pungent than those of summer fare when made with fresh herbs. The essential oils of dried herbs are so concentrated—dried herbs contain only ⅓ the oils found in fresh herbs—that far less is needed.

Dried herbs can be bought in bulk in most large grocery stores and co-ops, allowing you to buy only what is needed. But they can be almost as expensive as the ones in jars, which have often been irradiated. If you're a kitchen gardener, grow extra to dry and maybe experiment with making your own blends. Select some of the more fragrant varieties to grow in your garden, such as licorice tarragon, sweet Thai basil, or heady rosemary, and you'll have a better product for less than half the price of store-bought herbs. And even if you aren't a gardener, you can still buy them fresh at the farmers' market and dry and mix them yourself. By following a few basic steps, you'll be on your way to a winter pantry that rivals the finest spice shop in town.

Use a dehydrator to dry herbs whenever possible; its adjustable low temperature and circulating air shortens the drying time, limiting the loss of flavor, color, and overall quality. But if a dehydrator isn't in your pantry or your budget, all is not lost.

A microwave can be used, as can a conventional oven, gas or electric. For all drying methods, it's important the herbs are washed and completely dry before proceeding. Light, heat, and humidity depletes flavor (oils) and color and causes mold. Rinse in cold water and dry in a salad spinner or blot with paper toweling.

Drying Herbs in Conventional Ovens

Electric ovens have more consistent heat than gas ovens; an oven with a convection setting is best for maintaining a constant, low temperature while letting the air come in contact with all surfaces.

With minimal overlapping, evenly spread the leaves or stems on a mesh screen,* a cookie sheet, or an overturned shallow-sided pan and place in an oven at a maximum temperature of 180 degrees F for 3 to 4 hours with the door open, turning stems and stirring leaves at least twice during this time. If using convection, reduce the temperature by 60 degrees and the time about an hour, and keep the door closed.

*A mesh splatter guard works perfectly for this as long as it doesn't have any plastic or wood on the handle.

Drying Herbs in a Microwave

Place clean, dry leaves or stems on a paper plate or towel without crowding. Set microwave temperature at high, dry for approximate recommended time (see below), and turn stems and mix leaves every 30 seconds, depending density. Hissing or popping is water evaporating and will subside. To reduce water content and drying time, strip leaves from stems, especially dense, fleshy herbs: sage, rosemary, marjoram, etc. Leave delicate herbs like dill, fennel weed, and chervil on stems, and strip after drying.

Evenly space dried herbs on a cooling rack so air can circulate for at least an hour to ensure they're completely dry; loosely pack in glass jars, without crushing. Seal with tight-fitting lids and store in the dark, away from heat-generating appliances.

Approximate Times for Microwave-Dried Herbs

Evenly space on a single sheet of paper toweling or a paper plate without overlapping, and turn or mix every 30 seconds:

1 minute/leaves only:	thyme, tarragon, mint, Italian parsley, basil (small to medium leaves), chives (chopped), dill, and fennel weed (stem on)
2 minutes/leaves only:	rosemary, oregano, curly parsley, basil (large leaves), marjoram, bay
3 minutes/leaves only:	sage, borage, lemon verbena
Other herbs:	compare to those listed, with similar size and density.

Other Ways to Dry Herbs

Actually, the easiest and most economical way to dry herbs is the oldest; it just takes longer. Instead of making an investment in equipment, plus the cost of the energy consumed in operation—all in the interest of saving time—do as your forebears did and dry the herbs in a dark, nonhumid environment at room temperature. They used their fruit rooms and attics, but you can get by with a closet or cupboard as long as it's dark and dry.

Another ingenious method is to use small brown paper bags. Harvest the herbs with stems intact; wash, dry, and place in paper bags, tops first with plenty of headroom and ends sticking out. Gather the bag around the stems, securely tie with a long piece of string, and hang from a hook or broom handle positioned between two shelves. When dried, crush the bags by hand, untie, and remove the stems.

All herbs should be stored in dry, airtight containers in the dark. Tin cans or colored glass jars with close-fitting lids are great. When stored in this way, dried herbs will retain much of their flavor for a long time, but are best if used within 6 to 9 months.

Butternut Squash with Maple Syrup

Serves 4

We mix maple syrup, mustard, and cider with sautéed onions and rosemary for a quick pork roast baste and to add dimension to the flavor of baked beans and barbecue sauces. And in the classic combination that follows, butternut squash roasted with butter and maple syrup reaches a new level with generous grinds of black pepper.

1 medium butternut squash
4 tsp. unsalted butter
Coarse sea or kosher salt, to taste
Freshly ground black pepper,
    to taste
1 c. pure maple syrup

Preheat oven to 400°F.

1. Wash the outside of the squash; quarter, remove seeds, and stem. Lay skin side down on sided baking sheet.

2. Place 1 tsp. of butter, a pinch of salt and pepper, and ¼ c. maple syrup in each cavity.

3. Roast in the lower part of the preheated oven for 15 minutes, remove and brush the butter-pepper-syrup mixture over the squash. Return to the oven, and roast another 15 minutes. The maple syrup and butter will be absorbed into the squash, leaving a lovely sweet, peppery glaze.

Romanesco Broccoli Sauté

Surprise and delight your science-minded friends by serving Romanesco broccoli, with it's architectural light green florets that spiral to a point. Be sure to refer to it as "fractal food," the whimsical moniker conferred on it by cruciferous-eating mathematicians everywhere.

1–2 heads Romanesco broccoli,
    trimmed, with florets cut into
    1–2-inch pieces
¼–½ c. extra virgin olive oil
3–4 cloves garlic, peeled and cut
    into thin slices
Hot pepper flakes, to taste
Juice of 1 large lemon
Coarse sea or kosher salt
4 thick slices of toasted bread,
    rubbed with garlic,
    as accompaniment

1. Steam or parboil broccoli until bright green but still crunchy, about 5 minutes. Remove from heat, and take off the cover.

2. While broccoli is cooking, heat olive oil in a large sauté pan over low to medium heat, add garlic, and cook for 1–2 minutes, just until softened, but not browned.

3. Increase heat to high, add par-cooked broccoli florets, red pepper flakes, coarse salt, and lemon juice, and toss to coat. Serve with thick slices of toasted bread that has been rubbed with a bit of garlic.

Lena's Rutabaga Malt

Linda, AKA Lena, Shamburg

Serves 2

Lena, who is full of energy and goodwill, is also full of surprises. When we called to see if she'd give me the recipe for her rutabaga concoction, we learned Lena had come up with a host of other things too, including an environmentally friendly fire starter made completely from recyclable materials, eliminating the need for kindling—something that made Minnesota's forest rangers so happy they gave her an award. She was not the least bit hesitant to share her recipe, and will be publishing *The Complete Rutabaga Cookbook*. Lena's malt, and her recipe for rutabaga jam, will be included for all rutabaga enthusiasts to enjoy.

2 tbsp. rutabaga, peeled and
    cut into small chunks

1 scant tsp. canola oil

3 c. vanilla ice cream (not soft
    serve)

1 oz. real maple syrup

1 oz. malt powder

1½ oz. whole milk

½ c. whipped heavy cream,
    for garnish

Dash of nutmeg, freshly grated
    if available

Preheat oven to 400°F.

1. Spread rutabaga evenly on a baking sheet and lightly oil with scant teaspoon canola oil. Loosely cover with parchment or aluminum foil and roast until soft. Remove to a bowl and mash while warm. Chill until ready to use.

2. Place rutabaga in a blender or malt mixer with the next 6 ingredients, and blend. Use more milk to thin if desired. Serve in a tall malt glass and garnish with whipped cream and nutmeg.

October

Endive · Beets · Blue Cheese · Duck · Yak · Elk · Bison · Apples
· Roasting Chicken · Dried Rosemary

I confess to favoring October, but only after dark. You can have the sunny days and pretty colored leaves—it all stinks of sadness for me. I like Halloween, the Day of the Dead, the rusty tin skeleton I brought from Mexico clattering in the wind, nights that promise to be dark and mysterious, candles blown ghoulish, rich game dinners, spicy greens, blood-red beets, blue cheese, and poached apples dripping with cream and sparkling cider sauce.

Minnesota's Own—From Haralson to Honeycrisp™

Say "Red Delicious" to University of Minnesota fruit breeder David Bedford and you are likely to see a grimace cross his face. Developer of Honeycrisp™, the tasty apple that's captured the hearts and taste buds of Minnesotans, Bedford implies that a childhood distaste for the unappealing red fruit in his lunchbox was one motivation for breeding a better apple.

The Honeycrisp™ was introduced in 1991; the fact that it still seems new to us and is something of a novelty in grocery stores is an indication of just how glacially slow the business of breeding fruit really is. Left to its own devices, nature might have developed the Honeycrisp™ over thousands of years. The University's fruit-breeding program is a speedy process compared with that, but it still can take fifteen years for a new variety to get to market—in part because getting rid of the bad apples is done one bite at a time.

Bedford tastes 500 to 600 apples a day in search of one that will excel in a test of twenty criteria. In response to my widened eyes, he joked, "the first hundred are not too bad." He's looking for a big taste difference, one that will reach out and grab the general public, and only one in 10,000 is good enough to make the grade.

One might think that Bedford has the nose, or taste buds, of a wine connoisseur, who is trying to discern particular characteristics, but he downplays his skill, saying that even I could do the job.

The process begins when trees are cross-pollinated and bear fruit; then the seeds, which carry the genetic material and are the true hybrids, are harvested. The University plants 3,000 of these seeds a year, and when they've grown, it grafts the resulting plants to root stock that will bear fruit in a few years. Throughout that time, Bedford and his team observe the hybrids' winter hardiness, storage characteristics, and disease resistance because, like contestants in a beauty contest, the apples must excel in more than just what meets the eye. In the ninety-nine years that the University of Minnesota has been breeding apples, eighteen new apples have been introduced.

Once an apple is found, a name is given, and a patent applied for, Bedford extends the same methodical scientific process used for winnowing thousands of cultivars to developing a name for the apple—thousands of names are considered.

"People buy an apple on appearance, and name . . . which doesn't always tell you much, in part because patented names are required to avoid description." He gave the example of Zestar!™, a variety that was introduced in 1999, saying that it could not have been called "Zesty." Some apple varieties like Prairie Spy or the long-standing Minnesota favorite, Haralson, have names that are not descriptive at all. But apples that have been developed during Bedford's tenure—such as Honeycrisp™, whose crisp texture is a salient feature, and Snowsweet™, a winter-hardy northern apple with slow-to-oxidize white flesh—have names that bridge description and imagination.

When the new apple has a patented name, it is released to the nurseries. Two years later the new apple is finally announced to the public, but it will be a long while before you'll find it at the grocery.

Nurseries graft cuttings of the new variety onto dwarf stock, then sell the plants to growers who, faced with catalogs full of trees, may gamble on purchasing only a few. It then takes three or four years before there is fruit and seven before a good production level is reached. During that time, if word of a new great apple gets around, the grower may hedge his bets and buy a few more. If he is well stocked with apples at the time a new apple has captured the public's desire, he's sitting pretty. If not, it takes a few years to catch up, and during that time the apple's reputation may have changed for the worse, since the longer a variety has been on the market, the greater the changes from

When the bright green Granny Smith apple from New Zealand came along, displays that formerly held only Red Delicious gained eye appeal from the other side of the color wheel, and buyers who craved tart apples bought them eagerly.

Apples compared to apples. David Bedford, the University of Minnesota fruit breeder who developed the Honeycrisp™, talks about apples as if they were his children; he can tell an interesting tale about the unique lineage of every apple variety.

natural mutations, varied growing conditions, or market-driven "guidance."

Bedford says the "mindless march toward redder is better" has ruled the market and elevated the mealy and tasteless Red Delicious apple. Seven thousand, five hundred apple varieties are grown throughout the world, and two thousand, five hundred of those are grown across America. But since the 1960s and the ascendance of the modern supermarket, Red Delicious has reigned—the result of breeders and growers consistently choosing color over flavor in order to attract produce buyers.

"We're not sure the grocers have it right," he said. It's not that red in itself is inherently bad, but eye appeal is merely one characteristic. "I started this job twenty-nine years ago, and I can't make a redder apple." It's doubtful that he would want to try since, in general, appearance is of less importance to the University: "We would release an apple without good looks if it had great texture and flavor."

When the bright green Granny Smith apple from New Zealand came along, displays that formerly held only Red Delicious gained eye appeal from the other side of the color wheel, and buyers who craved tart apples bought them eagerly. Today's Granny Smith neither tastes nor looks like the apples that first came from New Zealand. Originally the apple was yellow, but mutations and market choices have resulted in the vibrant green color and a hard, woody texture. Despite the fact that it is less of an apple than it was, the apple still has appeal because of its more acidic flavor.

An interesting, but somewhat puzzling fact to Bedford is that the farther north you go, the more people like tart apples; perhaps that's why, as an apple market, Minnesota is unique. Here, as in much of America, grocery stores tend to carry apples grown outside the state, but in Minnesota's co-ops and farmers' markets there are twenty-five varieties, all locally developed and grown.

Of these, few are such striking successes as the Honeycrisp™. It has a remarkable seven-month shelf life and a texture, which Bedford says is from an exceptionally large cell size, that packs a burst of juice and flavor into every bite. And the overwhelmingly good reception it has enjoyed in the marketplace has pumped new life into what was, in places, a dying business.

Though he has plenty to be proud of, I wondered if Bedford's subject might lose some appeal after 500 to 600 bites every day, but as I was leaving he handed me an apple from the Research Station's cooler and said, "I must have eaten ten thousand Honeycrisp™ over the years and every one of them is good."

Sky Blue Waters: Great Blue Cheese

Cheesemakers know something the rest of us don't. If they didn't, their eyes wouldn't twinkle the way they do.

They look healthy and a bit younger than their years. A workroom atmosphere of 99 percent humidity and a little layer of butterfat gained from frequent taste testing would keep anyone's skin plump. Though aging like the rest of us, laboring over vats of milk keeps cheesemakers looking moist, pink, and relatively unwrinkled. This alone might make my eyes twinkle, but it's not the reason for their satisfaction. No, the twinkle in the cheesemakers' eyes comes from possessing a skill that is nothing short of magic.

Cheesemaking is a tricky process at best, taking years to learn; but once mastered, the cheesemaker's work is akin to alchemy: transforming a white liquid into a flavor-packed wheel that has the heft of a small treasure chest and the finish of a fine, hand-built vessel. Picture deep mysterious caves beneath a river bluff, racks and racks of wheels tended by men in white suits, and you're more likely to imagine "The Hall of the Mountain King" than a small blue cheese business in Faribault, Minnesota.

Now picture Faribault cheesemaker Jeff Jirik. His eyes twinkle, and they should. He knows the magic of cheesemaking well enough to impress cheese judges around the world, and he is doing it all in the Minnesota caves that the big cheese businesses passed up long ago.

To cheese connoisseurs, nothing is more magical than a big blue with its distinctly tangy flavor. Over a thousand years ago it occurred serendipitously, and someone ventured a taste. You can almost see early cheese aficionados in a cave somewhere, salivating over the last moldy crumb, and wondering how to duplicate that fabulous taste. Re-creating nature's best accidents is no mean feat.

The most famous blue cheeses—Roquefort, Stilton, Danablue, and Gorgonzola—are so highly regarded for their distinct regional characteristics, the European Union protects individual designations of origin in order to discourage copycats. At times, these cheeses were prohibitively expensive or importing them was not allowed.

In 1937 the first American blue cheese was made in Minnesota's own Faribault caves, and it quickly cornered the American market because of a wartime ban on the importation of European cheese. Treasure Cave® Blue Cheese, made in the caves now owned by Faribault Dairy, was produced by various companies for more than fifty years; the last of these, Beatrice Foods, gave up the Faribault facility in southeastern Minnesota for a more modern factory setting in Wisconsin.

Few businesses can claim so bucolic a setting as the Faribault Dairy. Downtown Faribault rests on the western bank of the Straight River, once the thoroughfare for French fur traders. Though the buildings are a mix of the old and the new, they conspire to create the comfortable look of a town from fifty years ago and across the river, the Faribault Dairy perches on a little flat land half way up an impressive sandstone bluff. The 1940s building is as white as a bottle of milk, and has the clean, no-nonsense look that a dairy should have, but hidden deep in the bluff beneath the dairy's unromantic exterior is a catacomb of caves dating back over one hundred years. The public is not allowed to visit the dairy, but the site is so interesting we decided to give our readers a look beneath the scene.

Autumn was giving winter a run for its money the day BJ and I went to the dairy. Just as we crossed the river, the sun punched a hole through a leaden sky, lighting the white uniforms of a couple of employees who were outside enjoying lunch and a treetop view of the river. We didn't know it then, but that was probably the only sunlight they'd see that day, since most of their working hours are spent below ground. Not that it's unpleasant, for the sandstone caves have a mystique of their own.

Jeff Jirik, Fairbault Dairy's CEO, met us above the factory and caves, in an office crowded with cheese awards and vintage photos.

"You begin with a cow," he grinned, hefting a 500-page cheesemaking manual.

Jirik's love affair with cheesemaking started in the 1990s while working in the Treasure Cave® Blue Cheese laboratory, and when the Treasure Cave® Blue Cheese operations were moved to Wisconsin in 1993, he went with the company, continuing his cheesemaking education for several years.

But Jirik, who grew up in a Czech community near Faribault, still had strong ties to the area and he never forgot the mystique or the excellent cheese-aging properties of the St. Peter sandstone caves.

The Fort Knox of Faribault: Deep inside the sandstone caves where Faribault Dairy ages their cheese, owner Jeff Jirik checks the progress of his treasure—St. Pete's Select® aged blue cheese.

In 2001 Jirik bought the Faribault site and began to manufacture his own cheese, which he dubbed Amablu® to stress its American origins. This is now the trade name for several high-quality blue cheeses: Amablu®, fairly young and easy on the taste buds; St. Pete's Select®, aged longer, tastes stronger, and able to make a true cheese lover smile; and Amablu® Gorgonzola, a sweeter, creamier, Italian-style blue cheese.

An almost reverent look crossed Jirik's face as he described the unique sandstone caves where Amablu® is aged. Found only in Minnesota and named for the town where it was first identified, St. Peter sandstone is composed of very fine glacially deposited beach sand that is 99.9 percent pure quartzite. The first of Faribault Dairy's caves was dug here by hand in 1854.

One noted characteristic of St. Peter sandstone is its ability to support an arch. At fourteen feet wide and twenty-two feet tall, these hand-carved caves extend up through the rock in graceful gothic arches. Beneath them, Faribault Dairy has nearly an acre of usable space filled with lovingly tended, gracefully aging blue cheese. Within the whitewashed walls that stretch up into the darkness is a strange hush. Jirik says that in this place the cares of the world are left behind.

Another of the sandstone's unique characteristics is its ability to transport water vertically and horizontally, enabling the caves to stay at 99 percent humidity without dripping. Ground water, which travels down to the cave wall, then out to the face of the bluff, transports the ammonia that is released in the cheese aging process from the cave's interior out into the fresh air.

The caves and their special atmosphere are only part of the story. From the amount of butterfat in the cow's milk, to the composition of the bacteria that forms the mold, cheesemaking is in the details, many of which are proprietary company secrets. One technique Jirik did reveal was the importance of an old-fashioned "cut."

Cutting is the process of drawing a comb-like rake through coagulating milk that creates clean edged curds on which the bacteria forms. When done by hand, irregular blue veins of mold weave their way through the cheese, making each crumble unique. Less artisanlike producers make cheese in which the mold is evenly distributed, resulting in a reliably even appearance and less distinctive taste.

At a production level of 950,000 pounds a year, Fairbault Dairy is a small but promising business. Their cheese astonished international judges, who chose Amablu® in a blind taste test for the 2002 World Cheese Awards, never thinking it was from America.

To Jirik it's not really a mystery. He is quick to point out a fact little-known to Minnesotans: Faribault is located at the same latitude as Roquefort, the home of France's signature blue cheese. There's that twinkle in the eye again.

Cheesemaking is a tricky process at best, taking years to learn; but once mastered, the cheesemaker's work is akin to alchemy: transforming a white liquid into a flavor-packed wheel that has the heft of a small treasure chest and the finish of a fine, hand-built vessel.

The Yak Man

John Hooper: Christmas Trees, Hoof Trimmer, Yak Consultant. Will Travel. So could read the business card for this quiet, unassuming businessman. The only clue to his unusual vocation is the "YAK MAN" license plate on his well-traveled SUV. If you're curious, Hooper will tell a tale that stretches from central Minnesota to the Tibetan Plateau where nomadic tribesmen call him "The Yak Man" too.

We met Hooper at the St. Joseph Farmers' Market not far from the tree farm and yak ranch he calls home, but you can find him standing behind a freezer full of yak meat at the St. Cloud or the St. Joseph farmers' markets with a photo album of yaks in his hand.

A self-appointed ambassador for the yak industry, Hooper has fun turning people on to what must be Minnesota's most unusual livestock. And, after chancing upon him at the St. Joseph Farmers' Market, we made what BJ and I thought would be a quick stop at his place to see a real yak. Before you could say Khyber Pass, we were bouncing across Hooper's pasture on a golf cart in the pouring rain, trying to get photos of the furry beasts before they turned their hooky horns our way.

We probably weren't in any real danger, because Hooper, who began his career trimming the hooves of cattle and now owns the largest yak herd east of the Rockies, knew his animals and kept several golf-cart lengths between us and the herd at all times. Without him though, we might have gone foolishly close because, despite weighing thousands of pounds, full-grown yaks dripping with dreadlocks look as cuddly as English sheep dogs.

Baby yaks have not yet grown their long, shaggy coats and resemble more common bovine calves, but are even more adorable. Before we left, we saw one close up while Hooper patiently bottle fed it—simultaneously calming the calf and Grace who barked crazily at the unfamiliar creature.

Hooper got into yaks when the U.S. government sent him to Indonesia in the late 1980s to train farmers to trim cows' hooves. From there it was a short but logical shift to Tibet and yaks, where he became a consultant to the nomadic tribesman, helping them improve the productivity of their herds.

As he huddled with the nomads in their wall-tents woven from yak hair, eating yak meat and drinking yak milk, Hooper saw that every part of the animal could be put to good use. He

Yak Man becomes Yak Mama. John Hooper, seen here hand-feeding a yak calf, knows this species so well he was once a yak consultant for tribesman in Tibet.

brought some of the Tibetan's handiwork home as mementos and now displays saddles, horn flagons, and tufted yak fur garments on the walls of his ranch-style home. These were common objects for the Tibetans, but with growing pressure from the Chinese government for herders to give up their animals and traveling ways, Hooper's "yakanalia" may soon become collectors' items.

Heeding the lessons of his former nomadic clients, Hooper lets no part of the yak go to waste. His herd doesn't produce enough milk for yak butter, a staple in Tibet and a hard-to-find luxury here, so he saves the milk and contributes it to a grateful and growing Tibetan community in North Minneapolis for their personal use. In turn, that community is a ready market for his various cuts and preparations of yak, which includes roasts, ground yak, and bratwurst. BJ and I experimented with a slow-cooked stew made from yak roast, but in the end we preferred yak brats accompanied by dark ale. Try them for a summer barbecue or check out more traditional preparations in Twin Cities restaurants that serve Tibetan food.

Apples of Your Eyes

Picking your own apples and then going home to make a pie is one of Minnesota's more idyllic activities. As the country's second-largest apple-producing state, Minnesota has an unusually wide assortment of apples, many of which were developed at the University of Minnesota's horticultural research center in Chanhassen, just west of the Minnesota Landscape Arboretum. In addition to selling fresh fruit, many of the more than one hundred Minnesota growers produce apple cider and other products; a number of them let you go into the orchards and pick. If you're not up to the task, the pick-your-own orchards will pre-pick for you.

While most orchards are open all week during the fall season, many pick-your-own places have activities on weekends for good old-fashioned fun. Check with the Minnesota Department of Agriculture—(651) 201-6114, www.minnesotagrown.com—or the current *Minnesota Grown Directory* located at MN Department of Agriculture, Minnesota Grown Program, 625 Robert St. N., St. Paul, MN 55155-2538, for a list of orchards.

Great Pumpkin Patches

One of the easiest and most enjoyable pick-your-own outings is hunting for the perfect Halloween pumpkin. There's little stooping down and no reaching up, and some farmers even make it easy to carry them away, offering hayrides to the pumpkin patch where they've cut the gourds from the vine and separated them by size into easily accessible piles. In early autumn this family-friendly weekend adventure can include petting zoos, corn mazes, and mugs of freshly pressed, hot apple cider. There are more than 140 farms and orchards that grow pumpkins in Minnesota, so it won't be hard to find a pumpkin patch near you. Check the list in the *Minnesota Grown Directory* or call the Minnesota Department of Agriculture to locate one in your area.

One pumpkin patch we really enjoyed was Minnetonka-Orchards near Minnetrista (www.minnetonkaorchards.com, 763-479-6530). Close to the Twin Cities, it's easy to find, welcomes children, has ample park-ing and bathrooms, and—most importantly—has plenty to do, see, and taste. Even well-behaved family dogs can join in the fun. On the weekends there are brats, burgers, and apple donuts to eat out-of-hand along with take-away treats such as fresh apple pie, dried apples, jams, and jellies. En route to the pumpkin patch, their hayride took a short detour into the woods where scarecrows and goblins had been tacked to the trees. The ride was long enough to put color in your cheeks and capture the spirit of Halloween. Once we got to the field, the kids went running to find their favorite pumpkins, the littlest of them invariably picking ones as big as themselves.

**Roasted Beet Salad
with Blue Cheese &
Curly Endive**

♦

Shortcut Cassoulet Exotica

♦

Poached Apple Supreme

♦

Roasted Rosemary Chicken

Roasted Beet Salad with Blue Cheese & Curly Endive

Serves
4 to 6

This salad has everything: sweet, salty, and sour tastes, soft and crunchy textures, and tons of eye appeal. Perfect when individually plated or on a buffet, it will convert the most ardent naysayer into a beet aficionado. For an exceptional presentation, consider using orange, yellow, and striped beets along with, or in place, of red ones.

2 bunches small beets (about 8–20, 1–2 inches diameter), washed and trimmed

1 small bunch each curly endive, romaine hearts, arugula, mesclun, or other crunchy, flavorful greens

1 c. walnut halves and pieces, roasted

½ c. blue cheese, about 4 oz., crumbled

1 pt. fresh raspberries, sorted and rinsed

1 medium red onion, peeled and thinly sliced, about 1 c.

1. Adjust rack to middle of oven and preheat oven to 375°F.

2. Evenly space the washed, trimmed beets on a 15x10x1-inch sided greased or oiled baking sheet or jellyroll pan, place in the middle of oven, and roast for 30–45 minutes; until slightly tender. Shake pan to loosen and turn the beets; cover with aluminum foil. Reduce oven temperature to 350°F, and continue cooking for 20 minutes.

3. While beets are roasting, wash, dry, and trim salad greens. Place in a single layer on cotton or paper toweling, roll up jellyroll style and refrigerate until ready to use. Make Raspberry Dressing (see recipe on page 97), and set aside at room temperature.

4. Remove roasted beets from the oven, keep covered, and let sit for 10–15 minutes. Use a table knife to peel the beets. The skins should slip off easily, but beware: they stain! If red fingers are a problem, try wearing lightweight surgical-type gloves. Slice beets into ¼-inch rounds, or cut into quarters. Place in stainless-steel or glass bowl, and set aside.

5. Wipe the roasting pan off with paper towels and spread the walnuts evenly over the top. Roast for 3–4 minutes, shaking the pan once during this time to ensure even roasting. Nut oils burn easily, resulting in a bitter flavor, so keep a close eye. If they get too brown, *start over.* Let the nuts cool completely before using.

6. Reserve a few walnuts, raspberries, and bits of crumbled blue cheese to garnish the top of the salad; set individual salad plates, or one large shallow service bowl on the counter.

7. Place half the dressing in the bottom of a large mixing bowl. Add crisped greens (gently tear any oversized leaves), fresh raspberries, crumbled blue cheese, walnuts, and onion slices. Carefully toss with clean hands, and place on platter or salad plates. Evenly distribute roasted beets on the tops of the salads. Garnish with reserved blue cheese, walnuts, and raspberries. Drizzle remaining dressing over the top. Serve with thinly sliced French bread and chilled dry, still, or sparkling rosé or white wine, or mineral water.

Raspberry Dressing

3 tbsp. raspberry vinegar

2 tbsp. seedless raspberry jam

1 tbsp. crumbled blue cheese

Salt and freshly ground black pepper, to taste

¾ c. canola, or other lightly flavored vegetable oil

2 tbsp. walnut oil, check for freshness*

1. Place vinegar, raspberry jam, blue cheese, salt, and pepper in a mini-processor, blender, or small bowl. Process or whisk until blended.

2. With motor running (or while whisking), slowly drizzle oils into the mixture. Process or blend until smooth. Taste for salt and pepper; adjust as needed.

*Nut and seed oils are very volatile and can go rancid quickly once opened and exposed to light. Buy in the smallest quantities possible, refrigerate or store in a cool, dark place, in colored glass or tin with a good seal.

French Fast Food:
Shortcut Cassoulet Exotica

Serves
8 to 10

This cassoulet is a classic French country dish the pioneers might've made. Don't be intimidated by the lengthy ingredient list; this recipe is really is fast compared to the traditional method, which can take up to three days. The key is *mies en place*, or the practice of prepping, measuring, and setting out all ingredients in order of use. Just clear the counters, set up your *mies*, start your oven, and you'll be done in no time.

5 slices thick-cut bacon, coarsely chopped

1 tbsp. olive oil

3 lbs. buffalo or yak loin, boned and cut into 1- to 1 ½-inch pieces; dried with
    paper towels

1 lb. elk sausage, cut in pieces

1 lb. pork sausage with garlic, cut in 2-inch pieces

2 c. yellow onions, chopped

2 c. dry white wine or dry white vermouth

3 tbsp. tomato paste

1 c. carrots, sliced in 1-inch pieces

1 large herb bouquet tied in a muslin sack or cheesecloth:

    6–8 parsley sprigs

    2 peeled carrots inserted with 4 whole cloves

    1 rib of celery

    2 bay leaves

1 tbsp. dried thyme

1 tbsp. freshly ground black pepper; salt will be added at the end of cooking

2 tbsp. Girardin Gardens roasted garlic

1 lb. pancetta, cut into ½-inch pieces

2 cans cooked Great Northern beans with their liquid

3 c. dry white bread crumbs

½ c. minced fresh or ¼ c. dried parsley

3 tbsp. olive oil

1 qt. hot beef, chicken, or pork stock, or a combination

1. Preheat oven to 325°F; position rack on lower bracket.

2. Place roasting pan over medium heat and add chopped bacon and olive oil. Add the cut bison or yak to the heated fat a few pieces at a time, browning on all sides and removing browned meat to a side dish before adding more. Add more oil to the pan as needed between batches.

3. Add cut sausages to roasting pan, brown on all sides.

4. Add chopped onion and cook until soft. Remove from pan and place in side dish with yak or bison meat.

5. Add the dry white wine or vermouth to the roasting pan with the tomato paste, increase heat to high and reduce to half volume; scrape the pan to loosen any tasty bits stuck on the bottom.

6. Return the browned bison or yak, sausages, and onions to the roasting pan, then add the carrots, herb bundle, thyme, pepper, and roasted garlic, stirring to coat. Add the pancetta and cooked beans with their liquid and stir to combine. Taste for seasoning and adjust, adding salt if needed. Press down on the mixture with the back of a spoon or spatula, and smooth the top.

7. In a separate bowl, mix the bread crumbs with the parsley and olive oil, and sprinkle half over the top of the roasting pan. Set rest of bread crumbs aside. Add half of the stock along with any meat juices that collected in the side dish, cover and place in the lower part of oven for 1 hour.

8. Remove lid, increase oven temperature to 375°F, and continue to cook casserole uncovered until bread crumbs have browned and formed a crust, about 20 minutes. Stir down most of the crust into the beans; baste with the liquid that rises. Top with last 2 c. of bread crumbs, add remaining stock, and continue roasting in oven until a sturdy crust forms again, about 45 minutes. Leave the final crust intact. Serve from its casserole, with a tart green salad, warm crusty French bread, and a good red table wine. *Bon Appetit!*

Pepin Heights™ bluff-top apple orchard south of Lake City was without question the most spectacular sight BJ and I saw while traveling Minnesota in search of local foods. We sought them out because we were hooked on the taste and quality of Pepin Heights™ fresh-pressed, preservative-free apple ciders and juices, found in local grocers' refrigerators in season.

The company's little apple store on Highway 61 presents a deceptively small and homey face to the kaleidoscope of day-trippers who arrive in sports cars, pickups, or flotillas of noisy Harley hogs each weekend in the fall. Not far away is the huge, but understated, state-of-the-art plant where Pepin Heights™ stores their apples—a full 20 percent of Minnesota's fresh apple stock—and makes the juice and cider BJ and I adore. Then there are the orchards, situated on the bluffs above behind locked gates, where apples grow closer to the clouds than the lake below.

Poached Apple Supreme

Serves 4

Our Poached Apple Supreme is made with three ingredients and a technique even a novice cook can master easily, but the incorporation of Pepin Heights™ Sparkling Apple Cider raises the humble apple to new heights. We oven-poached apples in the carbonated cider, then reduced the liquid and blended it with reduced heavy cream for a heavenly sauce that allows the flavor of fresh-pressed apples to shine through.

4 medium to large
  Honeycrisp™ apples
2 12-oz. bottles Pepin Heights™
  Sparkling Apple Cider
2 c. Land O'Lakes™ Extra-Heavy
  Whipping Cream

1. Preheat oven to 375°F.

2. Peel apples vertically, leaving stripes of skin for decoration; cut a thin slice from the bottom of each apple so it will sit level.

3. Place in a deep glass or ceramic baking dish; cover with sparkling cider and bake 40 minutes or until tender, basting occasionally.

4. While apples are poaching, pour whipping cream into a heavy-bottomed saucepan, place over high heat and reduce by half.

5. Remove apples from poaching liquid, set on a plate, and loosely cover with plastic wrap until serving. Pour 2 c. of poaching liquid into a heavy-bottomed saucepan and reduce by two-thirds. Blend reduced cider with reduced cream, return to heat, bring to a full boil, and remove from stove.

6. Pour into individual shallow serving bowls, place apples on top, and serve, passing the remaining sauce.

Roasted Rosemary Chicken

Serves 4

No time for cassoulet? Roast chicken is a fast seasonal alternative. When it comes to savory comfort foods, few are as simple or as easy.

1 4–4.5 lb. free-range chicken

Kosher salt

Freshly cracked black pepper

5–6 cloves garlic, peeled

2 tbsp. dried rosemary

Zest and juice of 1 lemon

Kitchen string

1. Preheat oven to 500°F.

2. Remove excess fat and innards from chicken cavity and discard; wash the inside and outside with cool water and pat all surfaces, including cavity, completely dry with paper towels. Salt and pepper the cavity, and set the chicken aside.

3. Mash the garlic cloves and a pinch of kosher salt with a mortar and pestle, a chef's knife, or in a mini food processor; add the dried rosemary, lemon zest, and a little more freshly ground black pepper, and mash to combine. Rub half of the seasoning mixture inside the cavity and insert remaining seasoning under the skin, breast, leg, and thigh. Squeeze half a lemon over entire outside of chicken, and tuck the squeezed half lemon into the cavity. Tie the legs together with kitchen string, and bend the wingtips back behind the neck.

4. Roast or rotisserie according to directions below. Then, remove from oven or rotisserie to a platter so juices can collect, and let rest on for 15–20 minutes before carving.

To Roast

Reduce the oven temperature from 500°F to 400°F; set the chicken on a roaster rack, breast side up, and place in the center of the oven with the legs to the back and the breast closest to the door. Roast until the internal temperature reads 160°F on an instant-read thermometer inserted between the leg and the thigh.

To Rotisserie

Insert the skewer securely through the chicken, and follow instructions for your oven or grill. Rotisserie until the internal temperature reads 160°F on an instant-read thermometer inserted between the leg and the thigh.

November

Potatoes · Kale · Carrots · Parsnips · Pork · Apple Cider · Pumpkin

November. Tender, green vegetables are long gone from the market stalls, leaving room for a regal procession of purple-trimmed kale, sunset-orange turban squashes—ruby red at the rim, rich earth-brown potatoes, smoked meats, and the ivory orbs and cones of turnips and parsnips. In the country, the conquering frost long ago crowned anything green with some shade of gold—from yellow ochre to auburn, and now the wind is picking up and ermine snow trims our footfalls, catching first on the corn stubble then filling in the furrows. The barn at the farm where we go to buy pork is awfully quiet this time of year, but the farmhouse kitchen windows drip with steam from an army of pumpkin pies camped, cooling in their tins, on every horizontal plane.

Bringing Home the Bacon

As a baby buckaroo, my dad, who was reared on a hardscrabble Norwegian homestead in western North Dakota, loved salt pork and potatoes in milk gravy. In pre-refrigeration days, everyone kept a few pigs, and their meat was preserved in crocks of salt brine; hence, salt pork. To get the salt out, my grandmother boiled the meat in milk, then made a gravy that my dad harbored a lifelong craving for—not a dish I've found in any cookbook.

If I could get past the idea of an all-white meal, or overlook the unappetizing appearance of cellophane-wrapped cubes of pork fat hiding in the far reaches of the meat case, I might try to reconstruct the recipe, but it would be hard to know where to start. What's labeled as salt pork doesn't look like a source of protein, or anything even remotely healthy.

Made from pork bellies, salt pork is similar to bacon but fattier and saltier, and it adds those very qualities, plus a little pork flavor, to old American standards like Boston baked beans. It must have put the same spin on the milk gravy too, drawing out the essence of the protein, fat, and salt—the good life—that people of the Depression era yearned for.

The problem with trying to duplicate the taste of something eaten during deprivation is that today we are no longer deprived in the same way. Most of the time we eat so high on the hog, and in such quantities, that we need to cut back on fat and salt; I would have to find my way back to the farm, pickle my own pork, and spend a year eating only my own produce before I could really appreciate, and approximate, my dad's favorite meal. This could well be one of those recipes that, once gone from memory, is lost forever, subjugated to the realm of mysterious culinary flavors of the past along with pheasant pie, turtle soup, and ham.

Ham? Most people think they know ham. But listen to astonished customers sampling country-cured ham from Neumann Farms at the Princeton Farmers' Market and you will see that they've never tasted anything like it before. The first time I ate Neumann Farms' pork, I was so impressed by its leanness and flavor that I had a similar, astonished reaction. Although Princeton is considerably farther than my average shopping trip, I'll drive miles out of my way to bring home their pork roasts, chops, and bacon.

That's what happens when you get hooked on fresh-from-the-farm food, and that's why we Minnesota food scouts have freezers.

The first time we drove to Princeton, a relative scarcity of homes along the highway fooled us into thinking we were entering a rural area, but we'd never really left town. Off the highway, signs of expansion are everywhere, with wooded parcels advertised as "Acreage, Lots for Sale" and many new homes dotting hills that were formerly rolling pastures. Fifty-five miles northwest of Minneapolis and the city has swallowed all but a few remaining farms around Princeton.

It was a blustery mid-June day when BJ, Grace, and I began our trip to Neumann Farms, with a quick stop at the Princeton Farmers' Market where we hurried to catch Ron Neumann before the wind brought the market to a speedy close.

The market was small that day, only a dozen farmers in a double row that stretched the length of a parking lot on the main street of a friendly-looking town. Vendors, who struggled to hold down awnings and keep pots of seedlings from blowing over, hustled to make quick sales in order to avoid hauling lettuce and strawberry jam back home again.

Although their signs were already down, it wasn't hard to spot the Neumanns by the easy confidence with which they were dismantling their professional looking rig. They had the appearance of people you might trust to collect market fees from vendors or run the local food shelf. Ron was tall and quiet, and Joyce was a friendly, talkative woman we'd first encountered over the phone. There aren't many folks who say "call anytime" and really mean it, but the Neumanns did.

We followed Ron's shiny black pickup to an orderly, prosperous-looking farm five miles from town and drove into a wide, open barnyard that looked as welcoming as the Neumanns themselves. Joining Joyce in her kitchen, we gathered around a counter island with mugs of coffee in hand and soaked up an atmosphere that bespoke homework sessions, family dinners, and community meetings.

Hogs that began as piglets on the Neumann family farm have been sweeping the 4-H awards at the Mille Lacs County Fair for years. Those piglets, along with thousands of their relatives, were coddled and nurtured by Ron Neumann, who strove for thirty years to produce only the leanest, healthiest animals. Raising more than two thousand hogs a year put him in a position to take the best from conventional farming, utilize the most current research in animal health and nutrition, and incorporate it into his own way of doing things. He developed a careful crossbreeding program and mixed hormone- and additive-free feed for each specific stage of the pig's growth. Ron maintained the spirit of independence that draws people to farming in the first place, so it's not surprising to find him making another kind of entrepreneurial effort in middle age.

The Neumanns ventured into direct marketing with a few sales from the farm, and within a couple of years had built a thriving little business at the farmers' markets in Princeton and Maple Grove. Customers were enthusiastic because it was easy to taste the difference from store-bought meat.

With a customer base established, Joyce, whose talent is in the kitchen, saw the opportunity to add to their revenue with her crowd-pleasing strawberry rhubarb pie. She baked a few pies, and by the end of her first full selling season, she'd sold more than four hundred, not all of them strawberry rhubarb.

Plans are as plentiful as piglets at Neumann Farms: Joyce, who was already selling small portions of baked goods—three cookies or two muffins to a bag—hopes to add a permanent stand on the farm, squash, corn, and pumpkin patches, and a larger selection of pies. When we last spoke, Joyce had just finished unpacking seven hundred pie pans, the result of a post-Christmas sale on aluminum cookware, which had entirely filled the trunk of her car.

> *If you haven't spent much time on a farm (and these days who has?) you probably don't know how real ham tastes or the recipe for salt-pork gravy—or that "going whole hog" means chops, hams, roasts, head cheese, pigs feet, sausage, and not just bringing home the bacon.*

Direct marketing wouldn't work for every farm family, but Joyce and Ron could be model spokespersons for the Pork Council—they meet the public with ease and answer even the most elementary questions patiently.

"Now and again, someone wants to buy a whole hog," said Joyce, "thinking they will fill their freezer with chops and bacon. I hate to disappoint them. I mean they are adults and all, it's just that they don't know that there's a lot more to a pig than chops and bacon."

If you haven't spent much time on a farm (and these days who has?) you probably don't know how real ham tastes or the recipe for salt-pork gravy—or that "going whole hog" means chops, hams, roasts, head cheese, pigs feet, sausage, and not just bringing home the bacon.

The King of Kale

If Gardens of Eagan, a thirty-year-old vegetable stand, went up in a puff of pumpkin dust, I'm not sure many drivers barreling down Diffley Road at fifty miles per hour would notice. But, if the Gardens of Eagan logo disappeared from the shelves of Lunds, Byerly's, and Whole Foods Markets, not to mention the Twin Cities network of natural food co-ops, buyers would tear their hair out trying to replace what has become a solid and reliable source of local organic produce.

We'd hoped to catch a dirt-under-the-fingernails-farmer fresh from the fields when our car skidded to a stop on the gravel drive in front of the vegetable stand and old frame farmhouse on Diffley Road. Instead we met a young, neatly dressed farm intern updating the company website on a laptop.

"Writing a book? You MUST speak to Martin," she said with the earnest manner and glowing enthusiasm of a recent convert.

Our interest was piqued, and soon we were driving farther south to visit Martin Diffley, owner of Gardens of Eagan, at his hundred-acre production plot in Farmington. It seemed odd that one small vegetable stand would require a production plot, but it soon became clear that the stand was something of a holdover from Diffley's parents' era, and the modern-day Gardens of Eagan was a large and successful wholesale operation.

The Diffley family had operated a vegetable farm in Eagan on the land surrounding the vegetable stand for many years. When burgeoning land development in the southern suburbs resulted in a $225,000 assessment for sewer and water, the Diffleys were forced to sell everything but the small plot that the vegetable stand and narrow, white frame house share. Martin Diffley, who had been farming the family land, could easily have been forced out of business.

Instead, Diffley regrouped, growing Gardens of Eagan produce on rented land in a dozen locations before purchasing 140 acres near Farmington in 1989. As an early proponent of the Land Stewardship Project, which promotes the preservation of urban land, and one who was instrumental in establishing organic standards for the state of Minnesota, Diffley spent years correcting and improving the soil on the Farmington land to achieve organic certification. In 2006 he faced another hurdle imposed by urban development when the Koch refinery proposed running a crude oil pipeline from Canada right through the land.

From coiffures to kale: During his time as a barber in New Orleans, former Minnesota farm boy Martin Diffley noticed the popularity of kale at the French Market and thought it had potential for northern markets too.

The Gardens of Eagan's production plot was located just beyond the southern shore of a sea of houses, where a glimpse of the horizon signaled the beginning of forty-acre-per-house zoning. Despite nearby urban sprawl, it was hard to believe that the Koch refinery was in the vicinity when we turned off the highway and drove over rolling hills and between lush vegetable plots into Diffley's farmyard.

Diffley, who had unruly black hair and ruddy skin—was he Irish—or French?—came to the door wearing something that looked like pajamas. After greeting us, he launched into a spellbinding monologue that did not let up until we left a couple of hours later.

Back in the 1950s, organic food wholesaling as we know it now wasn't on anyone's radar screen, but the Diffley family, for whom the Eagan thoroughfare is named, had already been feeding wholesome vegetables to Twin Citians for a hundred years.

The early Diffleys, who were indeed both French and Irish, homesteaded in the 1850s on the east side of Lake Calhoun, on land that was part of a "green ring" of truck farms surrounding the Cities. Both sides of the family produced vegetables that were sold at the original Minneapolis Farmers' Market until World War II.

By 1950 the green ring had moved farther out and Martin Diffley was just another farm kid who spent long, tedious summers doing chores on the 340-acre dairy and vegetable farm in Eagan where the roadside stand is now located.

When Diffley recalls those days, it's obvious that his vision for an organic veggie biz wasn't spawned in childhood. By summer's end he and the other vegetable farm kids were so bored that they were the only ones happy to get back on the school bus.

Hesitant to take over the family farm as a young man, Diffley traveled through several other interesting passages before taking his place as the heir to his portion of the vegetable kingdom.

He is a man of passionate interests—from politics to music, history to hairdressing or, to be more gender precise, barbering.

Along with vegetables, pacifism is at the root of his family history. It is a little known fact that there was a time when a professional barber could avoid conscription, and Diffley, whose father was also a barber, was deferred for four years during the Vietnam War.

While shaving sideburns and trimming mustaches, the Diffleys picked the brains of neighboring immigrant farmers who came to America with generations of growing expertise. They learned land stewardship and composting from Europeans whose organic farming practices were a long-standing tradition, rather than a newfangled trend.

Diffley gave us a little history of the back-to-the-land movement, beginning with the postwar years, when chemicals adapted from German chemical research for World War II were promoted for use in American agriculture. Agent Orange, used to defoliate Vietnam, had been originally developed as an herbicide in the 1940s.

At the same time, the diesel engine was developed, and then there was refrigerated cross-country trucking of vegetables from California, Florida, and Cuba. In 1972 the government first used the word agri-business (instead of agriculture) in their campaign to convert farmers to single-crop production, and suddenly there were soybean farmers, and corn farmers, and feedlots instead of a wholly diverse system.

"Basically, the 'culture' was gone from agriculture, because suddenly we wanted our neighbor's land more than our neighbors," said Diffley.

When the baby boomers began to have kids they began to question the safety of agri-business production methods. And the organic movement was on the horizon. In the 1980s, people began to ask for organic; by the late 1980s, the demand exceeded the supply. Since the late 1990s the business has grown 15 to 20 percent per year. Then multinationals bought in and organics were here to stay.

"In the seventies it was hard to get the market directors to spell organic properly, now most of the large food businesses like General Mills have organics in their portfolio because the money's there. Look at the prices of whole foods; the margins are much greater," said Diffley.

Today the organic movement makes it possible for small farms to survive on niche markets, with the largest growth in agriculture being in farms of under fifty acres that operate without subsidies.

While selling at the Minneapolis Farmers' Market, Diffley realized that building clientele was the future for his business. The Wedge, Seward, and Valley co-ops were on his way home, so he began to stop. And Brenda Langton of the vegetarian restaurant Café Kardamena began to highlight Diffley's vegetables. Those contacts paid off. Years later one of his original co-op customers, actually purchased Gardens of Eagan and continues to sell the produce under the Gardens of Eagan name.

We asked Diffley which of his crops had the most interesting story. "Kale," he said, without a moment's hesitation.

He recalled his years in New Orleans when, trading on looks that could be mistaken as Sicilian, he barbered sans license. While he was flying under New Orleans regulatory radar, he operated as "the only straight guy in a gay barbershop on the fringes of the French Quarter." Even in New Orleans, Diffley took note of anything that had to do with producing food. He was frequenting the French Market, making friends with growers of yams and Crowder peas, when he noticed that black people bought kale when no one else was eating it.

Kale comes from the *brassica* family; it predates domestication of cabbage, cauliflower, and broccoli. *Lacinato*, or Dinosaur Kale, was with us in the Fertile Crescent. But because it had such a low profile, kale was never hybridized like other commercial produce, retaining its high calcium content. When the food service industry began to substitute cheaper, durable kale for parsley, Garden's of Eagan was the first to grow it. And when it became a menu item in its own right they were the "Kings of Kale".

Before leaving, we took a walk out to Diffley's kale field. It was a sight to behold: richly colored curly leaves on plants that looked as if they'd been pumping iron. On one side there was a huge pile of tan kale stalks from an earlier year. He showed us how the stalks are strong enough to use as walking canes and woody enough to be used as a source of fuel. Of all the good things about kale, the best news for farmers is it sweetens with the frost.

Casually silhouetted against the field of emerald and amethyst, Diffley's slightly wild-eyed French-Irish looks and pajama-like style of dressing might not lead you to believe he is the last in a long line of Midwestern vegetable farmers or an urbane, seasoned entrepreneur. But it would take very little imagination to see him riding a Mardi Gras float in New Orleans as the King of Kale.

Make Space for a Modern-Day Root Cellar

For many midcentury babies, the term "root cellar" brings up the image of Dorothy in *The Wizard of Oz* struggling to open the slanted doors built into the hill behind Auntie Em's farmhouse as Toto sits patiently at her feet, a tornado threatening overhead, and inside the cellar everyone else sitting out the storm among the shelves of canned goods, baskets of onions, and shocks of corn. Well, at least they won't be hungry.

Way back when on the Northern plains, long before houses had basements and freezers had yet to be invented, pioneer vegetable gardeners countered the challenge of over-wintering produce from the short growing season by going underground. They grew hardy root vegetables and stored them outdoors in root cellars dug into hillsides, preferably south facing, where the underground air temperature remained constant, between 33 degrees F and 45 degrees F—close to the recommended safe temperature range of 35 degrees F to 40 degrees F used in modern refrigeration. With the ability to survive light frosts, root vegetables were something farmers could grow in quantity. Some root vegetables, like parsnips and carrots, were found to be sweeter when left in the ground through a frost or two.

When the practice of putting basements below houses became standard, many northern homebuilders took advantage of the space under outside stairwells and entryways to construct "fruit rooms." Dug into the ground beneath the front or back steps, these rooms became the twentieth century equivalent of urban root cellars. Now the fruits, vegetables, and canned goods could be accessed while wearing bedroom slippers, eliminating the need to don parkas and boots before going outside to get the shovel and dig. If you don't have a south-facing hillside or an exterior entry to build a proper root cellar or fruit room, but you do have a basement, it's easy to approximate one. Here's what you need to consider:

- Temperature should remain constant at 33–45 degrees F.
- Humidity, which varies for different vegetables, should be consistently high (see sidebar). Even if kept cool, vegetables will soften and shrivel up in a low-humidity environment.
- Light should be kept off the shelves and storage area.
- Proper venting and air circulation helps minimize deterioration. Some fruits and vegetables naturally give off gases, which can cause other stored produce to sprout prematurely or spoil; for example, the gases given off by apples encourage deterioration in potatoes. Shelves should be kept a couple of inches away from the walls for increased ventilation.

Properly stored beets, carrots, parsnips, onions, garlic, turnips, rutabagas, and potatoes can last several months. Carrots, parsnips, and like vegetables can be kept between layers of sand in crocks; square milk crates stacked are great for storing vegetables and encouraging circulation; similar crates are sold in stores like Target or Wal-Mart in the college-bound student area. Take care not to stack too many vegetables on top of each other, because those on the bottom will be smashed and break down. A good way to avoid this is always to remove vegetables from the bottom of the container first.

Optimum Storage Conditions for Vegetables and Fruits

Cold, very moist: 32–40 degrees F; 90–95 percent humidity:

Beets
Carrots
Celery
Chinese Cabbage
Celeriac
Salsify
Parsnips
Rutabagas
Turnips

Cold, moist: 32–40 degrees F; 80–90 percent humidity:

Apples
Cabbage
Cauliflower (short term storage only)
Grapes (40 degrees)
Oranges
Pears
Potatoes
Quince
Endive, escarole
Grapefruit

*November
Menu*

Kale and Walnut Sauté

◆

Roast Loin Pork with
Sparkling Cider Sauce

◆

Oven-Roasted Carrots
and Parsnips

◆

Roasted Pumpkin Pie
with Sour Cream
and Brown Sugar

Kale and Walnut Sauté

Serves
4 to 6

One year when everything else in her garden was caught by an unseasonably early frost, Shelley, in a fit of pique, decided to eat the ornamental kale edging. Here's what she came up with.

2 tbsp. sesame oil
2 tbsp. olive oil
4 c. chopped, raw kale with
   ribs removed
⅓ c. walnuts toasted
1 tbsp. soy sauce
¼ tsp. black rice vinegar (found in
   Asian groceries), or to taste

Heat sesame and olive oil over medium heat and sauté kale until limp but still bright green. Toss with toasted walnuts, season with soy and vinegar, and serve.

Roast Loin Pork with Sparkling Cider Sauce

Serves
8 to 10

For purposes of flavor, it's always best to roast meats with their bones. But when it comes to serving, the bones can present a challenge to the carver. Good news. Removing the bones from the meat and either tying them back in place before roasting or placing them alongside keeps most of the flavor but makes carving an easy task. If boning a roast is something you'd rather not tackle, have the butcher do it or show you how. Then next time you can economize by buying a bone-in roast and removing the bones yourself.

Slice the meat across the grain, reassemble it into the loin shape, and garnish with the Sparkling Cider Sauce. The addition of sparkling versus still cider adds a sharp but sweet element that complements the rich, roasted meat.

3–4 lb. boned, rolled pork loin, bone laid back in or tied to the side

1 tbsp. dried rosemary, pan roasted and crushed

4–6 cloves of garlic, smashed, peeled, slivered

Kosher salt, to taste

Freshly ground pepper, to taste

½ c. sparkling apple cider

1. Place rack in center of oven and preheat to 425°F.

2. Wash the pork loin and set aside. Roast rosemary in a dry skillet for 15–20 seconds. Roll garlic slivers in roasted rosemary, salt, and pepper. With the point of a paring knife, make ½-inch slits all around the roast and insert garlic slivers. Pat the roast with paper toweling to dry and generously pepper the surface.

3. Place roast, and bones if available, in a roasting pan just large enough to accommodate it. Roast uncovered 45–55 minutes, or until meat reaches an internal temperature of 170°F; meat might be slightly pink but will continue to cook while standing.

4. Remove roast and bones to a platter to rest and let the juices collect. Place roasting pan over high heat, and deglaze with ½ c. sparkling cider; remove from heat. Make Sparkling Cider Sauce (see sidebar).

Sparkling Cider Sauce
Makes 1 ½ c.

½ c. shallots, minced

Juices collected from platter

1–1½ c. sparkling cider

½ c. unsalted butter divided into 6 pieces, at room temperature

1. Add minced shallots and juices from the platter to deglazed pan, stirring with a metal spoon to loosen drippings.

2. Add 1 c. sparkling cider; return to the heat and reduce to a glaze; remove pan from heat; add softened butter piece by piece so it does not liquefy; mixture should have the consistency of a hollandaise sauce. Thin if necessary with additional ½ c. cider. Cover sauce to keep warm. Slice pork roast on the platter; dress with some of the sauce and serve immediately with remainder of sauce on the side.

Getting Down to the Root of the Matter: Oven-Roasted Carrots and Parsnips

Serves 8 to 10

Root vegetables are seldom on many people's top-ten vegetable lists, but this combination might just change their minds. They're simple, inexpensive, and elegant enough to serve at a cold-weather dinner party.

7–8 medium carrots, peeled, halved, and sliced into ½-inch pieces

7–8 medium parsnips, peeled, halved, and sliced into ½-inch pieces

2 tbsp. unsalted butter, melted

2 tsp. celery seed

1 tsp. coarse salt

Freshly ground black pepper, to taste

3 tbsp. minced parsley, to garnish

1. Preheat oven to 425°F.

2. Blot sliced carrots and parsnips dry with paper toweling. Place in a large bowl and drizzle with melted butter, celery seed, and salt and pepper, and toss.

3. Place on a 14x12-inch sided sheet pan, and roast on the lowest oven shelf for 15–20 minutes. Remove from the oven, and use a metal spoon or spatula to redistribute the vegetables to assure even browning. Place back in oven and roast for 15 minutes more.

4. Remove to dish or platter, sprinkle with parsley, and serve.

Roasted Pumpkin Pie with Sour Cream and Brown Sugar

Serves 4 to 6

Thanksgiving's in a couple of days, and it's your turn to bring the pie. And every year: pumpkin. Thanksgiving is not the day to disappoint the traditionalists at the table, nor is it a day for science experiments. This pie is easy, can be done in steps over several days, and is sure to impress and elevate all pumpkin pie palates.

1 small pie pumpkin (about 1¾ c.)
½ c. white sugar
¼ c. brown sugar
½ tsp. salt
1½ tsp. ground cinnamon
½ tsp. ground ginger
¼ tsp. ground cloves
2 large eggs
1 c. half & half or evaporated milk
Sour cream and brown sugar
 or course turbinado sugar, to
 garnish

Pastry

3 c. all-purpose flour
1 c. cake flour
2 tsp. salt
1 lb. well-chilled lard or vegetable
 shortening, or a combination,
 cut into quarters
¾ c. ice water

1. Preheat oven to 425°F; position rack in center of oven.

2. Wash pumpkin and cut in half. Scoop out seeds and place cut side down on a lightly oiled sided sheet pan. Roast until tender, about 1 hour.

3. While pumpkin is roasting, make the pastry and chill for 30 minutes. Roll into a 12-inch diameter circle on a lightly floured surface, place in a 10-inch pie tin, flute the edge, and return to the refrigerator to chill.

4. While the pumpkin is still warm, remove skin and place flesh in a large bowl and mash with a potato masher or press through a ricer. Add sugars, salt, cinnamon, ginger, and cloves and mix well. Doing this while the pumpkin is still warm releases the essential oils in the spices.

5. Beat eggs in a large bowl, stir in pumpkin and sugar/spice mixture, slowly pour in half & half or evaporated milk, and beat until smooth.

6. Pull center oven rack halfway out, place pastry shell in middle of rack, fill shell to crimped edges with pumpkin mixture, and gently push rack back into oven. Place a sheet pan on the lowest rack of the oven to catch any drips.

7. Bake for 15 minutes at 425°F. Reduce heat to 375°F and bake for 30–40 minutes or until a knife inserted in the center comes out clean. Cool on a wire rack. Serve garnished with sour cream and dark brown or coarse turbinado sugar.

Pastry

Makes 4 single pie crusts

1. Place flours and salt in a large bowl and whisk together.

2. Cut chilled fat in small pieces and add to flour. Quickly work flour and fat together with your fingertips until it resembles cornmeal; don't over mix—this will cause the gluten to develop, resulting in a tough crust.

3. Place a well-packed cup of flour and butter mixture in a mixing bowl, sprinkle with 3 tbsp. ice water, work gently to form a ball. More water may be needed depending on the humidity. Form into a 4-inch disk that is 1-inch thick, wrap in plastic wrap, and refrigerate for 30 minutes or until needed. Place extra mixture in a gallon-sized freezer bag and freeze up to 3 months.

4. Remove chilled dough to a lightly floured surface. Press down with palm of hand, and turn over to coat other side of pastry.

5. With a floured rolling pin positioned at the edge nearest you and using a gentle pressure, roll pastry out and away from you, lifting the pin just before reaching the opposite edge. This keeps the dough from becoming too thin around the edge. Rotate the dough 30 degrees and roll again. Turn dough over, lightly dust with flour, and repeat rolling, rotating, turning, and dusting until the dough reaches the desired size. Line a 10-inch pie tin with pastry and crimp edge as desired.

December

Pickled Herring · Beef · Garlic · Potatoes · Rutabagas · Frozen Green Beans
· Cabbage · Dried Apples

You can't count on snow in December. But traditions (no matter which ones) show up like clockwork, insisting upon resurrection, and pushing us into a breathless trot, as if we have been infected with some childish madness by the frisky winds and heavy gray skies. After a frantic search for family recipe cards, we find them where we first looked, and turn up all the lights to see if we can't make out Grandma's writing between the grease spots and crumbs. Then, because we are shopping for things they just don't make any more, we drive for miles to unfamiliar ethnic stores in distant suburbs searching for ingredients that we think might be right—though we're never quite sure. By now we are in the province of perfectionism, and what lies before us has nothing to do with economy or common sense. There will be endless hours of mincing and molding and shoving into tins that we will forget entirely when dear little Aunt Ruby—who says little and remembers even less—sits for Christmas tea in front of the fireplace, takes a bite, and then turns toward us with a slow and knowing smile.

The Last Lutefisk Supper

In Mexico I have seen men circulate among the tables in bars looking for tourists who are drunk enough to test their manhood by holding both the positive and negative poles of a battery. And shocking as that may be, it is almost more surprising that anyone who attempts to measure his testosterone in this way has to pay for it.

Characteristically understated, but unwilling to leave masochism entirely behind, the Minnesotan manner of testing bravado is reserved for sub-zero swimming and eating lutefisk.

Literally translated as "lye fish," many stories of the origin of lutefisk involve water and fire. Wood ash plus water equals lye, and lutefisk is simply cod cured with lye. One legend claims that lutefisk was created when marauding Vikings burned a village, including the drying racks where cod was being prepared for winter. It was raining when the starving villagers crept back from their hiding places, and their burned, now wet and reconstituted cod had the look of fresh fish. The first person who boiled and ate it was most certainly brave, and devotees of the gelatinous stuff are forever taunting their friends to reenact his courage.

The Scandinavians who brought lutefisk to Minnesota claim it is a special treat and feel deprived if they don't have it at least once between Thanksgiving and Christmas. Since most people want to avoid the scent of boiling lutefisk at home, it is most often served in churches, where a consensus of believers can be gathered.

Enthusiasts search the newspapers for notices of lutefisk dinners and plan ahead. And no matter how you feel about actually eating lutefisk, the dinners can be fun, since the Scandinavians (especially the older ones) come out of their hiding places to celebrate their heritage.

North America's largest lutefisk factory is in Minneapolis, and because of that, BJ and I decided it simply wasn't practical to provide a recipe; however, in the interest of reporting on a truly Minnesotan food experience, we stopped in to a lutefisk church supper in Little Falls one snowy evening.

Taking the Plunge in Little Falls

Pastor Larson of Bethel Lutheran Church in Little Falls looked stern as he climbed to his perch overlooking the sanctuary. The

> *"Beej, do you like lutefisk?" I ventured. "Me?" she said stifling a grimace. "Only if there is absolutely nothing else to eat, and it's too far to walk to Krispy Kreme."*

pews—packed with souls wrapped in mufflers and mittens, all hungrily anticipating lutefisk—fell silent.

"Everyone through four hundred fifty," he intoned, and the lucky ones made their way to the church basement. The hungry ones left waiting upstairs groaned and slid closer together for warmth on the now half-empty pews.

Even at peak Scandinavian efficiency, lutefisk, potatoes, and "secret" Swedish meatballs for 650 are far from fast foods. It was dark outside when we finally took our places in the serving line and prepared to partake of the second most holy meal for Scandinavian immigrants—the first, of course, is served at the communion rail on Sundays.

Steaming stainless-steel chafing dishes were manned by perspiring male parishioners, whose red vests and aprons further accentuated their flushed faces. By comparison, the plops of potatoes and gelatinous globs of lutefisk conspired to make an almost perfectly colorless plate. At this point in the evening, the potatoes were broken and the lutefisk was more than a little lumpy, but the room radiated with warm spirits.

There weren't many seats left, but people moved over to make room, and we settled over our plates, more interested in the dinner conversation than in the food. Our good-natured tablemates told tales of old-country Norwegians, chuckling over their difficulties with inheritance issues.

"Folks get so mad and hold grudges for such a long time, that the following generations don't know they're related. So, then they go off and get married," said one third-generation Norwegian. "And everybody gets mad all over again."

I was pushing the all-white meal into patterns on my plate, when I began to suspect that I might not be alone in my sufferance.

"Beej, do you like lutefisk?" I ventured.

"Me?" she said stifling a grimace. "Only if there is absolutely nothing else to eat, and it's too far to walk to Krispy Kreme."

Having said this, she turned back to her plate of lutefisk and meatballs with Iron Range resolve.

"Why not just eat the meatballs?" I wondered aloud.

I know lots of people who like meatballs, but the few who claim to like lutefisk have a veiled look in their eyes as if to say, "If this wasn't a pledge of allegiance to Grandpa Thor and the old country, I'd hate it too."

Some people claim lutefisk was never even eaten in Norway at all; that it was strictly a food of Norwegian-American immigrants. But I'd once asked this question of an authority, Chris Dorff, CEO of Olsen Fish Company in Minneapolis—the largest producer of lutefisk in North America. As head of a business that has been going since 1910 and turns out a half a million pounds of lutefisk yearly, I figure Chris has heard all the theories and every joke about lutefisk at least twice.

He said, "I chuckle when I hear that one. Records of reconstituted cod, prepared with the addition of birch ash, first appeared in Norway around the year 1000, at a time when people all over the world routinely preserved fish by salting and drying. We get cod from Norway, and I talk to those guys every other week; they still eat it. In fact lutefisk is served in Oslo's finest restaurants all the time."

That may be, but when I'd visited my Norwegian relatives in their resort hotels near Lillehammer, there was nary of whiff of lutefisk coming from their kitchens, and I suspect my cousins are not alone in sidestepping the tradition.

My suspicions were confirmed that evening at Bethel Lutheran Church when we met a Swedish exchange student who said she was sampling lutefisk for the first time. I had the satisfaction of seeing what my face might have looked like when Grandma first served it to me.

"My people don't eat this at home!" the student protested.

"So, if the real Scandinavians like her don't get into it, how can this lutefisk supper thing survive?" I asked the die-hards on either side of me.

"If you look upstairs," said one of our tablemates, "you'll see it's more Germans and Poles than Norwegians."

"They can't help it," another grinned.

The Communion Wafer Factory

"If you're writing a book on foods, you'd better not forget spiritual sustenance," a lady in the Fishing Museum in Little Falls told us with a cunning smile. We'd gone into the museum hoping to get information on trout farms but got hooked by word of a communion wafer "factory" instead. This latter term, we found out, is not popular among the Franciscan Sisters at the nearby Convent of St. Francis who had been making the spiritual repast for more than one hundred years, and considered the baking of unleavened bread by the Altar Bread Department to be the Lord's work.

Short, bespectacled, and cheerful, Sister Anne agreed to let us take a tour of the convent and watch the making of communion wafers in the Franciscan Sisters' commercial kitchen. It was evening and few sisters were in evidence when she showed us the needlework room, library and music room with its darkened large-screen TV, gift counter—donations are always welcome—and chapel with long-unused confessionals stacked high with sheet music. Like someone who, despite having lost weight and diminished in size, still wears their old far-too-roomy clothes, the Convent of St. Francis had a yawning feeling.

The Convent buildings, which once housed an orphanage, school, and a hospital, are a large imposing presence on the outskirts of Little Falls. Sixteen nuns started the community in 1891, and by 1969 their numbers grew to five hundred. Attrition has reduced their flock to fewer than two hundred sisters, most of whom are in their 70s and 80s but still work in hospitality, spiritual guidance, health care, and international missions.

In the convent's commercial kitchen, Sister Anne showed us how the dough was poured onto, and baked in, a machine that resembled a lefse iron. Before being made into wafers, the individual sheets of the unleavened bread were steamed in a proof box. Then, closely set 1⅛-inch circles were stamped out with a hand-operated die press, leaving tiny kite-shaped leftover bits between. With the press, it took the nuns an hour and a half to cut 12,000 small wafers; the larger 2¾-inch hosts were individually cut for priests in Catholic churches. Once a host of wafers was assembled, a priest would bless them, then they were stored to safeguard them from humidity until shipping. Over 150 parishes of Episcopalians, Lutherans, Methodists, and Catholics from across America ordered white or whole wheat altar breads made by the Sisters.

Though they still distribute to their church customers, we were sad to learn that since we visited them, the Sisters have stopped baking the altar bread. School-aged children in First Communion classes used to go and see the sisters make the communion wafers, and they too might have been touched by the same things we were. It was a gentle art—a humble service performed with the loving hands of people who practiced an unabashed recycling ethic; they used hospital x-ray boxes and Pringles Potato Chip cans to store the wafers and made cinnamon and sugar snacks from the unblessed leftover scraps.

"I don't need a computer," Sister Anne had said as she opened a file box containing addresses for the convent's customers. She had not been put off by our curiosity and generously shared the recipe, which, we were gratified to see, was made with local ingredients:

Cold water · 5 lbs. Dakota-made wheat flour · 5 lbs. Dakota-made white flour

Yield: 13,000 communion wafers

Sister Anne stamps out communion wafers: small wafers are ecumenical; the large ones are for Catholic priests.

With the closing of the Altar Bread Department, we wondered if there was another way for people to experience the Sisters' mission of hospitality. Happily, there is. They have a 40-acre farm, called Clare's Well, which welcomes overnight visitors. With accommodations in either cabins or the farmhouse B&B, it is a quiet place where reflection, nature, and the Franciscan Sisters environmental ethic are at work. The Sisters grow all their own food and have their own cookbook, and although they are on the electrical grid and use it in part, they primarily heat the farm with a geo-thermal system of pipes dug deep into the ground. For a donation, guests are welcome to eat with the sisters or, if preferred, simply enjoy the woods, lake, or the farm's many animals. On the Franciscan Sisters website (www.fslf.org) the name Clare's Well is explained as being "inspired by Clare of Assisi, a 13th-century woman, saint, mystic and friend of Francis" and reflects "the Franciscan virtues of a loving respect for all creation, joyful hospitality and solidarity with the marginalized." On the same page is an unattributed saying: "Wisdom is simple and deep within you. Drink from your own well."

117

Seed Caps and Cowboy Hats— Thousand Hills Grass-Fed Beef

In Cannon Falls, a town in a state where seed caps are the norm, Todd Churchill's cowboy hat sticks out like a steeple. It's a statement that suits his lanky, country-fresh looks and rings of the romance in his calling. A contemporary cowboy of sorts, Churchill is the CEO of a modern-day cattle company. Modern in this case means old-fashioned, because the name, Thousand Hills Cattle Company, was biblically inspired and its methods smack of the Old West, when free-ranging, grass-fed cattle were the rule rather than the exception.

But Churchill has an up-to-date mission that goes well beyond selling steak. Armed with an array of facts and figures about diet, environmental practices, and conventional beef production methods, he converts consumers to sustainable eating practices as purposefully as any missionary preaching in the wilderness. Except, there is no wilderness here anymore and Churchill, neither cattle baron nor butcher, is but one person in a growing network of like-minded Minnesotans giving their all to make a go of grass-fed beef.

One raw, gray early winter day, we drove to Cannon Falls and found Thousand Hills' tiny, overflowing office in the corner of a metal prefab building.

Once inside we huddled near the door, trying to make ourselves as small as possible while five young men jostled each other for access to computer screens, reference books, and bulletin boards. On the wall next to us, a posted list of corporate goals ran the gamut from expanding into bison, poultry, and eggs to finding time for vacations.

Though struggling with the company's new software program and other growing pains, Churchill took lunch in one hand, cell phone in the other, and found a quiet corner in the neighboring banquet hall, where he launched into his corporate story.

Raised on an Iowa farm, and with a family in cattle ranching, Churchill came to Minnesota by way of St. Olaf College. After graduation, he married, bought a small farm, and built a financial consulting business. He was serving as a CFO to a number of small businesses, among them Lorentz Meats in Cannon Falls, when the idea for Thousand Hills came, or rather was delivered, to him. Mike Lorentz showed him an article in the *New York Times* exposing what's wrong with corn-fed beef. It changed Churchill's life.

As a financial consultant, Churchill could make an educated guess about the potential market for organically produced meat, and with his farming background, he thought he knew enough about cattle to identify animals that would make good eating while they were still on the hoof. Churchill believed that if consistently tender grass-fed beef could be supplied, then a market would follow.

Tender beef is partially a matter of breed and build: small- to moderate-sized British-bred cattle have the right ratio of yield to bone, while the American beef industry is built on large, easily fattened French breeds. Churchill would need to find farmers willing to make a significant departure from conventional cattle raising, and even with the right genetics, not all cattle would make the grade—it would take an educated eye to choose the best animals.

No single farm could produce enough meat to consistently keep grass-fed beef in stores, and most farmers would need an incentive to grow and feed animals in a certifiably organic manner. But 100 percent grass-fed beef could command a high enough price to make the conversion to grazing profitable for the farmers.

Unless you understand the difference, it's easy to gloss over the phrase "100% Grass-Fed Beef" prominently located in the middle of the Thousand Hills label. All cows are grass-fed initially, but in the final two to six months, feedlot cows are switched to corn in a super-fattening program that makes them gain weight with astonishing speed. Corn is not a natural fodder for cows, and the quick weight gain it promotes is so disturbing to the ruminants it weakens their immune systems, necessitating the administration of antibiotics, which are then passed along to us in the meat. It takes only two to four weeks on corn to negate any health benefits the cows gained from eating grass.

The feedlot system was built by economics, and the resulting low prices made eating meat affordable for more Americans in the latter part of the twentieth century than at any other time in history. But it is now theorized that the type of fat found in corn-fed beef has an imbalance of Omega 3 fatty acids, which is linked to a full menu of health ailments, such as obesity, heart disease, and diabetes.

Thousand Hills' cows are "source verified," meaning everything from genetics to veterinary care is tracked and every cow is personally inspected by Churchill or one of his partners. Farmers who join the program read and sign a three-page document of protocol prohibiting chemical use on pasturelands or the feeding of hormones, antibiotics, animal by-products, and grains except for flax.

As a whole, more than twenty farmers participating in the Thousand Hills program have converted more than 600 acres of cropland into pasture, planting it with rye, brome, timothy, and other grasses; and in addition to getting a good price for their cattle, they benefit from lower fuel and equipment costs.

The Thousand Hills cattle we saw with Churchill were short, fine boned, and frisky, and though no one would wish to share their destinies, they were, for the moment, in fine circumstances, grazing over rolling grass-covered hills on a farm outside Cannon Falls where they were being "grass finished."

Beef raised on pasture, by the very same method dating back to Methuselah, has major environmental benefits: turning land back into pasture significantly reduces erosion, cuts out chemicals used on annual crops, pulls more carbon dioxide out of the air, and requires minimal consumption of fossil fuels. So in theory, nothing could be better than grass-fed beef, right?

All true, except for the fact that our first experiment with grass-fed beef had been a disaster. BJ and I bought a variety of cuts, not from the Thousand Hills program, but directly from a farm. We'd heard grass-fed beef should be cooked quickly to keep it tender, so we gave the steaks a good test run on the grill. But grilling failed with this beef. We tried every method we knew, including stewing and braising, but even the most extreme tenderizing techniques produced meat that, though flavorful, so fatigued the jaw we couldn't convince the dog to finish it. With all the arguments in favor of grass-fed beef (and the horror stories about conventionally produced beef), BJ and I wanted to be proved wrong. Churchill didn't know about our

As much at home on the prairie as on the range, Todd Churchill of Thousand Hills Cattle Company brings his cowboy ways and knowledge of grass-fed beef to his business in Cannon Falls.

previous experience, but if he had, he might have felt some pressure to produce a tender cut of meat; fortunately, he did, and we were able to begin our experimentation with grass-fed beef in earnest.

The results? There was some variation in the tenderness of Thousand Hills' beef, but never once did we approach anything like the shoe leather we'd bought freelance from the farmer.

As for flavor, there really is a distinct difference. I convinced a meat-hungry seventeen-year-old boy to try a grass-fed steak. He got so excited, he began to sell the idea of grass-fed beef back to me.

"This is how a steak's supposed to taste," he raved. "Regular steak shows you what meat's supposed to taste like, but it's a faint, watered-down version. This is the real thing."

It's safe to say that this Minnesota kid will never wear a cowboy hat or a seed cap or, for that matter, the toque of a chef. But he's into food. He asks for hand-crafted sausages from Clancy's Meat Market in Linden Hills (where grass-fed beef is a mainstay), tries his hand at making pasta, and loves the Mill City Market on Saturdays almost as much as a meal of pizza and vinegar-flavored potato chips in front of the latest video game.

Despite the latter—he is, after all, a teenager—his appetite for reading ingredient labels and books like *Fast Food Nation* makes him more akin to his Minnesotan elders. Not only will he go for a new kind of steak but, if he likes it, he won't think twice about paying a little bit extra for the real deal.

Take this kid's educational background, level of discernment, and healthy skepticism, multiply times many, and you have Minnesota: the kind of place where a maverick like Todd Churchill can give big beef businesses a run for their money.

Lorentz Meats

Thousand Hill's beef processor Lorentz Meats was mentioned so often in our conversations with Minnesota food producers that BJ and I began to suspect if something were to happen to this high-quality abattoir, Minnesota's most unusual specialty meats, from yak roast to pheasant sausage, would disappear from the market. The Lorentz family's livelihood was, in fact, once threatened, and the solution they cooked up not only saved the company, it made their name known to farmers across the Midwest.

In 1968 Ed and Mary Lorentz bought a defunct locker plant in Cannon Falls and, with sons Rob and Mike, began providing custom meat processing to local farmers and sportsmen. From the beginning, Lorentz's was a busy plant and by the 1980s was growing and processing over a million pounds of meat a year, when, with little warning, the farm crisis cut business by 75 percent.

The Lorentz family response was innovative; they diversified and offset the slump in their meat processing by selling "'home-made' made" chicken pies, bologna, and plate lunches at their deli counter and adding a catering business. At one time the deli was so popular with locals that once when BJ and I stopped during the lunch rush, we found ourselves waiting in line. After carving out this niche for themselves in deli and catering operations, the Lorentzes rebuilt their custom meat processing business, and eventually closed the deli's retail operation, but they never forgot their hard-learned lessons.

The family's now multifaceted business continues to thrive and grow, in part because the next generation took an interest in teaching other food producers how they weathered the crisis. Sons Mike and Rob reasoned that helping present and potential customers diversify could bolster both their business and that of the farm economy as a whole; and they could teach processing-plant customers how to develop new products and increase profits by selling directly to consumers, as they had done with their deli business.

Rob Lorentz worked to develop a new state inspection system that allowed farmers to sell beef, pork, and poultry directly to the public. To promote the new system, the company offered Branding Your Beliefs, a sixteen-hour business course on the ins and outs of private branding. Though private branding wasn't a good fit for every farmer, dozens were inspired to branch out from commodity farming into home-based businesses.

Another forward-thinking outreach program spawned by the Lorentzes teaches farmers about grass-fed beef, an industry in its infancy. Along with a cattleman from Argentina, Mike Lorentz team teaches Grass-fed Production School, a program developed by *Stockman Grass Farmer* magazine that helps farmers produce marbled grass-fed beef for niche markets. A quick Internet search reveals Lorentz's achievements: dozens of privately branded grass-fed beef producers credit the Cannon Falls meat processor on their websites. More evidence can be seen in the profusion of private-label bacon, yak, elk, and pheasant sausage sold at farmers' markets across the state.

In Keeping with the Season: Standing Rib Roast

Serves 8

All holidays seem to be steeped in food traditions, but none more so than Christmas. The traditional entrée in an English household is standing rib roast with Yorkshire Pudding. An elegant rib roast with a savory pudding is the centerpiece on our Christmas table too, but we've surrounded it with Minnesota vegetables: rutabagas, cabbage, and garlic from the root cellar and garden green beans that we froze last summer.

5–6 lb. standing rib roast, with ribs and exterior fat intact, at room temperature

3–4 cloves garlic, peeled and slivered

Kosher salt and freshly ground black pepper, to taste

1–2 c. red wine or an equivalent amount of beef stock

1. Place oven rack at the second level from the bottom; preheat oven to 500°F.

2. Using a sharp knife, separate the fat layer from the meat in one piece. Turn the roast over and remove the rib bones in one piece. Tie both back in place with kitchen string. A roast prepared in this way can be carved easily and with little mess. Have the butcher do this if you are unfamiliar with the process. Dry the surfaces of the roast with paper toweling and place in a 12x14-inch roasting pan, bone side down and fat side up. Lift the fat and season the meat with slivered garlic, kosher salt, and black pepper, then retie to keep the fat in place during roasting. Roast in the center of the preheated 500°F oven for 30 minutes. Reduce heat to 325°F and roast for 15–20 minutes, or until the internal temperature of the meat reaches 135°F.

3. Remove the roasting pan from the oven and transfer the meat to a serving platter, bone side up; cut kitchen string and discard. Loosely cover with foil, shiny side down, and let rest in a warm place for 15 minutes before carving; make the pan sauce while the roast is resting.

4. Deglaze the roasting pan, using the method described in "The Art of Deglazing" on page 122. Strain through a fine sieve into a measuring cup or a glass-lipped bowl, taste, and adjust seasonings. Pour half into a sauceboat for the table and spoon the rest over the individual servings.

December Menu

Standing Rib Roast

♦

Roasted Garlic Custard

♦

Potato Rutabaga Soufflé

♦

Green Beans Hazelnuts

♦

Christmas Coleslaw

♦

Festive Apple Cake with Hard Sauce

Some of the best dividends of roasting are the juices that collect and build up in the bottom of the pan, but you'll need a bit of skill to reap these delicious rewards. Start by removing as much fat as possible. The easiest way to accomplish this is to tilt the pan so the fat and juices collect in one corner. The fat will rise to the top and the heavy, flavorful liquid, or in cooking parlance, the "fond," will remain at the bottom. Skim the grease with a large metal spoon and discard. Any remaining fat can be blotted from the surface with a piece of folded paper towel. Don't worry about removing too much volume, because you will replace it with stock, wine, or both.

Place the roasting pan over medium-high heat, add the wine, stock, or both, hold the pan firmly, and vigorously scrape the flavorful bits from bottom of the pan. Pour all of the liquid into a wide 2 c. measuring cup, and skim again. If not using immediately, refrigerate in a tightly closed glass container up to 2 weeks or freeze, up to 6 months.

Carving the Roast

To carve the roast you will need:

- Sharp, flexible slicing knife, not serrated
- Long-tined meat fork
- Additional warmed platter or stacked dinner plates
- Absorbent towel to place beneath the platter

Remove the aluminum foil from the roast and carefully pour excess plate drippings into the extra sauce. Place the platter of meat on the towel. Remove ribs in one piece; cut between bones to separate, placing them on the additional warmed platter. Slice across the grain in ¼- to ½-inch-thick slices and put on the platter with the bones, or on individual plates, passing bones separately.

Roasted Garlic Custard

Serves
6 to 8

Oven roasting is a no-fuss method for preparing vegetables, and it brings out their sugars, supplanting any bitterness. Had Ebenezer Scrooge eaten more roasted garlic, he might've been a bit less cantankerous at Christmas. Serve this on Christmas Day, and his ghost, along with those of Tiny Tim and Christmas Past, might be hovering at your table hoping for a taste. You can roast the garlic a day ahead of time and keep it refrigerated until you are ready to prepare the custard.

4 firm, large heads of garlic

1 c. unsalted chicken
stock, heated

1 tsp. unsalted butter

½ tsp. salt

¼ tsp. freshly ground white pepper

2 large eggs, room temperature

1 large egg yolk, room temperature

⅔ c. half & half, warmed

1 c. whole milk, warmed

2 tbsp. unsalted butter

4 tbsp. coarse bread
crumbs, toasted

Boiling water, for baking

1. Preheat oven to 350°F.

2. Remove excess loose peel from the heads of garlic; slice off the top quarter of each. Place each, root end down, on a square of aluminum foil; pull corners up and twist; roast in the center of the preheated oven for 30–45 minutes, depending on size and freshness of the garlic. When the garlic is fully roasted, the packet should be soft and pliable, like a tube of toothpaste.

3. Peel aluminum foil back, and twist into a knob at the root end; place on a dinner-sized plate. Run hot water over the flat side of a chef's knife. Garlic sugars developed during roasting are sticky; moisture makes extraction less messy. Grasp the foil-covered garlic in one hand, and the wet knife in the other. With the sharp edge of the knife away from you and the dull edge toward the root, press down on the roasted garlic head with the broad side of the blade, tilt the blade up, and push out with the back edge; the roasted cloves should slip easily onto the plate. Remove any remaining garlic skin with wet fingers.

4. Remove the garlic from the foil, and squeeze the flesh out onto a plate, taking care to remove any skin that may stick to it. It's easier to do this while the garlic is still warm.

5. Reduce the oven temperature to 300°F. Heat the chicken stock, butter, salt, pepper, and roasted garlic, and simmer for 30 minutes, or until the liquid is reduced in volume by three-fourths. While the stock/garlic mixture is reducing, combine the half & half with the milk in a medium saucepan and warm over medium heat.

6. Beat the eggs and yolk together in a small bowl until light. Add a bit of the warmed cream and milk, blend thoroughly, then pour the mixture from the bowl into the remaining cream and milk in the saucepan. This technique is called tempering and helps keep sauces from curdling or separating.

7. Add the garlic/chicken reduction to the tempered cream, eggs, and milk, and blend well.

8. Put a strainer in a larger container and pour the mixture through it, using the backside of a metal spoon or the bottom of a ladle to press the liquid through. Scrape any excess from the underside of the strainer, and whisk into the custard mixture.

9. Butter 6 4-inch or 8 3-inch ramekins, coat with toasted bread crumbs, and evenly space in the bottom of a deep-sided baking pan. Ladle custard mixture into the prepared ramekins, carefully place the pan in the middle of the preheated oven, and add boiling water to ¼ inch below the top of the ramekins. Bake in the water bath for 30 minutes until firm, slightly puffed, and lightly browned, or until a knife blade inserted into the custard comes out clean. Place the hot ramekins on a doily or napkin-lined plate and serve.

What They Don't Know: Potato Rutabaga Soufflé

Serves
6 to 8

Rutabagas are one of the most maligned vegetables grown, and it's a bad rap. If you passed on Lena's Rutabaga Malt—and shame on you if you did—you might try rutabagas in this combination. Just call it by its *nom de plume—Soufflé*—and you'll get this one past your doubting family and guests, no questions asked, and be showered with praise.

4 tbsp. or ½ stick unsalted
  butter, melted

1 c. red onion, minced

1 c. unseasoned bread crumbs

3 c. cooked baking potato, mashed

3 c. cooked rutabaga, mashed

4 large eggs, well beaten

1 c. half & half

1 c. Parmesan cheese,
  freshly grated

6 tbsp. parsley, minced

2 tsp. salt

1½ tsp. white pepper

½ tsp. freshly grated nutmeg,
  optional

1. Preheat oven to 375°F; place rack in center.

2. Sauté the minced onion in 1 tbsp. of melted butter. Let cool.

3. Grease an 8 c. soufflé or casserole dish with ½ tbsp. of the melted butter, and cover buttered surface with ⅓ of the bread crumbs. Set aside.

4. Place mashed potatoes and rutabaga in a large mixing bowl, and mix until thoroughly combined.

5. In a separate bowl, beat eggs together with half-&-half, ¼ c. Parmesan cheese, and 2 tbsp. of minced parsley. Add the sautéed onions, salt, pepper, and nutmeg, mix well, and add mixture to potatoes and rutabaga. Beat with a wooden spoon for 1–2 minutes; this helps the potato mixture rise a bit in the oven.

6. Turn mixture into prepared casserole or soufflé dish. Place remaining melted butter, minced parsley, Parmesan cheese, and bread crumbs in the mixing bowl, combine, and spread on the top of the soufflé. Bake for 30–40 minutes. The mixture should puff up a bit and be golden brown on top.

Green Beans with Toasted Hazelnuts

The holidays call for special ingredients, but every dish need not be complicated. Our holiday hazelnut green beans pair last summer's frozen homegrown beans with roasted hazelnuts and exotic hazelnut oil found in the specialty department of finer grocery stores. If you can find hickory nuts, this dish is even more festive.

½ c. hazelnuts

1 lb. frozen green beans

2 tbsp. hazelnut oil

Coarse sea salt and freshly ground
    black pepper, to taste

1. Place rack in center of oven, and preheat to 400°F. Spread hazelnuts in a single layer on a sided sheet pan, and roast for 10–12 minutes, or until buttery smelling; watch carefully so they don't burn. After the nuts are roasted, gather them in a clean dish towel and rub gently to remove the skins.

2. Bring 4 qt. water to a boil and add a generous pinch of salt and the frozen beans; cook uncovered at a full boil for 5 minutes. Drain beans well, shaking to remove as much excess water as possible.

3. Place hazelnut oil, salt, and pepper in a large bowl; add drained beans, mix well, then transfer to a large serving dish. Sprinkle with toasted hazelnuts, salt and pepper to taste.

It's Beginning to Look a Lot Like . . . Christmas Coleslaw

Serves
6 to 8

All the colors of the season come together in this refreshing holiday version of a summer staple. It's fast and inexpensive; can be done for a crowd, and travels and holds well for holiday potlucks. More than just a holiday side dish, this pretty, wholesome salad can be made ahead and presented at any time of year. In winter this vitamin C–packed slaw helps clean up some of those excess fats and sugars we consume, boosting our immune systems when we need it most.

3 c. finely shredded green cabbage (about 1 small head)

1 c. white onion, thinly sliced (if onions are too strong, soak in cold water for 20 minutes and drain well)

1 bunch curly parsley, tops minced

½ c. dried cranberries or cherries

1 tsp. caraway or celery seed

3 tbsp. apple cider vinegar

2 tbsp. water

1 tsp. coarse sea or kosher salt

Freshly cracked pepper, to taste

2 tbsp. canola oil

1 tart green apple, skin on

1 tart red apple, skin on

1. Remove any brown or spotted loose outer cabbage leaves, and cut the head into quarters through the core end. Cut the core away from each chunk and finely slice the cabbage by hand, or shred in a processor. Place in a large bowl and add onions, chopped parsley, and dried cranberries or cherries.

2. Pan-roast celery or caraway seeds in a dry, small sauté pan over high heat for a minute or two, just until seeds start to pop and/or release their aromatic oils. Place vinegar, water, caraway or celery seed, salt, and pepper in a blender/ processor or small bowl. Slowly add oil through top/tube, or whisk in by hand. Taste, adjust seasoning, and place in a large mixing bowl.

3. Core apples and cut in half from the top to the bottom. Thinly slice the apples, leaving a strip of skin showing on each. Add to mixing bowl with vinaigrette, and toss to coat. Add cabbage mixture, mix well, cover, and refrigerate for several hours, or up to 1 day. Re-toss and serve in a white, green, red, or clear ceramic or glass bowl. Garnish the top with some additional chopped parsley.

Homemade for the Holidays: Festive Apple Cake with Hard Sauce

Serves 10

This is a truly old-fashioned holiday dessert. Its flavor benefits from being made in advance; it keeps and travels well, and leftovers make an easy transition into trifles or crumbles. Best of all, this cake's sweet aroma is reminiscent of the season. If time is an issue, make this cake up to three days in advance and hold at room temperature in a tightly sealed tin container, or wrap tightly in food film, then aluminum foil and refrigerate; or make it three weeks ahead, wrap as for refrigeration, place in a zip-lock-style bag and freeze. Thaw overnight in the refrigerator. Always let it come to room temperature and warm it in a low, 300°F oven for 10–15 minutes before garnishing and serving.

⅔ c. whole milk

1 c. molasses

2 tsp. baking soda

½ c. safflower margarine

½ c. firmly packed dark
   brown sugar

2 large eggs

4 c. all-purpose flour, sifted

¼ tsp. ground cloves

½ tsp. ground ginger

1 tsp. ground cinnamon

½ tsp. salt

2½ c. golden raisins

1 lb. dried apples, coarsely
   chopped

½ c. brandy

¾ c. toasted, chopped walnuts

1. Preheat oven to 325°F.

2. Mix milk, molasses, and baking soda in a medium bowl, and set aside. In a large bowl, cream the margarine until fluffy. Add brown sugar; mix again. Add 2 well-beaten eggs, mix to combine.

3. Sift flour with cloves, ginger, cinnamon, and salt. Set aside.

4. Place raisins and apples in a glass or nonreactive metal dish. Heat the brandy in a microwave for 30 seconds; pour over raisins and apples. Steep for 5–10 minutes to plump. Reserve ¾ c. plumped fruit and ½ c. toasted walnuts for garnish.

5. Alternately, in three additions each, add the milk mixture and flour/spice mixture to the creamed margarine, sugar, and eggs. Fold in the plumped apples and raisins and the toasted walnuts.

6. Turn mixture into a greased and floured 9-inch Bundt™ or tube-cake pan. Cover the top with a double thickness of waxed or parchment paper large enough to overlap the pan by several inches. Secure the paper by tying with string.

7. Stand the cake in a deep roaster and add hot water to halfway up the side of the pan. Bake for 2½–3 hours, or until an inserted toothpick comes out clean. Carefully remove the cake from the water; cool to lukewarm before removing the waxed/parchment paper. If serving right away, make the hard sauce while the cake is cooling; recipe follows. If making in advance, let cool completely before wrapping for storage, refrigeration, or freezing. Make the hard sauce while the cake is warming in the oven.

8. Turn the cake out onto a serving platter larger than its diameter and surround the base with the remaining fruit and nuts.

9. Cut the cake into generous pieces, place on dessert plates, and garnish each with hard sauce, fruits, and nuts.

Hard Sauce

1½ c. light brown sugar
½ c. unsalted butter, softened
⅓ c. heavy cream
2 tbsp. brandy

Using an electric mixer, cream brown sugar and butter until fluffy. By hand, slowly beat in cream and brandy, and mix until smooth. Keep warm in a *bain Marie* or water bath until service.

January

Gouda Cheese · Smoked Whitefish · Bison · Onions · Carrots · Dried Fruit

After all is said and done, Minnesotans seem a little uncomfortable with the overabundance of the holidays. So after working ourselves into a frenzy in an attempt to make the season's events perfect and plentiful (but not embarrassingly extravagant, mind you) we utter a collective sigh of relief and turn back to the basics in January. Nothing fancy, please. Soup and sandwiches for Sunday supper will be just fine, thank you very much. Oh, but we could add a little smoked whitefish spread for starters and make our soup a stew (let's use the frozen ground bison from the trip to the buffalo ranch), then guild the grilled cheese with aged Gouda we've been saving, and dress up Grandma's fruit soup with a little sherry for dessert . . .

Finding Faith in Center City

Whenever I drive back from Taylor's Falls on Highway 8, I make a habit of pulling my rusting Honda out of the seemingly unending line of late-model SUVs for a brief detour into Center City. In moments, this still-extant fragment of small-town life transports me to another era—when every barn glowed at milking time, lakes were for nothing more than the serious business of fishing, and the big city was much farther away.

If you drive too quickly along the hillside road overlooking North Center Lake you'll miss Center City's historic district—a string of small-town-sized Victorian houses that ends at Chisago Lake Lutheran Church, a towering brick structure that holds dominion over the community from its command post atop the highest hill in town. From there you can see that there is a second lake, and the two are divided by a road and a row of narrow buildings that clings to the larger lake's precipitous edge. I never seem to see anyone, and after wondering about life in this lovely setting for a moment or two, I usually turn around and head back to the highway.

One Sunday afternoon in autumn, I made a lengthier stop. Long shadows and the last golden rays of a rapidly sinking sun made me want to put the brakes on the upcoming workweek and—even more—the upcoming winter. This time I drove beyond the sunlit hillside to the two or three blocks of slightly scruffy homes that make up the interior core of Center City's historic district. I had pulled in behind the church and stood looking out over the lake when, suddenly, my lone Honda was joined by a half dozen cars of similar age that screeched to a halt and expelled a dozen hot, sweaty-looking fellows, all wearing oversized t-shirts that said "In Cod We Trust" on the back.

My private, rather melancholy moment must have taken on a suspicious air. They looked at me curiously, inquiring how they might help, so I, thinking quickly, asked if I might see the inside of their church. The t-shirt wearers conferred, and pretty soon someone was dispatched to get the pastor and his key.

From their t-shirts I guessed that these were Scandinavians, which explained why they stood watch silently while I waited, as if guarding their church from my unexpected presence. After a very long pause, I asked about the beautiful scene that

> *"In Cod We Trust" was the team's slogan, the fishy t-shirts their uniforms, and from the pride with which they were worn, I'd wager that this parish's lutefisk supper would be worth visiting at Christmastime.*

spread out in front of us. They pointed out landmarks on the glowing hillside just to the west: first the old church cemetery, then the new one with its cross-shaped planting of columnar cedars, and the church's handsome white frame parsonage, where we could see that someone was arriving to fetch the pastor. Presently he came with the key, and the parishioners disappeared down the stairs to the church's parish hall, but not without extending a polite invitation to attend their Sunday-after-baseball supper.

It seems they'd just returned from a game—a Chisago Lake Lutheran special, played according to rules from the 1880s, whatever those are. "In Cod We Trust" was the team's slogan, the fishy t-shirts their uniforms, and from the pride with which they were worn, I'd wager that this parish's lutefisk supper would be worth visiting at Christmastime.

The significance of the 1880s became clear when I learned that the church was built twice during that decade. Only six years after its completion in 1882, the original brick church was struck by lighting and destroyed by fire. An identical copy was built within the year.

The inside of Chisago Lake Lutheran was definitely worth the wait. Once the massive doors were opened, a flood of afternoon sun pulled me out of the dimly lit entrance hall into a sanctuary luminous with tawny, carved wood and delicate Swedish colors.

"They've really done a good job painting it," the pastor said, carefully distancing himself from wholly un-Lutheran pride. (Earlier when I'd complimented him on the parsonage, he'd said with modesty, "It's just a hundred years old.")

131

Pastor Lundstad-Vogt told me you could still hear Swedish spoken downtown here until the 1970s. "There used to be a 5 a.m. service for milkers on Christmas," he said. "I'm glad they don't do that any more."

I could see a candlelit sanctuary: the scent of manger straw mingling with milk, Christmas trees festooned with garlands, and pews packed with broad-shouldered farmers—hats respectfully balanced on their knees. And back on their farms, I imagined barns full of seriously mad cows with bursting udders.

"This was the largest rural congregation in America at one time," said the pastor. "All Swedes; all dairy farmers." Surprisingly after five generations of dairy farming among the Scandinavians, one local farmer swapped cultures, went to Holland, and learned cheesemaking from the Dutch.

In 1978, with dairy prices down, Mary and Joseph Eichten, who had dairy cows just down the road, enrolled in a cheesemaking program at the University of Minnesota that then sent them to Holland for six weeks where they learned to make authentic Gouda, which is actually pronounced "howda." They learned their lessons so well that today even the Dutch recognize Eichten's production quality, awarding the Minnesota-made Gouda 98.7 points out of 100 in a field with their Dutch cousins and uncles. The Eichten product line now includes eight different aged and young Goudas, low-fat and Baby Swiss, Parmesan, Romano, cheese curds, and Tilsit, formerly an exclusive European export now made in the United States only at Eichten's Hidden Acres in Center City, Minnesota.

It takes 125 pounds of milk to make one 10-pound wheel of Gouda, and that's more pre-dawn milking than any cheese-producing family, even one with eight kids, can manage. By out-sourcing their milk production to neighboring farmers, and filling their then empty fields with bison—a lower-maintenance livestock—the Eichtens were on their way to the smörgasbord of cheeses and meats they produce today. Low-fat and low-cholesterol, buffalo were a perfect pairing for cheese production since they consumed whey, a byproduct of cheesemaking that formerly went down the drain.

Visit on an open-house weekend, and you can see the entire scope of the Eichtens' operation: There are hay rides into the buffalo fields, cheese production tours, and samples of buffalo and elk in every form from patty to link. These days Eichten's products can be found everywhere, from local farmers' markets to the fancy cheese section at local co-ops and grocery stores. You can arrange to have your office party catered through Eichten's or stop into their new Bistro for a beer.

Beneath the giant mouse at Eichten's Center City location, I found a veritable Disneyland of cheese- and livestock-related items with everything from cheese and meat to keychains and t-shirts—a far cry from the days when the only product Center City farmers traded in was milk.

As I drove away that evening, I thought a lot about those Swedish dairy farmers and how surprised they'd be to see the "Got Milk?" billboards, reminding twenty-first-century Minnesotans about the other white stuff—the kind you drink, not shovel.

Smokin' the Waters

Every good Minnesotan has eaten smoked fish at some point. As a kid, I was fascinated when my dad would come home from an extended summer fishing trip or a frosty January Saturday on the ice and fire up Grandma's old Cold Spot refrigerator out by the garage. Back in the 1950s, old refrigerators recycled as backyard smokers were Northland standards, and every avid angler boasted that his smoked fish, "the best you'll ever eat," resulted from his own special blend of wood.

Even though the equipment has changed—those small white enamel Kelvinators have become big stainless-steel commercial smokers subject to state regulations—the techniques and woods used are still pretty much the same.

The smoked fish found in most markets today are salmon, trout, or whitefish, which are fleshier with higher oil content than other freshwater species. As with most rich foods, a little goes a long way. Smoking adds density and moisture, giving the fish a flavor that is more of the land and less of the lake.

The smoked fish processors we visited covered the waterfront: from the brand-spanking-new, stainless-steel smokers operated by Duluth's Northern Waters Smokehaus, to the decades-old creosote-lined ovens behind Russ Kendall's Smokehouse on the North Shore at the mouth of the Knife River.

We tried them all, and our friends did too. Great Waters Smokehaus got the highest marks for full-service gourmet picnic supplies, and Morey's, whose product line is shifting from smoked fish to pre-packaged filets in sauces, is a nice addition to the freezer for busy days. But Kendall's got the most votes from our reviewers for fish that brings to mind the cold, smoky North Shore air in every delicious sliver.

Northern Waters Smokehaus

Northern Waters Smokehaus, the brainchild of Eric Goerdt, a former member of the U.S. Coast Guard who harbored a passion for gourmet food, is on the lower level of the Dewitt-Seitz Marketplace in trendy Canal Park. Northern Waters smokes fish fresh out of Lake Superior, farmed and wild-caught ocean fish, and local, sustainably raised meats. Their deli case featured a four-flavor smoked Atlantic salmon filet with black pepper–coriander, dill, Cajun, and traditionally smoked sections in colorful alternating stripes.

You can sit at tables in the shop and have one of the daily specials, but we preferred to raid their refrigerated cases for picnic fixings and, in addition to smoked fish, came away with proscuitto, bison jerky, and local cheeses.

Morey's Seafood Markets

As legend has it, Morey's Seafood Markets in Motley, Minnesota, got its start when a fish-laden truck from Chicago broke down outside of town and Ed Morey traded a load of corn for the soon-to-be-spoiled fish. That was back in 1937, and the Morey family has been mongering fish ever since. Ed Morey's entrepreneurial ability parleyed Morey's into one of the upper Midwest's largest fish importer's and purveyors of fish products. Morey's still has markets that are filled with everything from herring to lox, but now there's a line of wholesale products with the Morey's name on it too. We visited the plant, which is under separate ownership, behind the store in Motley and saw semi loads of frozen salmon, wall-sized smoking chambers, and mountains of packaged, seasoned fish filets.

Russ Kendall's Smokehouse

If the creosote-soaked walls of Kendall's in Knife River could talk, oh, the history they would tell. Located along the North Shore of Lake Superior, the legendary smokehouse is out back of the roadside bar and market, long a fixture along this stretch of Highway 61. The rich black patina from the smoking chambers extends onto all surfaces near the smoke room, giving great contrast to our exterior photos, where gray gulls sit on the cold roof, patiently waiting for their shore lunch. In the market you'll find smoked Lake Superior ciscoes, trout, salmon, and white fish; herring; and Kendall's specialty—brown sugar trout and salmon, plus a great variety of cheeses, gifts, antiques, and home-smoked beef jerky.

Northern Waters Smokehaus
Dewitt-Seitz Marketplace
394 Lake Avenue South
Suite 106
Duluth, MN 55802
(218) 724-7307
(888) 663-7800
www.NWSmokehaus.com

Morey's Seafood Markets
P.O. Box 2508
Brainerd, MN 56401
(218) 829-8248;
(800) 548-9630
orders@moreysmarkets.com
Morey's Seafood International
   LLC
P.O. Box 248
Motley, MN 56466
(800) 808-3474
www.moreys.com

Russ Kendall's Smokehouse
149 Scenic Dr.
Knife River, MN 55609
(218) 834-5995

Buffalo Gal

I f the only buffalo you've seen are on the nickels in your pocket, maybe it's time to take a closer look at the herbivores grazing in your own backyard. Cows were once the biggest bovines seen in Minnesota, but the increasing popularity of bison as a lean, flavorful alternative to beef is tempting more cattle farmers to develop buffalo herds. Despite their familiar and distinctly American profile, buffalo remain enough of a rarity in Minnesota that the sight of a herd makes drivers pull off the road for a better look.

Bison farmers know this, and they have turned buffalo meeting and greeting into an ag-attraction to boost sales of bison steaks, jerky, and chili. While there are a number of farms where you can visit buffalo, we found that Money Creek Buffalo Ranch in Houston, Minnesota, home of Buffalo Gal meats, covers every angle, from online shopping to opportunities for a ranching vacation.

Buffalo Gal's big claim to fame was Cody, a one-ton, seven-foot bull who played the buffalo lead in *Dances with Wolves*. Not content with mere movie star fame, Cody made commercials, traveled to Washington for the unveiling of the new nickel, marched in parades, and became a petting zoo favorite on the ranch.

Sadly, Cody died in 2006 at age nineteen, but his spirit lives on in Cody II, another trained buffalo, who we found tethered next to the drive at Money Creek Buffalo Ranch near a bronze statue of his namesake. Even though he was lying down, placidly chewing, Cody II was nearly eye level to those of us in the car, and if that was not unnerving enough, the rope he was tied to stretched across the road blocking our way. We could have driven over the low end of the buffalo's tether, but not without giving him a rather nasty tug.

Moments later, our retreat was blocked by a UPS truck whose driver was just as wary of the massive woolly creature as we were. Neither the driver, BJ, Grace, nor I knew that in the right hands, Cody II was as docile as a stuffed animal; so we sat there eyeing him until the UPS guy got the idea of honking the horn.

Cody didn't budge, but the horn roused the Buffalo Gal herself, owner Valerie Shannon, who came running down the drive to uncork the bottleneck. A vivacious Southern charmer, Shannon threw her arms around Cody and gave him a kiss before

> *He told her the best way to handle buffalo is to let them think everything is their idea. Valerie chuckled and BJ rolled her eyes as if to say, "only a guy would think that's original."*

leading him across the road, and motioning for us to drive up to the barn.

A wriggling Australian shepherd herded our car, barking happily at Grace, BJ's service dog. The pup's bright blue eyes and fluffy speckled coat had petting zoo cuteness that was right in line with the miniature ponies, tame deer, and other animals that shared the barnyard with Cody II. Valerie kenneled her dog so Grace could join us for a tour of the ranch. But Grace had other ideas, and tore off, proudly returning moments later completely covered in buffalo dung. The perfect hostess, Valerie took it upon herself to hose down the dog, joking, "If I didn't have buffalo shit to clean up, I'd be out of a job."

Valerie had come to Money Creek a few years back as a sort of modern-day mail order bride. She'd met Mike Fogel, owner of the ranch and Cody, over the Internet. He saw it as a sign that her online moniker, Stands With a Fist, was the name of a character from *Dances with Wolves*; she took to the idea of raising buffalo, instead of living on a hobby farm in Alabama and working in the hospitality industry. Her first Minnesota winter was miserable from the combination of cold weather and light deprivation, but by spring she'd decided she loved Mike more than she hated winter.

When Grace was cleaned up, we took a closer look at the buffalo. A pasture next to the barnyard held a couple dozen bison that looked much jumpier than Cody II, who was back sitting in his spot next to the drive. They snorted and stomped when Grace came near. She was oblivious to the fact that wolves are a bison's only natural enemy, and no matter how much buffalo poop they roll in, dogs are more like wolves than buffalo.

There's a tense, untamable wildness to most buffalo that makes them seem almost prehistoric. Unless you're dealing with a saddle-broken pet like Cody, they are dangerous. There were four times more deaths and injuries to people from buffalo than bears in Yellowstone Park between 1978 and 1992. Even when Valerie had us pose for pictures hugging Cody II, I knew that if she weren't there, we wouldn't be either.

Valerie has enough "Buffalo Gal" in her to actually saddle and ride the bison, but it's her husband, Mike, who really communes with them. After twenty-nine years in the business, Valerie said Mike had become so like the buffalo, they had become kindred spirits, and when Mike was in a bad mood, no one could even touch Cody. He told her the best way to handle buffalo is to let them think everything is their idea. Valerie chuckled and BJ rolled her eyes as if to say, "only a guy would think that's original."

Valerie drove us up on a ridge high above the ranch where the buffalo cows were raising their calves. Money Creek Buffalo Ranch is just a few miles from Scenic Highway 16 and the Root River State Trail, on which bikers, hikers, and skiers can follow the Root River for forty-two miles through marshes and farms, and over bluffs that offer wide, breathtaking views of landforms cascading down into the river bottoms. We climbed through woods and fields until we reached a lofty pasture where the herd was silhouetted against a background of sky and clouds.

A blazing late afternoon sun made the little buffalo calves glow bright orange as they nestled against the dark humped forms of their mothers, who watched us warily from behind a high barbed-wire fence while they continued to graze. Money Creek Ranch's herd of more than three hundred buffalo range freely year-round, are never castrated, given hormones, or de-horned. Theirs is not the largest buffalo herd in America, and it's kept that way in part to keep a healthy grazing system that sustains the ranch. When they need greener pastures, the cows and calves gather near a fence, and just to make sure they think it's their idea, Mike and Valerie move them only after they've stood there for two days.

We paused to admire the herd then drove a little farther to take a look at the ranch's vacation rental, Cody's Cabin. Mike and Valerie had built the little log house on a prominent lookout spot and planned to retire there someday. In the meantime it's for rent at rates comparable to most vacation home rentals. The rustic, open main-floor kitchen, eating and lounging areas, and the sleeping loft above have a view across a deep ravine and of the buffalo cows and calves on their hilltop a quarter of a mile away.

It was a lovely hideaway and one of the all around best venues for agri-touring that we've encountered in Minnesota. For vacationers it's a chance to see how a real working ranch operates and mix the experience with canoeing, hiking, cross-country skiing, or biking. Mike and Valerie's mellow, hospitable manner makes it easy for visitors to participate in life on the buffalo ranch as much or as little as they'd like.

Buffalo Gal produces more than thirty products, and we couldn't leave before buying a few of them. BJ and I had eaten buffalo, which is lower in fat, calories, and cholesterol than beef, pork, or chicken, but we wanted to see if Money Creek Ranch's meat was discernibly different. Their prices are comparatively reasonable because they avoid middlemen by selling online. We splurged and bought tenderloin, rib-eye steaks, and ground bison. To sweeten the deal, Valerie threw in a pint of Buffalo Gal Chili with cheddar cheese and a pound of ground wild boar, suggesting we mix bison and boar into meat loaf—the best, she claimed, she'd ever eaten. Wild boars are raised at Money Creek too, but we didn't hear much about them since Grace began to fidget. Valerie took note, and to Grace's delight, a sample of Buffalo Gal's newest test product, bison jerky for dogs made from buffalo liver, was added to our purchases as well.

Thanks to the Money Creek Buffalo Ranch tours, and Mike and Valerie's public relations efforts at state fairs, stampedes, and rodeos, buffalo are a bit more familiar, and a little less intimidating to many of us. The big bison had totally captured BJ, Grace, and me, and we were all a little sorry to leave Mike, Valerie, and their buffalo educational efforts behind. It would have been fun to hang out at the ranch a little longer and watch other people react to the giant beasts, and to see if the UPS driver would get around to kissing Cody II on the nose next time his truck rolled up the drive.

Where the Buffalo Roam

In the 1950s, the buffalo was an animal every American child could name by sight. Its iconic image graced the reverse side of the 1920s and 1930s Indian-head nickels we stashed away with those turn-of-the-century-issue silver dollars we'd get for our birthdays, and the noble beast could be found stampeding away, across our black-and-white television and movie screens, with cowboys, Indians, and cavalry in hot pursuit. By the 1960s, most of those images had transformed with the times: Thomas Jefferson's head and Monticello replaced the Indians and buffalos; live, color television was filled with crowds of protesters charging toward police; the good guys traded their white hats for white dinner jackets; and the buffalo no longer roamed, having been hunted away, almost into oblivion.

Today Minnesota is home to enough American Bison producers that the old buffalo ballad "Home on the Range" might've been written about our state. The Minnesota Buffalo Association (MnBA) was established in 1993 as a nonprofit organization and is dedicated to both preserving the American Buffalo as an historic national species and promoting it as a nutritious food. The MnBA actively oversees and ensures bison are raised and cared for according to the highest ethical standards and maintains a comprehensive website, www.mnbison.org, listing buffalo herd locations and producers across the state. Many of these have their own websites filled with additional information specific to their operations. You'll find everything there is to know about bison and bison products, including educational, nutritional, and historical information; places to buy buffalo meat, with preparation tips and recipes; tanned hides and custom-made clothing; and places offering guided tours and strictly controlled hunts.

Three we visited and enjoyed were Eichten's Cheese & Bison, located north of the Twin Cities outside of Center City, www.specialtycheese.com; J & L Bison Ranch outside of Willmar, www.jlbison.com; and Buffalo Gal outside of Houston, www.buffalogal.com. To find locations close to you, visit the Minnesota Buffalo Association website.

A Superior Snack: Lake Superior Smoked Whitefish on Hardtack

Serves 10 to 12

Come Big Game Day, the food should be easy, stand on its own, and hold up on a buffet. Smoked fish does all this, and it's yards healthier than the usual couch potato fare. This unusual tangy spread had our tasters cheering long before halftime. This is best prepared a day ahead so the flavors can marry.

1 lb. smoked whitefish, from Lake Superior, if you can get it
½ c. mayonnaise
1 c. cream cheese, room temperature
1 tbsp. coarse ground mustard
1–2 dashes hot pepper sauce, or to taste
Sea salt, to taste
2 tbsp. chopped fresh parsley leaves, or 1 tbsp. dried
1 tsp. malt vinegar
½ c. thinly sliced celery heart
¼ c. minced red onion

1. Remove any skin and bones from the fish and flake the meat with a fork. Place in the bowl of a mixer with the paddle attachment; add mayonnaise and cream cheese, and beat on high until well blended.

2. Scrape the bowl down and add mustard, vinegar, pepper sauce, and parsley; blend again. Taste and add more pepper sauce and salt as needed.

3. Pack into a serving bowl or container, cover with food film, and refrigerate.

4. When ready to serve, remove from refrigerator, and stir with spoon or knife. Garnish with a scattering of sliced celery heart and minced red onion, reserving the remainder. Place the garnished bowl of whitefish on a glass serving tray or platter; surround with hardtack or cracker of your choice. Serve as a buffet item with reserved celery heart and red onion on the side.

January Menu

A Super Bowl Every Sunday

Lake Superior Smoked Whitefish on Hardtack

♦

Bison Chili

♦

Gouda Grilled Cheese

♦

Fruit Soup

Home from the Range: Bison Chili

Serves
8 to 10

After a visit to Money Creek Ranch, we had a mini chili cook-off, pitting my buffalo tenderloin and wild boar chili against Buffalo Gal's. Though delicious, the color of Buffalo Gal's chili wasn't overly inviting, while my version of bison, boar, and salsa chili with Mexican chocolate and beer got exceptional marks from our taste-testers. Later I substituted ground pork for wild boar. It is as flavorful as wild boar, combines perfectly with the bison and is much easier to find. The thickener for the chili is *masa harina*, the traditional flour used in Mexican cooking. Make this ahead during the slow, early days of the New Year and freeze until the Friday before kick-off.

2–4 tbsp. canola oil

½ lb. pancetta, diced into small pieces

2 medium yellow onions, or 1 large, peeled and chopped; about 2½ c.

5–6 garlic cloves, peeled and minced

1½ lbs. bison tenderloin or sirloin, cut in 1-inch cubes

1 lb. beef round steak, cut in 1-inch cubes

2 tbsp. chili powder

2 tsp. ground cumin

2 tsp. ground thyme

2 tsp. thyme leaves

2 tsp. unsweetened cocoa powder, Mexican if available

1½ tsp. kosher salt

1 tsp. hot paprika

¼ tsp. cayenne pepper

1 large ancho chili, seeded and finely chopped

1 fresh jalapeño pepper, seeded and minced

1 fresh Serrano pepper, seeded and minced

12 oz. dark Mexican beer

3 tbsp. tomato paste

1 16-oz. bottle medium hot salsa

¼–⅓ c. *masa harina*

1. Place 2 tbsp. of canola oil in a large, heavy frying pan or cast-iron skillet over medium heat. Add diced pancetta and cook until crisp and lightly browned, about 5 minutes. Remove from pan and place on paper toweling to drain.

2. Add diced yellow onions to skillet and continue cooking on medium until soft, about 2 minutes. Add minced garlic and increase heat to medium high; cook until onions are slightly browned. Transfer sautéed onions to Dutch oven.

3. Dry off cubed bison and beef; place dried spices in a medium-sized bowl and mix together; add dried cubed meat and toss to coat. Sear the meat in the skillet in batches, turning the meat as it browns and adding small amounts of canola oil as needed, so spices won't burn. Transfer to Dutch oven. Add minced fresh peppers to the last batch of meat, stir to coat before transferring to the Dutch oven.

4. Deglaze skillet with the beer. Bring beer to boil; add tomato paste and continue to cook over high heat until liquid is reduced and slightly thickened. Transfer beer and tomato paste mixture to Dutch oven.

5. Stir in salsa, cover, and simmer for 1½ to 2 hours.

6. When meat is tender, remove about 1 c. of liquid to small bowl, mix in ¼ c. *masa harina*; stir until smooth. Pour the mixture back into the chili pot, and stir to combine. Cook for another 5–10 minutes until chili thickens. Serve with sides of sour cream, grated sharp cheddar cheese, chopped cilantro, minced green onions, and beans. The chili may seem really hot on first taste but will mellow if made a day or more in advance.

To Bean or Not To Bean: Pinto Beans

Let your guests decide. I serve beans in a separate bowl that can be added to the chili, eaten on the side, or left out altogether.

1 lb. dried pinto beans, picked
    over and rinsed
Soft or spring water, for soaking
4 strips thick sliced bacon, or ½ c.
    pancetta, chopped
2 cloves garlic, peeled and minced
1 tsp. granulated sugar
Salt, to taste

1. Place beans in a bowl or container 3 times their size. Cover with soft or spring water and place in refrigerator overnight.

2. To cook the beans, place bacon or pancetta in a Dutch oven over medium heat, and cook for 3–4 minutes, until fat is rendered out. Add minced garlic and sauté for about 1 minute or until lightly browned.

3. Drain and rinse the beans, and add to bacon. Pour in enough cold water to cover the beans by 3 inches, and bring to a boil over high heat. Reduce heat to low, cover and simmer for 2–3 hours, until beans are tender.

4. Add the sugar and salt to taste, and continue to cook, uncovered, for 20–30 minutes to reduce the liquid.

Gouda Grilled Cheese

2 1-lb. loaves light rye bread, sliced; save the end pieces for another use

4 tbsp. unsalted butter at room temperature

Coarsely ground mustard

2 lbs. thinly sliced Gouda cheese

1. Lay out the slices of rye bread 6–10 slices at a time. Spread the top surface of each with softened butter, stack together, set aside, and repeat until all 24 slices have been buttered on one side.

2. Again, lay out 6–10 slices at a time, unbuttered side up and spread each with mustard. Stack and set aside.

3. Heat 1 large or 2 medium heavy-bottomed sauté pans over high heat. (If you have a cast-iron griddle that covers two burners at once, even better.)

4. After several minutes, turn the heat down to medium. Place as many slices of bread, buttered side down, as will fit in the pan without crowding. Cover each with 2½ oz. thinly sliced Gouda. Top with second slice of bread, mustard side down, buttered side up.

5. Grill until undersides are golden brown. Turn sandwiches and repeat. Add more butter to the surface of pan and adjust the heat as needed.

Fruit Soup

Serves
4 to 6

Fruit soup: it's not just for Scandinavians. This dessert was served on both the Norwegian and German sides of my family, and I've learned it's a Polish favorite too.

1 c. pitted prunes, diced

1 c. dried apricots, diced

2 medium green apples, pared
   and chopped

1 cinnamon stick

2 cloves

1½ c. water

1 tbsp. instant tapioca

2 tbsp. dry sherry

Whipped or sour cream for garnish

1. In a 2 qt. saucepan, combine prunes, apricots, apples, cinnamon stick, cloves, and water. Simmer for 20 minutes, or until the fruit is tender and the liquid is the consistency of thin syrup.

2. Stir in the instant tapioca and bring to a boil.

3. Reduce heat to low, and cook until the soup is slightly thickened, stirring with a wooden spoon to keep the fruit sugars from sticking to the bottom and burning,

4. Remove cinnamon stick and cloves. Stir in sherry. Serve in individual bowls with whipped or sour cream.

February

Cheese · Rosemary Croutons · Frozen Roasted Tomatoes · Frozen Basil · Pasta · Heavy Cream

Despite an occasional shot at 28 days, February is a month that is seemingly without end in Minnesota. Spring appears to be so wearily distant, it's not even worth flirting with the thought. This is a month that requires mettle: Take a decisive about-face from those thermal-paned windows, march straight to your pantry, and prepare to sacrifice the treasured tail-ends of last summer's produce. Then ring up your closest friends and plan a party. Share your best aged cheese, the last of your oven-roasted tomatoes, and deplete your hoard of precious chocolates. Afterward, when the candles are extinguished and the guests, who have been carefully re-packaged into coats, scarves, and mittens, are sent away home with hugs and kisses, use your dishtowel to wipe a peephole through the steam on the kitchen window and look to see if merry March isn't on the way.

Love Tree Farms

If Dave and Mary Falk had a different animal for every business idea they've entertained, they'd be living in a zoo. They very nearly are anyway.

With 250 head of sheep, 24 dogs, an assortment of horses, goats, a llama, and a ferret, Love Tree Farms qualifies, at least, as a menagerie. Add in the Falks' "yours, mine, and ours" children, place them all on their farmstead at the crest of a hill littered with the residue of Dave and Mary's ingenuity, and you have Love Tree Farms: suppliers of sheep's milk and lamb, breeders of livestock guard dogs, wannabe wine and cheese tour operators, environmental activists, tire recyclers, and producers of some of the finest artisanal cheeses found in the Midwest.

Their trade name may sound romantic, but aside from Dave and Mary themselves, there's very little about a small dairy and cheese business that qualifies as such. Between birthing animals in the night, standing appointments in the milking parlor, and outsmarting coyotes, dairying is daunting. Still, the grind hasn't dampened their creativity, and they continue hatching new plans while scrambling to keep up with the old ones.

Mary was standing uncharacteristically still when we arrived on her Grantsburg, Wisconsin, farm one late spring morning. Wearing a hot pink t-shirt with the slogan "Strong woman worth many sheep" emblazoned on it, she stood frowning with her fists on her hips.

A well wall had collapsed that morning, requiring an emergency call to the repairman. Mary fumed as the guy attempted to fix the problem. As anyone without city-supplied water knows, fixing a troublesome well is an expensive proposition. Expecting that our plans for a tour might dry up as decidedly as the water supply, we edged away to give Mary room for the bad news and waited next to a stock pen in the shade of her barn.

Beyond the fence, spring lambs huddled in the shade of a giant tree. Farther off, framed by the view of a distant lake, a team of guard dogs made lazy loops around a clutch of ewes. Grace yammered in the car, and in response, a score of temporarily unemployed sheep dogs went wild in their pens.

The heat slowed us down, but Mary, leaving her plumbing problems behind, was back in action. She came sailing across the yard and motioned for us to follow. So began a two-hour, breathless commentary about all the plans for Love Tree Farms that were gestating, thriving, or lying around abandoned.

Following food from the market back to the farm is as much of an adventure as a visit to an artist's studio. It's just as hard to tell what sort of studio lies behind a painting in a gallery as it is to know how a farm will look from a head of cauliflower. Love Tree Farms is a cipher: gigantic bundles of tires, a field of sheep watched by huge, block-headed dogs of unidentifiable breeding, the cheese cave—which did not appear to be a cave at all, but a building with grass growing on top, and, lying everywhere, rolls of white plastic fencing. But, just as an artist's studio, cluttered with the debris of seemingly unconnected bursts of creativity leaves an overwhelming first impression, after a longer look, a progression of ideas emerges.

Good sheep cheese comes from quality milk, and that's where Dave and Mary's story begins. Twenty years of sheep herding and plenty of genetic tinkering later, Love Tree Farms had its own brand of good milking sheep. Half Lacaune and half East Friesian, they are far from uniform in appearance. Black, white, curly, horned or hornless, with floppy ears, to our untrained eyes the sheep that were fanned out in the meadow looked more like a mixed deck of cards than a single suit.

To the local coyotes and bears, however, all sheep look uniformly tasty. So, with a vested interest in protecting their flocks, Dave and Mary turned their attention to breeding the perfect guard dog. By crossing Italian Maremma, Polish Tatras, and Spanish Mastiffs, they bred a large dog that was frightening to predators, but gentle with children. One of Love Tree Farms' many businesses was born. There were twenty-four guard dogs on the place when we visited; an overlap in family planning had resulted in three simultaneous litters.

Next came the cheese. Without natural caves for aging, Dave and Mary put their heads together and figured out how to build them. Inspired by Spanish architecture, they poured concrete to create beehive-shaped rooms with vent holes at the top. Wanting a more pleasing patina on the cave walls, Mary began to experiment. She painted the first twelve-by-sixteen-foot cave pink, but wasn't happy with the result: it looked like plastic. She stuccoed over the paint, and it looked like aging plastic. Undaunted, she covered the amalgam with orange shellac. The result looked so much like water damage, she had to convince the health inspectors it was merely surface decoration.

We crowded into the center of the small moist dome and looked up toward the daylight that filtered through a fan system above our heads. Shelves of ripening cheese ringed the interior—large globes of orange velvet, creamy white cakes, smooth golden loaves, and mossy green bricks. Mary brushed her hand across one wheel of cheese and a ¾-inch halo of dark green mold laid down like iron filings, suddenly bereft of magnetic charge.

There's a quotient of serendipity to making cheese: the cheesemaker presents the cheese in an environment with the correct temperature and humidity, and the mold comes to dinner. From the thousands of strains that float in the air, certain molds form an affinity for a particular cheese. The resulting flavor is as much determined by the ingredients that go into the cheese as by the particular strain of mold that grows on it, and each individual color on the cheese bricks represents a different strain of mold.

The bulging shelves in Love Tree Farms' cheese cave were only partially comprised of cheese from the farm. The rest had been consigned to them for aging, one of Love Tree Farms' newest enterprises.

With typical enthusiasm Dave and Mary had built large caves because, at the time, they had a burgeoning wholesale cheese business. But trying to meet the demand from stores for their cheese was killing them and it became apparent that raising more sheep to get more of the quality milk their cheese required was hardly the way out of the dilemma. They decided instead to cut their herd in half, begin selling through the farmers' markets and use the extra time and shelf-space to babysit other people's cheese. Since cheese needs frequent hand-tending, this allowed their customers to concentrate on other aspects of their businesses.

Other endeavors in Dave and Mary's entrepreneurial portfolio were just as ingenious: there was the sheep's belly wool, good for repelling pests, which Mary marketed as garden mulch. "I've never seen a squirrel or a rabbit attack a sheep since its wool is so stinky. Nothing will come near it." Unfortunately, her car got stinky too.

The lone llama we saw that day had a similar story. Dave and Mary's large circle of friends and family often lobbied for wine and cheese excursions into the nature preserve that borders the farm, but after hearing about bears, they worried about chance encounters. The couple envisioned picnic-packed llamas who can frighten bears merely with their spit, said to have the power and accuracy of a BB gun. Love Tree Farms' llama safaris are still under development, in line behind other farm projects, like new cheese caves and a swimming pool.

Our favorite Dave and Mary scheme was the tire-recycling program. They rented a machine that bundled tires into bales and ran an ad in the local paper offering to recycle old tires for a fee. The idea proved to be so popular that the bundling machine rental was repaid, and then some. Now they have gigantic rubber bricks, earmarked for use as building blocks for new caves.

"We plan to stucco them, and the new caves will look like they belong to Fred and Wilma Flintstone," said Mary.

Our tour ended in her kitchen with a taste of Love Tree's signature Trade Lake Cedar raw sheep's milk cheese. Dave came in from the field where he'd been tending lambs and played with his pet ferret as we talked.

Mary fondled the cheese, removed its decorative cedar branch wrapping, then cut and presented it to us with ceremonial style. The taste was powerful. It was made from spring milk, but our mouths filled with autumnal flavor and aromas—walnut and smoky cedar—that cried out for a glass of port.

Love Tree Farms' cheese has attracted a lot of attention among chefs and in cheese competitions. We asked Mary which of all her successes was her proudest moment. Without missing a beat she said, "Making the house payment each month." After a little thought she came back with, "Don't know about my proudest moment, but I can tell you about my most astonished one."

In 1998 she'd been playing with goat's milk and made some cheese for fun. On a whim, she entered it in a competition. During the award ceremony she was so busy talking with a friend she didn't even know she'd won the American Cheese Society's Best of Show.

The whimsical farm that lies behind this extraordinary cheese is not open for public tours, but it is an inspiration to anyone who's ever tried to make a living on a less-traveled road. Love Tree Farms is at the St. Paul Farmers' Market on Saturdays year-round, the Mill City Farmers' Market on Saturdays from May through October, and the Kingfield Farmers' Market on Sundays from May through October.

Farmstead *Fromage*

In Minnesota, Love Tree Farms' artisan-made cheese would be licensed as Farmstead cheese. Huh? If all "Farmstead cheeses" are considered to be "Artisan cheese," then why aren't all "Artisan cheeses" classified as "Farmstead cheese"? Confused? So were we until someone broke it down for us. While both are crafted by hand in small batches, Farmstead designation is reserved for cheese made on the same farm where the cows, sheep, or goats are milked, and in Minnesota this requires a special license.

In our travels, we visited two farmstead-cheese producers: Shepherd's Way Farms near Northfield and Green Pastures Dairy in Carleton.

Shepherd's Way Farms owner Jody Ohlson-Read and husband Steven Read nearly lost their whole operation to a fire in 2005. Friends and family came to their aid, and with community support they've maintained their niche in the artisan-cheese market. Notable are their creamy Queso Fresco de Oveja, fresh, light with a memorable tangy flavor, good served alone with white wine or as a substitute for ricotta; Friesago, a semihard cheese described by the makers as "reminiscent of Manchego or Parmesan"; and Big Woods Blue, the farm's most expensive cheese, which uses a live-culture blue-cheese mold.

In the Twin Cities, Shepherd's Way Farms sheep cheese can be found at the Mill City Market during the summer season, in natural food stores, co-ops, cheese shops, and fine restaurants such as the Bayport Cookery in Bayport and Restaurant Alma in Minneapolis. Set in rolling farmland seven miles southeast of Northfield near Nerstrand Big Woods, Shepherd's Way is well-equipped to handle tours, welcomes them by appointment, and even offers an occasional cheesemaking class. A 1940s barn that's been updated with a glass-fronted walkway along one side makes it easy for visitors to see the sheep-milking parlor and the cheese-production and aging rooms. Use the email link on their website to inquire about tours: www.shepherdswayfarms.com.

A drive north on I-35 brings visitors to Green Pastures Dairy and the Hedquist family in Carleton. The name, Green Pastures, is the basis of the Hedquists' farming philosophy—when the cows are moved to fresh pastures every day in spring, summer, and fall, they produce milk with the highest vitamin and mineral content.

The day we visited, the cheese-aging room was full to the ceiling with uniform, beautifully handcrafted red and black wax-covered raw-milk cheese, among them a variety of flavored, three-year-aged Goudas, fresh and cheddar-style. From January 1 through May 1, Green Pastures is open by appointment only; after May 1, a store and small café is open for business. Otherwise their cheese can be purchased online, by phone, or at the Duluth Farmers' Market: www.greenpasturesdairy.com.

Multicultural daycare for cheese: Love Tree Farms rents shelf space and provides TLC for gouda, cheddar, and chevre from other area cheesemakers.

Dry Weather Creek Farm

In my house, love and birthdays mean one kind of cake: devil's food. My never-fail 1950s recipe calls for buttermilk, which, BJ says, is why it's invariably moist. Otherwise the ingredients are ordinary: cocoa—which makes a cake dark as the finest Belgian chocolate—eggs, butter, flour, and leavening. Simple. Even the frosting is ordinary, plain old whipped cream, sweetened with a little powdered sugar. I might decorate it with some mint leaves and a violet or two, but that's it. It never fails, never falls, and always ends up the same way: perfect.

This year that cake made a liar out of me. I baked it for a newly heartbroken friend who couldn't have cared less about anything, much less her birthday, until she blew out the candles and took the first bite. Then BJ had some, I had some, and Grace begged, but none of us were sharing. Before we knew it, half that cake was gone and our faith in love was a tiny bit restored, if in no other way than in the love of friends. I never thought there was a way to improve it, but my foolproof cake was better than ever, and I didn't even know why.

But BJ did, and she volunteered a little lesson in baking: it was the freshly milled flour we'd brought back from Dry Weather Creek Farm out near Milan, because the fresher the flour, the more consistent the crumb. There are bakers, she claimed, that would drive halfway across the state for ingredients such as Dry Weather Creek's freshly milled flour.

Impressed that such a treasure lay in my larder, I rummaged around until I spotted the flour. Elegant in the simplicity of its brown paper bag, Dry Weather Creek's product was illustrated with a lone stalk of wheat underscored by the phrase, "organically grown and certified" in good sturdy sans serif type.

Funny how packaging can send you sailing down memory lane just as surely as an old top-ten hit. In my mind's eye, behind the brown paper bag stretched miles of fields, baked to a golden brown in the hundred-degree heat, where BJ, Grace, and I drove in hypnotic circles trying to locate the flour miller. Blame it on the extreme temperature that day or the flat farmland near Montevideo, but to us Dry Weather Creek Farm was as hard to find as water in the desert.

When we pulled into the drive, farmers Mark and Wendy Lange took off their work gloves and offered us a place in the shade of a huge old tree behind the farm's two-story frame house. They got Grace a pan of water and cold drinks for us, then we all melted into the cool, at first almost too hot to talk.

We hoped we weren't interfering with their schedule too much, but the Langes looked grateful for the break. As they recounted their lengthy list of chores, we realized how rare it was for them to pause for anything other than exhausted sleep. They seldom stopped. Their workday began at dawn and ended at 10 p.m., fumbling in the kitchen for food, with absolutely no naps in between. It had been like that since they took the plunge and moved onto Mark's grandfather's farm to make a go of it with hand-ground flour and goats' milk.

Heidi notwithstanding, Mark and Wendy may be the two most romantic characters who ever milked a goat. He was a Norwegian bachelor, wannabe farmer, and she a country girl from Michigan when they met over the Internet, fell in love, and dreamed up a wonderful new life together.

Running against the tide of farmers who've been forced off farms into towns, they researched their plan carefully, taking courses in business management, touring successful farms, and trying business models on paper, before quitting their jobs.

The Langes had settled on growing and milling organic wheat, corn, and oats for direct sale in Willmar and Montevideo, when they gleaned that relying solely on their own grain was too risky. So they offset their shiny new milling equipment by grinding grain for other area farmers, but the books still didn't balance. Ultimately, they diversified by selling goats' milk. When milk sales slowed, they sold goats to local Hispanic and African populations for meat.

In six years' time, the Langes had built a new barn, developed a herd of fifty-plus goats, purchased state-of-the-art flour milling equipment, and gained organic certification for land that had been farmed conventionally for generations. No wonder they were willing to sit a bit when we arrived. But it wasn't long before they were back on their feet, giving us a thorough tour.

Sheltering trees, a towering barn, and a slight swale between the house and the outbuildings surrounded a farmyard that had embraced people and animals since Mark's grandfather started the farm one hundred years ago. Riding horses grazed on pasture, miniature ponies nestled in a cozy straw-filled shed, and a herd of goats, accessorized with name tags and chain link collars, all turned to examine the visiting city folks.

The new frame building where the Langes produce their stone-ground flour was cool and dry, occupied by little more than their shiny new milling equipment. The phrase "stone-ground" brings millstones of yore to mind, but modern stones are encased in stainless steel. There was a different machine for each step in the process: one that separates the wheat from the

In six years' time, the Langes had built a new barn, developed a herd of fifty-plus goats, purchased state-of-the-art flour milling equipment, and gained organic certification for land that had been farmed conventionally for generations.

chaff, one that scours, and two that actually grind. Since grain will last longer when stored in its whole form, Irish oatmeal, whole wheat, and unbleached white flour are ground to order. With only three other stone-ground mills in Minnesota, Dry Weather Creek's reputation is growing steadily, turning out four or five hundred pounds of flour a month—more in winter.

Given the hurdles and frustrations of a start-up business, some might say the Langes traded their old jobs for more work than ever. The two of them seemed to love farm life and each other with an intensity that kept them from noticing long hours. As it turned out the Langes' marriage was not the stuff of fairy tales—they closed the dairy and parted as friends a year or so later—but the lift Mark and Wendy gave us was very real. When I remember how our spirits improved from the foolproof devil's food birthday cake, I like to imagine the Langes slipped a little of the midlife romance we all deserve into every bag. Such nice people. We're thinking of sending them each a cake.

You can purchase Dry Weather Creek flour in natural food outlets in Montivedeo, Milan and Morris, and taste the farm's creamy corn grits at the Brasa restaurants and the Red Stag Supper Club in the Twin Cities. Artisan bakers from much farther away would love to use it, but the weight makes it too expensive to ship. Like BJ said, some will make pilgrimages west to buy flour. I know I will before the need to make another pain-relieving cake arises.

Rosemary Croutons

1 lb. loaf sourdough bread

½ c. extra-virgin olive oil

1 tbsp. dried rosemary, crushed

1. Preheat oven to 300°F.

2. Trim crusts from bread; cut into 1½-inch slices; cut slices into 1½-inch cubes. Spread bread cubes evenly over 2 sided sheet pans, and place in oven for 10 minutes. Pull pans out once during this time and redistribute cubes so they dry uniformly; the croutons should not brown.

3. While croutons are in the oven, warm olive oil in a small pan over low heat. Add crushed rosemary; heat just until fragrant.

4. Remove dried croutons to a large mixing bowl. Sprinkle with warm rosemary oil and toss to coat. Place back on sheet pans; increase oven heat to 425°F. Return croutons to oven until lightly browned, stirring once.

5. Spear croutons with fondue forks or bamboo skewers for dipping into the fondue.

Cheese Fondue with Rosemary Croutons

Serves 4

Traditionally, fondue is made from two parts well-aged Swiss Gruyere and one part Emmenthaler cheese. This all-Minnesota version uses equal proportions of Eichten's Swiss (aged or Baby) and Tilsit, both of which are produced on their farm outside of Center City. Serve with blanched broccoli florets and Rosemary Croutons. Tart apples are a nice option as well.

8 oz. Eichten's aged or Baby Swiss, grated

8 oz. Tilsit, grated

3 tbsp. cornstarch

½ tsp. sweet paprika

¼ tsp. freshly grated nutmeg

⅛ tsp. ground cayenne

1 clove garlic, peeled and halved

1¾ c. dry white wine

1 tbsp. fresh lemon juice

2 tbsp. brandy

¼ tsp. baking soda

6 c. Rosemary Croutons (see sidebar)

1. Toss grated Swiss and Tilsit, cornstarch, paprika, nutmeg, and cayenne together in large bowl, and set aside.

2. Rub the inside of a fondue pot with halved garlic; discard the garlic, and add the wine. Place fondue pot on a stove burner and heat uncovered on low heat just until bubbles begin to appear.

3. Add shredded cheese to the pot one handful at a time while stirring constantly in a figure-eight pattern. The cheese should be melted and the mixture smooth before each addition is made. Add lemon juice, and stir for 15 minutes. Slowly stir in brandy, then baking soda; the fondue should be creamy, not lumpy or stringy. If mixture thickens, stir in a little more warmed white wine.

4. Light the alcohol burner for the fondue pot. Set pot over lit burner and adjust flame so fondue stays just below a bubble. It should never boil. Serve with Rosemary Croutons.

Now, That's *Amoré!*: Pasta *Pomo D'Oro*

Serves 4, or 2 for dinner and a midnight snack

Pomo D'Oro: translate the Italian word for tomato into English, and you get "love apples." Say "tomato," and "spaghetti" comes to mind. Think "spaghetti," and Italy pops into the picture. Italy? *Amoré*: love. Ah *"Pomo D'Oro"*; the word just speaks of romantic possibility.

For a fast and easy Valentine's Day dinner, spice up these plum-shaped apples of love with some fresh basil and garlic, a soft dusting of freshly grated Parmesan, and a good pinch of hot red pepper flakes. Just cue Dean Martin, dim the lights, and pop the cork on the Prosecco.

½ c. extra-virgin olive oil

2–3 cloves fresh garlic, crushed (not minced)

6–8 fresh basil leaves, depending on size

8–10 oz. oven-roasted tomatoes (see the instructions in "Oven-Roasted Tomatoes" on page 65) or 1 32-oz. can ripe plum tomatoes, fire-roasted if possible

Coarse salt, to taste

Dried hot chili pepper flakes, to taste

1 lb. dried semolina spaghetti or linguini

Freshly grated Parmesan cheese, for garnish

1. Heat the oil in a medium or 8- to 9-inch sauté pan over low to medium heat. Add crushed garlic, heat until it begins to brown, and discard. Tear basil leaves into small pieces and add to oil; remove pan from heat so basil doesn't burn.

2. Cut larger oven-roasted tomatoes in half. Place oven-roasted tomatoes in hot oil, lower the heat and return pan to the burner. Cook briefly until the tomatoes plump. If using canned tomatoes, place tomatoes in a large bowl, and crush with the back of a mixing spoon or ladle. Add to oil and basil. Return to heat.

3. Bring to simmer, add salt and hot chili peppers to taste. Simmer for 2–3 minutes; remove from heat; taste for seasoning and adjust. Recipe makes enough for 1 lb. of dry pasta.

4. Cook spaghetti according to package directions, and drain.

5. To serve, place ⅓ of the warm sauce in the bottom of a large mixing bowl, add drained pasta, and toss to coat. Add another ⅓ of the sauce and freshly grated Parmesan. Toss, and place equal portions into 4 or 2 bowls.* Top with remaining sauce and grated Parmesan. Garnish each serving with a fresh basil leaf.

*Leave remaining pasta in the mixing bowl, dust with Parmesan; put 2 forks in with the pasta; cover and refrigerate next to the Prosecco, if there's any left. Now, that's *Amoré!*

151

Chantilly Cream

1 c. heavy (whipping) cream
2 tbsp. sugar
½ tsp. vanilla extract, seeds
    from ½ vanilla bean, or
    ½ tsp. vanilla powder

Whisk the cream, sugar, and vanilla in a large bowl until soft peaks form. The cream should hold its shape but still be satiny in appearance.

Heartbreak Cake

Serves
1 to 8

This surprisingly moist, rich, and dark chocolate cake goes together quickly; even your chocoholic friends will never guess it's made with cocoa.

½ c. unsalted butter
1½ c. granulated sugar
2 large eggs, at room temperature
2 c. unbleached all-purpose white
    flour, stirred or sifted before
    measuring
1 tsp. baking powder
1 tsp. baking soda
¾ c. buttermilk
⅛ tsp. salt
1 tsp. vanilla
½ c. cocoa mixed with ½ c.
    hot water

1. Preheat oven to 350°F; adjust oven rack to middle.

2. Place butter and sugar in a mixing bowl, cover, and bring to room temperature. Beat eggs in a small bowl, cover, and set aside.

3. Combine flour and baking powder, and sift into a separate bowl.

4. Stir baking soda into buttermilk.

5. Cream room temperature butter and sugar until light and fluffy. Mix in beaten eggs.

6. Alternately add dry ingredients and buttermilk to the creamed butter/sugar, beating well after each addition.

7. Add salt, vanilla, and cocoa/hot water mixture, beating well after each addition.

8. Pour into 2 greased and floured 8-inch layer cake pans. Bake for 30–40 minutes.

9. Frost with Chantilly Cream (sweetened whipped cream) or a favorite chocolate buttercream frosting.

March

Potatoes · Dried Leeks · Roasted Tomato Juice · Horseradish · Shaker's Vodka · Dried Parsley · Porketta · Italian Rolls · Buttermilk · Cream Cheese · Apples

Promises, promises. By the end of March, spring *will* be here, and all across the state people are planning overly ambitious gardens. They sat home quietly studying their seed catalogues in late winter and, inspired by beauty shots of all the "new" heirloom varieties, ordered enough seeds to fill egg cartons and seed trays that covered their work benches and overflowed onto their washing machines. By month's end, the really eager ones will be on hands and knees planting those seedlings into the earth where they just might freeze, nature's way of returning an inflated garden plan back into one of manageable size. We're on our knees too—studying maps, planning our first trips into the countryside and generally giving thanks for another spring. But it's still too early to get fresh produce, and much of our cooking is based on held-over-winter freezer and root cellar foods. In honor of the season, we dreamed up a sprightly green edamame dip from frozen soybeans. We'll follow that with spicy porketta sandwiches (obtained on our first trip north) and hearty potato soup with a brilliant, flavor-packed tomato aspic on the side for color. For dessert: rich, carmel apple cheesecake.

Keeping it on the Farm

Carnival-colored squash, purple broccoli, black cherry tomatoes, and white pumpkins: the produce for sale in today's farmers' markets seems to have had a makeover, and we think the growers have a new look too. The farmers we interviewed in the course of writing this book were, by and large, young, college-educated, and ready to swap steady paychecks for a chance to live in the country. They'd give us impromptu tours, whip out laptops to show pictures of last year's crops, follow *New York Times'* food columnist Michael Polan, apply for grants from the Land Stewardship Project, and join organizations such as Pride of the Prairie and Midwest Food Alliance. Many of these young, "green" farmers are reinventing the wheel, since chemical-free farming was a rarity in their parents' generation. One young woman who was struggling with steep slopes and exhausted soil said it all when she told us plaintively, "We don't have any teachers any more."

Dave and Florence Minar of Cedar Summit Farm bridged the gap. Not only were they a little older, but, after farming conventionally most of their adult lives, they'd made a complete about-face by transforming their farm into a sustainable grazing operation and starting a creamery. The process started slowly more than ten years ago, but by the time we visited, their perky green and yellow Cedar Summit Farm logo could be seen on glass bottles and cartons of non-homogenized milk and cream in more than eighty area stores. They were the area's only certified organic creamery that sold milk from grass-fed cows, and that put them firmly at the forefront of Minnesota's locally grown movement.

Our first phone contacts with Cedar Summit were so calm and unhurried, we could tell this company wasn't like the start-up businesses we'd visited. A polite young man referred us deferentially to Dave, who heard us out patiently, promising to call back as soon as he knew his schedule. He did, within the hour. When the day came and Dave had run to Northfield for supplies, making him a few minutes late, another young man called to inform us. In the end we arrived at the farm just outside New Prague at about the same time.

The new red building housing the farm, store, and creamery had an expectant, businesslike appeal, standing as it did in full sun near the road, a discreet distance from the shady lane that led to the Minars' house and barn. Inside the store, there was a window into the creamery through which visitors viewed a circuit of shiny steel pipes, where milk was heated, cooled, and came out à la Louis Pasteur.

We were greeted by Dave's wife, Florence, a kind-faced woman who was tall and gray-haired, and who wore loose-fitting jeans and a t-shirt as easily as any teenager. She was the sort of person with whom everyone stands on comfortable ground. She didn't bat an eye while we, with the enthusiasm of truffle pigs, nosed through shelves, coolers, and freezers full of locally produced products. Next to the front door, a glass freezer case of Cedar Summit ice creams stood waiting to catch someone with a sweet tooth. Chocolate, vanilla, strawberry, and a flavor of the day were all available as single, double, or triple scoop cones.

Cedar Summit's signature green-lettered glass bottles shared the shelves with cookbooks and Pastureland butter from a regional dairy consortium; with spun, combed, and liquid honey from a New Prague neighbor and freshly milled flour from Milan; with frozen chickens and sausages from Caledonia and spices from the Twin Cities.

When Dave arrived, he began to describe the people behind the products, and it became clear from his quiet enthusiasm that he and Florence knew, and probably mentored, all of them.

As a mother and a teacher, Florence was already in the business of passing ideas from one generation to the next. Dave's thinking must have been the same, because Cedar Summit's creamery came into being as a direct result of this couple's plans for the future. After buying the farm from Dave's parents in 1969 and working it for more than twenty-five years, the Minars just couldn't see spending their grandparenting years in back-breaking, knee-wrenching work. Either they would sell or make the place into something sustainable that could be continued by their five children.

It would take radical changes, but they had already taken a momentous first step when, after a farm accident with chemicals in 1973, they stopped farming with pesticides. Later, they decided to put their animals on pasture, going against the conventional practices of the day.

It was a beautiful system: the cows would feed themselves, and the land would be in better shape; there were consumers ready to

Keeping it in the family: Dave and Florence Minar are the entrepreneurial model for their children and other young dairy farmers, encouraging them to follow in their footsteps by avoiding the middleman and selling directly to the consumer.

pay for organically grazed beef and dairy products if they could find them. It turned out there were double health benefits: the vet bills dropped by 90 percent, and Florence learned that eating meat and drinking milk from grass-fed animals was preventative medicine against a host of chronic ailments.

In the late 1990s, the Minars were still selling their milk through conventional channels, but realized that if they could market their own organic, grass-fed dairy products and sell directly from the farm, a unique market niche could be theirs. The financial investment was daunting: new equipment to process and bottle their own milk and a new milking parlor to save their backs and knees. All this at a point when the farm was nearly paid off and most people would be thinking of retirement.

If their children had shown no interest in the idea, the Minars would not have gone ahead. They were in a unique position with five children who, along with their four spouses, wanted to capitalize on Dave and Florence's dairy expertise and keep the farm in the family. Each of their offspring brought a different talent to the table. As a whole, the family had the bones of a corporate structure; marketing, finances, graphic design, computer operations, and office and dairy management could all be handled by a different person. They used family-owned farmland that was in the path of development on the outskirts of New Prague as collateral, and the dairy business was off to the races.

Eventually people outside of the family joined in. When we visited a young couple was living on the farm, interning to become farm managers. Though Dave is a graduate of ag college, this kind of hands-on farm schooling means more to Dave and Florence than a formal education.

"We teach them exactly what we want them to know, and that sometimes includes business advice," said Florence.

Months after visiting the Minars at Cedar Summit, we chanced across them at a Minnesota Slow Food dinner held on a farm near Lake City. A spinoff of an international movement that began in Rome in the 1980s, Slow Food was formed to challenge "fast food" by demonstrating how wholesome, local foods are delicious, beneficial to health, stimulate farm economy, and sustain the environment. Ralph Lentz, the farmer who hosted the Minnesota Slow Food dinner, added to the experience by talking about his grazing practices and waterway management, and leading tours into his fields.

A string of late-model cars, many of them hybrids, were parked along the fence outside the entrance to the farm. Inside the yard a line had formed near the farmhouse kitchen door, and plates of ramps (a kind of wild onion), elk, and wild rice were handed around. The diners gathered beneath the shade of trees that rimmed a small pond were a mix of young, or young-at-heart, Twin Citians and farmers.

An old fashioned cut-glass dish on a table with fresh-baked bread showcased butter from Cedar Summit Creamery, and a little ways beyond, Dave Minar's wide-brimmed straw hat could be seen nodding in the center of a circle of Slow Food devotees. Without even hearing the conversation, I had a clue to its content.

When we'd visited he'd said, "So many young people ask for advice, hoping to do what we've done. We ask them, 'Who is your market?' and they give us that deer-in-the-headlights look."

Frequent open houses and regular store hours make Cedar Summit and the Minars accessible to visitors. Whether you'd like to see what's new among locally produced foods, follow the steps from cow to carton of cream, or simply stop in for a cone of the most sinfully rich ice cream imaginable, Cedar Summit is reason enough for a pilgrimage to New Prague.

Seeds of Change

As a child I spent hours in the backseat of my parents' car while our family crisscrossed the United States, staring at farm fields, identifying crops, and linking them to the surrounding topography. Peanuts grew in the red soil of the South, winter wheat on the dry plains of eastern Washington, and corn, potatoes, and soybeans began to show up when we were close to home in the Midwest.

From the dinner table I knew how most of the crops were used, but soybeans were an enigma. Adults referred to them in the abstract, as in soybean futures, or answered my queries with vague references to "industrial" oils. Later I learned to eat tofu, and though I knew intellectually that it was made from soybeans, the link between the white tub of protein I bought at the grocery and the rows of leafy bean plants I'd passed on the road was far from clear. It was not until I tasted soybeans under the unfamiliar name of edamame (ed-duh-mommy) in a Japanese restaurant that I really identified with soybeans.

Lo and behold, soybeans that one can actually eat! And what's more, the way the Japanese served them, steaming hot in their pods and sprinkled with sea salt, was delicious—right up there with potato chips for finger-licking good. There are some lovely acronyms for beans that you shuck: shuckies, shell-outs, shelly beans, or shellies. You can imagine why I like them. And I liked them even better when I learned that edamame are healthy, a perfect protein high in isoflavins, filling—which makes them great for dieting—and far easier to digest than other beans. As far as I was concerned, the only thing wrong with edible soybeans was that they were hard to find.

Grocers replied to my inquiries for edamame with puzzled looks, but I finally found some in the freezer case at a high-end organic food store. Frozen edamame came already shelled or in the pod, and depending where you shopped, and where the beans hailed from, they were sometimes outrageously pricey—which was hard to square with my childhood assessment of the vast acreage devoted to soybeans.

How puzzling in Minnesota, where the word *soybeans* was on every farmer's lips, that people rarely ate them. It is, of course, hard to imagine Scandinavians getting their mouths around the word *edamame*, but they could have called it something

> *How puzzling in Minnesota, where the word* soybeans *was on every farmer's lips, that people rarely ate them.*

else—like "soyafisk" or "beanakake." Some varieties of soybeans are tastier than others, but in essence, edible soybeans are a young, green version of the same beans that are grown for ink or paint, which, from my childhood survey, appeared to grow just fine in Minnesota. I decided to test the ease of growing edamame myself, and as my gardening has unpredictable results, planned to set a pack aside, with the hope of giving it to a more experienced farmer who might test them for me.

It never occurred to me that the seeds would be hard to find. None of the garden centers had ever heard of them, and the companies listed under seed in the yellow pages were selling grass seed or industrial quantities of the other kind of soybean for agribusiness. I left messages on half a dozen answering machines and heard back from only one, who not only knew about edible soybeans, she had them in stock. "You should have come to me first," said the woman at the Southside Farm and Garden Store.

Billed as an old-fashioned farm and garden market, with the farm side of things leaning heavily toward household pets, I realized, when I arrived at the store on 38th Street, that I had gone to her once before for another hard-to-find-item—the sparkly ball toys my cat seemed to prefer and no one else in town seemed to carry.

The store had been there for ages, and the neighborhood around it had gone downhill, so its exterior, which had been a whimsical mix of floral embellishment and hand-printed signs, was now bracketed by iron bars and a chainlink fence. I poked my head inside the fence, and there on the seed spinner, flanked on all sides by mouth-watering pictures of heirloom vegetables from Seed Savers Exchange in Iowa, was a packet of edible soybeans. Pleased to find the seeds, I bought several and planted some (which, as a testament to my gardening skill, never sprouted).

Seed Savers Heritage Farm and Gardens is nestled in the hills that surround Decorah, Iowa.

Sometimes it pays to let the professionals do what they do best. Next year, I might work my way through the list of CSAs in the *Minnesota Grown Directory*, find one, and let them do all my gardening. CSAs are becoming more sophisticated all the time: drop sites are more convenient, some provide food throughout the winter, some offer the option of meat or baked goods, and some sell half shares to accommodate smaller households. Many have thoughtful, fact-filled websites too. One is Pastures A Plenty, a grazing operation, which delivers pre-ordered pork packs, free-range chicken, and eggs by truck to stops around the Twin Cities as well as Litchfield and Hutchinson.

And talk about sprouting: the 2009 *Minnesota Grown Directory* (with over 300 total members) lists forty-five CSAs, up from only ten in 2005. I wonder how many of those made their names with elegant, old-fashioned vegetables offered by Seed Savers Iowa-based operation that has packaging and catalogues as rich with pattern and color as Dutch still-life paintings. The place had been mentioned by growers so often as a source for seeds, it seemed to be beckoning us from its headquarters down near the Iowa border.

Seed Savers Exchange is a nonprofit organization that stores endangered seeds from plants that are no longer being grown, having been left behind by fashion and current agricultural trends. Their meticulously maintained 890-acre farm is a hymn to biodiversity, and a value-packed daytrip destination; visitors can hike in the forests, picnic in the orchards, see a storehouse that holds more than 20,000 seeds, and tour the Heritage Gardens, where 10 percent of the seed repository is planted each year, thereby continuing the strain.

In early summer we made the trip south to Iowa, passing long, uniform stretches of Minnesota corn and soybean fields along the way. As we neared the hilly outskirts of Decorah, it poured, and we drove in a rain-drenched rag of haze until we glimpsed the saturated red of the Heritage Farm's buildings nestled among verdant showcase gardens. The main visitor center building housed a conference center and a store with gifts for gardeners, colorful books, and, of course, seeds . . . hundreds of them, all with striking professional photographs that seemed to announce, "I am not your average, garden-variety vegetable." On a walkway beneath the building's eaves were planter boxes with seedlings to buy—a good choice for those whose luck with planting seeds equals mine.

In the rich, black dirt outside the front entrance of the visitor center was a woman on her hands and knees deftly inserting bedding plants into a tapestry-like edible garden. Focusing over her shoulder with my camera, I couldn't decide which segment to photograph, each one was more beautiful than the next. The gardener turned to us with a peaceful smile, and revealed that she was Diane Ott, the founder of Seed Savers Exchange. Though we were poking a hole in her busy day, Ott paused and talked long enough for us to get a glimpse of the resolve that had taken this woman from the simple act of saving her grandfather's morning glory seeds to the large and respected nonprofit organization it is today.

BJ was particularly excited to see Seed Savers firsthand, having learned of it years earlier from her elderly farmer cousin on the Iron Range. When she mentioned his name and connection to heirloom potatoes, Ott knew right away who BJ was talking about, saying "We still sell his potato seed."

In the store, BJ was like a kid in a candy shop when confronted with racks and racks of seeds, all in alphabetical order. She'd gathered an armload by the time she reached *S*, and there they were—edible soybeans in three varieties: Agate, Shirofumi, and Envy. Envy? Few farmers in Minnesota could be feeling that about edible soybeans. Hardly anyone seemed to want to grow them.

The long drive back home took us through thousands of acres devoted to soybeans, not one of which would make it to a table near us any time soon. We felt a bit like the Ancient Mariner, who, though surrounded by water, water everywhere, could never find a drop to drink.

Seed Catalogs

By March, winter has usually worn out its welcome in Minnesota. But if recent vernal equinoxes are any indication, the time to exchange the snow shovel for a garden spade hasn't quite arrived, so we must wait and dream. Way back when, in another century, the seed catalogs began trickling in after the New Year, and by March our mailboxes could compete with December's toy catalogs and holiday cards.

The more established catalogs were no-nonsense and straight forward, until the 1980s produced a crop of vendors with new looks and marketing approaches to one of man's most fundamental endeavors. Highly styled photographs replaced forward facing shots, copy became quote worthy, and the explosion of heirloom seed varieties threatened to overtake the tried-and-true yellow sweet corn, Idaho russets, and beefsteak tomatoes that we'd all grown up thinking were our only options. The advent of the Internet changed it all again, making it easy to browse and order, without generating a lot of extra paper, which I have to admit is a good and responsible thing.

Today websites abound, many dangling promotional carrots for us to take advantage of. A search for seed sources suited to Minnesota's climate zones yielded a list of 127,000 possibilities. Many continue to produce catalogs, but need to charge a small fee. Still, there's something to be said for putting your feet up, in some cozy slippers of course, enjoying a cup of hot tea, and perusing the pile of seed catalogs in your lap while the cold March wind blusters about outside. Below is a list of ten websites worthy of any Minnesota gardener's consideration.

Seed Sources for Northern Gardens

Seed Savers Exchange
www.seedsavers.org

Organic Agriculture Resources
    Suppliers Seed Sources
http://extension.agron.iastate.edu/
    organicag/seedsources.html

Gurney's Seed & Nursery
www.Gurneys.com

Park Seed®
www.ParkSeed.com

University of Minnesota Plant
    Information Online
www.plantinfo.umn.edu

Minnesota DNR: Native plant suppliers
    and landscapers
www.dnr.state.mn.us/gardens/
    nativeplants/suppliers.html

Spring Hill Nurseries
www.SpringHillNursery.com

Tomato Bob's Heirloom Tomatoes
www.tomatobob.com

Organica Seed
www.organicaseed.com

The Cook's Garden
www.cooksgarden.com

March Menu

Edamame Dip

♦

Potato Leek Soup

♦

Virgin Mary Aspic

♦

Porketta Sandwiches

♦

Caramel Apple
Cheesecake

Yummy Edamame Dip

Makes
3 to 4 c.

Thanks to frozen edamame, this flavor-filled spring-green dip can be served throughout the year. It comes frozen with or without the pods, which are inedible. In summer we serve it with big round slices of daikon radish, new carrots, and celery; in fall, try slices of tart apple. And in keeping with eating fresh foods in season, in winter substitute dried cilantro and crushed red pepper flakes for the Hungarian pepper and cilantro.

3 c. frozen soybeans, cooked;
   shelled and steamed if fresh
   and still in pods
½ c. red onion, minced
2 tsp. hot Hungarian pepper,
   minced
2 medium-sized cloves of garlic,
   minced
1⅓ tbsp. apple cider vinegar
1½ tsp. freshly squeezed
   lime juice
4 tbsp. fresh cilantro leaves,
   coarsely chopped
1½ tsp. fine sea salt
1 tsp. whole cumin, pan roasted
   and ground
1 c. cooked Great Northern
   beans, drained
2⅓ tbsp. extra-virgin olive oil
2 tbsp. water, as needed

1. If using frozen edamame, cook according to package directions.

2. Put edamame, minced red onion, hot Hungarian pepper, and garlic in the food processor, and pulse to purée.

3. With the motor running, drizzle in the cider vinegar, followed by the lime juice. Scrape down the sides of the bowl. Add cilantro, sea salt, and cumin and blend.

4. Add the Great Northern beans and olive oil in three parts. Scrape the sides of the bowl, taste for seasoning, and adjust as necessary. Add up to 2 tbsp. of water until mixture reaches desired consistency.

5. Cover and refrigerate for about an hour, taste, and re-season, if needed.

Late-Winter Elegance: Potato Leek Soup

Serves
4 to 6

This wholesome, chunky Irish standard is perfect for chilly Minnesota evenings—it begs for thickly sliced and buttered homemade bread, dark ale, and a roaring fire—but you can also serve it in summer as the French do, puréed and chilled. For a textured, peasant-like purée, only blend half the soup.

7 tbsp. unsalted butter, divided

1 tbsp. dried chives; in summer use 4 tbsp. fresh, reserving 1 tbsp. for garnish

5 leeks, white part only, sliced and washed

1 medium-sized carrot, trimmed, scrubbed, and thinly sliced

2 Idaho or yellow-flesh potatoes, peeled and thinly sliced

1 qt. chicken stock; homemade is best (see chicken stock recipe in "Taking Stock While Making Stock" on page 163)

3 tbsp. all-purpose flour

1 c. whole milk, room temperature

Coarse salt and freshly ground black pepper, to taste

1. Melt 4 tbsp. unsalted butter in a large skillet over medium-high heat; add chives, leeks, and carrots and sauté until soft.

2. In heavy 3–4 qt. saucepan, cook sliced potatoes in chicken stock until tender. Add sautéed leeks and carrots to potatoes and cook 5–10 minutes.

3. Melt the remaining 3 tbsp. butter in the same sauté pan in which you cooked the leeks and carrots; stir in the flour, and cook over medium heat until it smells nutty. Do not brown. Add milk slowly and stir until thickened. Add salt and pepper.

4. Stir 1–2 ladles full of chicken stock/potatoes and leeks into the white sauce; cook for 1–2 minutes, then stir contents of skillet back into the larger soup pot. Cook until thick. Taste and adjust seasonings. Serve sprinkled with remaining chopped chives.

Summer Variation: For a delicious summer soup, purée the soup in a food processor with 3 tbsp. fresh chives. Garnish with an additional 1 tbsp. fresh chives.

Taking Stock While Making Stock

Whoever said April was the cruelest month missed Minnesota in January. It's the time of year when winter gets really cold and feels as if it will stay forever. But Minnesotans have a sure-fire remedy for this: hot soup. Being folk of hearty Midwestern stock, they won't settle for the kind that comes in a can. Oh no, they do it the way Grandmother did back in the old country: start with stock.

Stock is one of the most essential elements you can have in your larder. Consider future uses, and make extra. Freeze it in a variety of sizes from quarts for soups to pints for pan and pasta sauces, or reduce it to a demi-glace and freeze in ice cube trays. One cube dropped in at the end will add depth to any number of meat, vegetable, fish, and poultry dishes. Having stock in your freezer in winter might be better than having it in the market.

Chicken Stock (Makes 3 quarts)

3–4 lbs. chicken parts and/or bones

1 c. yellow onion, outer skin removed, roughly chopped

1 c. unpeeled carrot, roughly chopped

½ c. celery, roughly chopped

1 sprig of fresh or 1 pinch dried thyme

Several sprigs fresh parsley, or a generous pinch dried parsley

1 bay leaf, broken in half

1 tbsp. black peppercorns, crushed

4 qt. cold water

1. Preheat oven to 400°F.

2. Rinse chicken parts and bones and pat dry. Place in shallow roasting pan with chopped onion and carrot. Roast for 15–20 minutes, or until chicken is golden brown.

3. While chicken is roasting, put celery, thyme, parsley, bay leaf, peppercorns, and 4 quarts cold water in a stockpot.

4. Transfer browned chicken, carrots, and onions from roasting pan to stock pot, place over high heat and bring to a boil. Set roasting pan aside.

5. Deglaze roasting pan while stock is coming to a boil by placing pan over burner on high heat. Add 1–2 ladles of the liquid from the stock pot to the roasting pan. Bring to a rapid boil, scraping all the browned bits from the bottom of the pan. Add entire contents of roasting pan to the stockpot; continue cooking stock as directed. Once stock comes to a boil, reduce heat so liquid is just below a boil, sending just a few bubbles up at a time. Cook in this manner for at least 2 hours.

6. Strain the stock through a sieve or colander, pressing down on vegetables to extract as much juice as possible. Discard solids and refrigerate stock until fat hardens. Remove fat before using or freezing. If not using for a day or two, leave fat in place and tightly cover container with food film.

Beef Stock (Makes 3 quarts)

3–4 lbs. meaty beef bones
1 c. onions, outer skin removed, and roughly chopped
1 c. unpeeled carrots, roughly chopped
1 c. celery, roughly chopped
1 c. chopped tomatoes, canned is fine
1 sprig of fresh or 1 pinch dried thyme
Several sprigs fresh parsley, or 1 generous pinch dried parsley
1 bay leaf, broken in half
1 tbsp. black peppercorns, crushed
4 qt. water

1. Preheat oven to 400°F.

2. Place meaty bones in shallow roasting pan with chopped onion and carrot. Roast for 15–20 minutes, or until beef is golden brown.

3. While beef is roasting, place remaining ingredients in the stockpot.

4. Transfer browned meat, carrots, and onions to stock pot; place over high heat and bring to a boil; set roasting pan aside.

5. Deglaze roasting pan while stock is coming to a boil by placing pan over burner on high heat. Add 1–2 ladles of the liquid from the stock pot to the roasting pan. Bring to a rapid boil, scraping all the browned bits from the bottom of the pan. Add entire contents of roasting pan to the stockpot; continue cooking stock as directed. Once stock comes to a boil, reduce heat so liquid is just below a boil, sending just a few bubbles up at a time. Cook in this manner for at least 2 hours.

6. Strain stock through sieve or colander, pressing down on vegetables to extract as much juice as possible. Discard solids and refrigerate stock until fat hardens. Remove fat before using or freezing. If not using for a day or two, leave fat in place and tightly cover container with food film.

Vegetable Stock (Makes 3 quarts)

2 leeks, cut in half lengthwise and washed

2 large onions, peeled and quartered

4 carrots, unpeeled and cut in half

2 celery stalks, cut in half

6 cloves garlic, unpeeled

3 shallots, unpeeled

1 c. mushrooms, trimmed, or mushroom stems, or ¼ c. reconstituted dried mushrooms
with their soaking liquid

4 tbsp. extra-virgin olive oil

10 sprigs fresh parsley

2 or 3 sprigs fresh thyme

10 peppercorns

2 qt. water, plus up to 4 c. additional water

½ c. dry white wine

1. Preheat oven to 400°F.

2. Place leeks, onions, carrots, celery, garlic, shallots and mushrooms in a shallow-sided roasting pan, and drizzle with olive oil. Place in the center of the oven, and roast ingredients for about 45 minutes, shaking the pan and turning the ingredients once or twice during this time.

3. While vegetables are roasting, place parsley, thyme, and peppercorns into a stockpot with 2 qt. cold water.

4. Transfer roasted vegetables to stock pot; place over high heat and bring to a boil; set roasting pan aside.

5. Deglaze roasting pan with white wine by placing pan over burner on high heat. Add 2–4 c. water, depending on the size of the pan; bring to a boil, scraping all bits of vegetable from the bottom of the roaster. Add this mixture to the stockpot, bring to a boil and reduce heat to a simmer. Cook for 1½ hours, strain to remove solids and refrigerate or freeze.

Not Your Grandmother's Gelatin Salad: Virgin Mary Aspic

What would a major holiday dinner be without a "molded salad"? Here in the Midwest, it's a time-honored tradition, along with a relish tray featuring carrot and celery sticks and those soft, pitted black olives. As kids we liked the sweet, green "jiggly-thing" filled with grated carrots or the orange one with whipped salad dressing and canned Mandarin orange slices, but did you ever see any of the grown-ups wolfing it down? Not until now. Here's one that will appeal to the child in every adult. Try it at Easter, Christmas, or even on a hot Sunday in August.

6 c. thick tomato juice, homemade if possible

Bouquet garni:
3-inch piece of celery stalk
1 large or 2 small, bay leaves
3–4-inch strip of lemon peel
3–4 parsley stems

2–3 dashes Worchestershire sauce, or to taste
3–4 dashes Tabasco™, or hot pepper sauce of choice, or to taste
3 packages unflavored gelatin
½ c. celery hearts, cut into fine dice
1-inch piece of lemon peel, plus remaining zest of whole fruit
1 tbsp. Italian parsley leaves, minced; save stems for inclusion in
    bouquet garni
1 tbsp. grated horseradish, or to taste
1 tbsp. freshly squeezed lemon juice
5 or 6 romaine leaves, cut into a fine julienne
Zest of one lemon, for garnish
2 c. Remoulade, recipe on page 167
Shaker's™ Vodka

1. Put all but ½ c. of the tomato juice in a heavy-bottomed saucepan. Securely tie ingredients for bouquet garni together with a long piece of cotton string, tie the loose end to the handle of the saucepan, and toss the bundle into the tomato juice. Add several dashes each Tabasco™ and Worchestershire to the tomato juice mixture, stir to combine; bring to a low boil, lower heat, and simmer for 5 minutes.

2. While tomato juice is heating, soften gelatin in reserved tomato juice and set aside.

3. Blanch celery hearts in a small saucepan with piece of lemon peel and the minced parsley for 1 minute. Drain and move to an ice-water bath. Soak in ice water for 1–2 minutes; this stops the cooking and fixes the bright colors. Drain and spread out evenly on paper toweling; roll towel to absorb excess moisture from parsley.

4. Remove bouquet garni from heated tomato juice, taste, and adjust sauces and seasonings, add horseradish, lemon juice, and dissolved gelatin; stir to combine and transfer to a glass or stainless-steel bowl. Loosely cover the bowl with plastic wrap to allow some of the steam to escape while chilling.

5. Refrigerate bowl for several hours or until salad begins to set. It should be about half congealed. Fold in blanched celery hearts, parsley, and remaining lemon zest. Pour aspic into a lightly oiled tube-type salad mold, cover tightly with plastic wrap, and refrigerate until fully set, about 6 hours or overnight.

6. Make Remoulade Sauce, following recipe on this page.

7. To serve, lightly wet the serving platter with a damp cloth—this will help anchor the salad; the platter should be 2 inches larger in diameter than the molded salad. Wipe the outside of the mold with a hot cloth, and run the tip of your index finger around the edges of the gelatin to help loosen the aspic. Give the salad a good shake and invert onto the damp serving plate. Place julienned romaine in the center of the mold and top with some of the Remoulade; serve the remaining sauce on the side. Tuck the rest of the romaine around the perimeter of the aspic, and garnish with finely grated lemon zest. Serve with iced shot glasses of Minnesota's own Shaker's™ Vodka.

Remoulade Sauce
Makes 2 c.

Traditionally made with chopped pickles and served with crab and shrimp, this sauce is a winner with our spicy tomato aspic and, like the aspic, can be made ahead. The flavor of both salad and sauce benefit from being made a day in advance.

2 tbsp. fresh parsley leaves, chopped

3 tbsp. green onions, white and green parts, finely chopped

1½ c. mayonnaise

2 tbsp. olive oil

1 tbsp. fresh lemon juice

2 tsp. Dijon mustard

2–3 dashes Worcestershire sauce

Hefty pinch of cayenne pepper

Combine all ingredients, and let sit 30 minutes so flavors will blend. Taste, add salt if needed, and adjust other seasonings. Cover and chill until served.

In my hometown of Hibbing, there are three men whose Iron Range roots and achievements make the local crowd proud; but I'm not talking about Roger Maris, Kevin McHale, and Bob Dylan. No, people still refer to these other guys solely by their first names: Jeno, Vince, and Leo, almost like they were close family friends. Though Maris, McHale, and Dylan might have walked the same city streets and sat in the same classrooms as those other three, they were just kids by the time Paulucci, Forti, and Fraboni become household names in Hibbing. Jeno Paulucci, Vince Forti, and Leo Fraboni had taken what their immigrant Italian parents taught them and set up shops on Third Avenue East. Jeno moved Chun King to Duluth in the 1960s, where eggs rolls morphed into pizza rolls; and the resulting line of Italian food was renamed for his mother, becoming Michelina's Frozen Italian Entrées. Vince's Sunrise Bakery and Leo's Fraboni Sausage and Meats remain on the north end of Third Avenue, near and dear to Hibbing hearts and stomachs; something, I'm fairly certain, with which those other guys would agree.

There is another first-generation Italian whose early life ties to Hibbing should be noted. As a young man he left northern Minnesota and its less-than-desirable climate for the warmth of the West Coast, where he successfully applied the grape-growing lessons he learned from his immigrant father; in time these became the standards of American viticulture. Early on, and well into the 1960s, he kept Iron Range Italian winemakers supplied with trainloads of ripe grapes delivered to the California Wine House, just behind Third Avenue on the north end of town. His name? Robert Mondavi.

Porketta Sandwiches

Serves 8 for sandwiches

Open the lunch pail of an Italian miner on the Iron Range early in the last century, and the tantalizing aroma of porketta would likely rise to greet your nose. While many Italian immigrants brought their version of this highly seasoned, economical cut of pork to the area, Hibbing's Leo Fraboni and his family's sausage company get the credit for turning it into a staple for the thirty-nine other ethnic groups who call the Iron Range home. Served hot or cold, this sandwich favorite has migrated south and is now made by butchers in the Twin Cities for a price. Follow the recipe below to retain both the authentic Italian flavor and economy that made this roast so helpful in difficult times.

4 garlic cloves, peeled, crushed, and minced

2 tbsp. kosher salt

2 tbsp. freshly ground black pepper

½ c. fennel seeds, dry roasted and crushed

¼ c. olive oil

2 tbsp. dried fennel weed, crumbled

4 lbs. pork butt, boned and flattened (Don't know how or want to? Ask the butcher)

Sunrise Bakery Italian hard rolls

Mustard

Pickles

1. Finely mince the garlic with the salt and pepper; place ½ c. fennel seeds in a dry sauté pan over medium heat, and pan roast until oils are released—do not burn. Remove from heat and crush in a mortar and pestle or spice grinder.

2. Combine crushed fennel seeds with the garlic, salt, and pepper mixture, olive oil, and fennel weed. Rub on both sides of the pork; roll and securely tie with cotton butcher's string. Wrap the roast in parchment or waxed paper and place in a large zip-top bag. Refrigerate 24 hours in the lower part of the refrigerator.

3. Remove roast from bag and paper, place porketta on a rack in a shallow roasting pan and bring to room temperature. Preheat oven to 425°F and adjust the rack to the lower third of the oven. Roast in the center of oven for 2–2 ½ hours, or until temperature registers 165°F. Cool to room temperature with string on. Remove string, slice thin, and serve on Sunrise Bakery Italian hard rolls with mustard and pickles on the side.

Delight for Non-Dieters:
Caramel Apple Cheesecake

Serves
12 to 18

From all outward appearances, this might look like your ordinary, everyday cheesecake, but looks can be deceiving. Cut a slice and reveal an inside marbled with caramel, then take a bite and savor the layer of cinnamon sautéed apples hiding between the cake and the crust. Words of warning: the substitution of low-fat cream or ricotta cheese will diminish the delight in this dessert! Make this recipe a day ahead, as it needs to chill in the refrigerator overnight.

Crust (Makes one 9-inch crust)

3 tbsp. unsalted butter, softened

3 tbsp. granulated sugar

1 large egg yolk, slightly beaten

1 c. bleached all-purpose flour

¼ tsp. salt

¼ tsp. baking powder

½ c. oven-toasted walnuts,
   finely crushed

1 9-inch springform pan

1. Preheat oven to 350°F (325°F if using convection). Position rack in lower third of oven.

2. In a medium-sized bowl, cream butter and sugar together until light and fluffy, add the egg yolk, and beat until smooth.

3. In a separate bowl, mix flour, salt, baking powder, and walnuts. Fold into the creamed mixture; it will be on the crumbly side.

4. Firmly press into the bottom of a 9-inch buttered springform pan; make sure it's spread evenly to the edge. Bake for 15–20 minutes. While the crust is baking, prepare apple garnish.

Assembling the Cheesecake

1. Preheat oven to 325°F; position rack in center of oven. (300°F if using convection)

2. Tightly wrap aluminum foil around the bottom of the spring-form pan so it covers the sides by at least 1 inch. Spread the sautéed apples evenly over the top of the crust, and pat into place. Pour the plain batter over the apples and tap the pan to even it out. Spoon the caramel batter over the plain batter in circles, leaving a fair amount of white batter exposed. Swirl the caramel batter into the plain batter with a table knife to achieve a marbled look, taking care not to disturb the layer of apples on the bottom.

3. Place filled springform into a large roasting pan, and add ½ inch warm water. Bake in the center of oven for about 1½ hours (if using convection, 1 hour at 300°F); the top should be nicely colored, the cake set, but the very center should still be a bit loose. Remove from the water bath, place on a rack until completely cool; the center might sink a little and the perimeter edges remain up; this is normal.

4. Wrap the cake, still in the pan, and chill overnight. Unmold on a flat serving plate, run the blade of a long, thin slicing knife under hot water and slice while the cake is still cold. Allow to warm almost to room temperature before serving.

Apple Garnish

2 large firm apples like Honeycrisp© or Haralson, peeled, cored, and thinly sliced
2 tsp. ground cinnamon
2 tbsp. unsalted butter

1. In a large bowl, toss the apple slices with the ground cinnamon.

2. Melt butter in a skillet over medium heat and sauté the apples until soft. Set aside.

Plain Batter

1½ lbs. cream cheese (not low-fat) at room temperature
½ c. granulated sugar
1 tsp. pure vanilla extract
3 large eggs

1. Place softened cream cheese in mixer bowl, and, using a paddle attachment if you have one, beat on low for 30 seconds. Scrape sides of bowl.

2. With the mixer on, add the sugar in a steady stream; mix again for 30 seconds and scrape the bowl.

3. Add the vanilla, then eggs one at a time, mixing after each addition.

Caramel Batter

1 lb. cream cheese (not low-fat) at room temperature
½ c. dark brown sugar
1 tsp. pure vanilla extract
1 tsp. cinnamon
1 tsp. molasses
2 large eggs

Prepare as for plain batter, adding cinnamon and molasses after the vanilla and before the eggs, mixing after each addition.

Contact Information

See the Minnesota Department of Agriculture's *Minnesota Grown Directory* (available free at co-ops and farmers' markets) for a guide to farmers, markets, and garden centers across the state.

Growers and producers mentioned in *The Minnesota Table:*

Alexis Bailly Vineyard
Contact: Nan Bailly
18200 Kirby Avenue
Hastings, MN 55033
(651) 437-1413
www.abvwines.com

Bar 5 Meat & Poultry
Contact: Laura Wemeier
(507) 964-5612
www.localfoods.umn.edu/bar5poultry

Bethel Church Little Falls
901 W. Broadway
Little Falls, MN 56345
(320) 632-2316
bethellittlefallsa@usfamily.net

Cannon River Winery
Contact: John & Maureen Maloney
421 Mill St. W.
Cannon Falls, MN 55009
(507) 263-7400
info@cannonriverwinery.com
www.cannonriverwinery.com

Cedar Summit Farm
Contact: Dave & Florence Minar
25830 Drexel Avenue
New Prague, MN 56071
Phone: (952) 758-6886
FAX: (952) 758-6197
www.cedarsummit.com

Chisago Lake Lutheran Church
1 Summit Ave.
Center City, MN 55012
(651) 257-6300
www.chisagolakelutheranchurch.org

Clare's Well
13537 47th St. N.W.
Annandale, MN 5530
(320) 274-3512
clwell@lakedalelink.ne
www.fslf.org/clareswell.html

Dry Weather Creek Farm
Contact: Mark Lange
(320) 269-9617
dwcreek@mvtvwireless.com
www.localfoods.umn.edu/dryweather

Eichten's Hidden Acres
Contact: Eileen Eichten
16440 Lake Blvd.
Center City, MN 55012
(651) 257-1566
www.theeichtensbistro.com
www.specialtycheese.com

Faribault Dairy Company, Inc.
Contact: Jeff Jirik
222 3rd Street N.E.
Faribault, MN 55021.
(507) 334-5260
info@faribaultdairy.com
www.faribaultdairy.com

Forest Mushrooms
(320) 363-7956
(888) 363-7957
www.forestmushrooms.com

Gardens of Eagan
25494 Highview Ave.
Farmington, MN 55024
(952) 985-7233
www.gardensofeagan.com

J & L Bison Ranch
5650 N.W. 41st Ave.
Willmar, MN 56201
www.jlbison.com

Lena's
Contact: Linda "Lena" Schaumburg
6344 Merchant St.
Askov, MN 55704-4280
(320) 838-3784
www.lenasofaskov.com

Lorentz Meats
705 Cannon Industrial Boulevard
Cannon Falls, MN 55009
(507) 263-3618
www.lorentzmeats.com

Love Tree Farms
Contact: Mary & Dave Falk
www.lovetreefarmstead.com

Minnesota Grown Directory
www.minnesotagrown.com

Money Creek Ranch
Contact: Valerie Shannon
(507) 896-2345
www.buffalogal.com

Neumann Farms, Inc.
Contact: Joyce & Ron Neumann
Princeton, MN 55371
(763) 389-4512
rneumann@izoom.net
www.neumannfarmsmn.com

Pastures A Plenty Farm & Co,
4075 & 4077 110th Ave. N.E.
Kerkhoven, MN 56252
(320) 367-2061
www.pasturesaplenty.com

Prairie Haven Farm
Contact: Lori Pint
(612) 877-2059
lori54@bevcomm.net

Produce Acres
Contact: Russ Willenbring
(320) 685-3257
www.produceacres.com

Schmidt's Meat Market
319 Pine St.
Nicollet, MN 56074
(507) 232-3438
www.schmidtsmeatmarket.com

Seed Savers Exchange
3094 N. Winn Rd.
Decorah, IA 52101
(563) 382-5990
www.seedsavers.org

Shepherd's Way Farms
Contact: Steven & Jodi Ohlsen-Read
(507) 663-9040
farmfriends@earthlink.net
www.shepherdswayfarms.com/
index.cfm

Simple Harvest Farm
Contact: Kathy & Nick Zeman
9800 155th Street East
Nerstrand, MN
www.simpleharvestfarm.com

St. Joseph Farmers' Market
(320) 845-2280
www.stjosephfarmersmarket.org

Thousand Hills Cattle Company
Contact: Todd Churchill
P.O. Box 68
Cannon Falls, MN 55009
(612) 756-1346
www.thousandhillscattleco.com

University of Minnesota
Research Station
Contact: David Bedford
www.apples.umn.edu

White Earth Land Recovery Project
& Native Harvest
Contact: Winona LaDuke
607 Main Avenue
Callaway, MN 56521
(888) 274-8318
www.nativeharvest.com

The Yak Man
Contact: John Hooper
(320) 685-4489
yak-man@yak-man.com
www.yak-man.com

Index

4-H, 12, 65, 104

Alexis Bailly Vineyard, 34–37, 70

Anne, Sister, 117

Asian vegetables, 61–63

asparagus, 9–11, 14, 20, 30–32, 74

Bailey's Raspberries, 31–32

Bailly, David, Nan, and Sam, 36

Bar 5 Meat & Poultry, 27, 64–65

Bayport Cookery, 147

Bedford, David, 89–91

Berry Hill Farm, 32

Bethel Lutheran Church, 115–16

Blue Roof Organics, 45

Brasa, 149

Buffalo Gal, 134–36, 138

Bush, George H. W., 9

Café Kardamena, 106

California Wine House, 168

Cannon River Winery, 34–35

carving instructions, 122

Cedar Summit Farm, 155–56

Cermak, Larry, 64

Chisago Lake Lutheran Church, 131–32

Chun King, 168

Churchill, Todd, 118–19

Clare's Well, 117

Common Ground Garden, 45–46

Convent of St. Francis, 117

Cook's Garden, The, 159

deglazing instructions, 122

Diffley, Martin, 105–6

Dorff, Chris, 116

Doyle, Kevin, 20

Dry Weather Creek Farm, 148–49

drying herbs, 84–85

Dufner, Angeline, 20–21

Duluth Farmers' Market, 147

Eichten, Mary and Joseph, 132

Eichten's Hidden Acres, 132, 136, 150

Falk, Dave and Mary, 145–46

Faribault Dairy Company, Inc., 92–93

Fogel, Mike, 134–35

Forest Mushrooms, 20, 46

Forti, Vince, 168

Fraboni Sausage and Meats, 168

Fraboni, Leo, 168

Fred's Bread, 20

freezing basics, 33, 50–51

frozen beans and other vegetables, 28, 38, 50

Gardens of Eagan, 105–6

Great River Gardens, 30–32

Green Pastures Dairy, 147

Gurney's Seed & Nursery, 159

Her, Ying, 61–62

Holl, Lorene, 27

HoneycrispTM apples, 89–91

Hooper, John "Yak Man," 94

Hungarian Pepper Bacon, 27, 64

J & L Bison Ranch, 136

Jirik, Jeff, 92–93

Kingfield Farmers' Market, 146

LaDuke, Winona, 73–74

lamb, 12–14, 16–17, 47, 65, 78, 145–46

Land Stewardship Project, 105, 155

Lange, Mark and Wendy, 148–49

Langton, Brenda, 106

Lena's Scandinavian Gifts, Coffee Bar, and
    Garden Center, 76–77, 87, 125

Lentz, Ralph, 156

Lorence's Berry Farm, 30, 32

Lorentz Meats, 118, 120

Lorentz, Ed, Mary, Mike, and Rob, 120

Love Tree Farms, 145–47

Lundstad-Vogt, Pastor, 131–32

lutefisk, 115–16, 131

Maloney, John and Maureen, 34–35

Mancini's Restaurant, 35

Michelina's, 168

Midwest Food Alliance, 155

Mill City Farmers' Market, 119, 146–47

Minar, Dave and Florence, 155–56

Minneapolis Farmers' Market, 9, 62, 64, 106

Minnesota Buffalo Association, 136

Minnesota DNR (Department of Natural
    Resources), 75, 159

Minnesota Grown Directory, 158

Minnesota Landscape Arboretum, 95

Minnesota Mycological Society, 22

Minnesota Slow Food, 156

Minnesota State Fair, 52

Minnetonka Orchards, 95

Mondavi, Robert, 168

Money Creek Buffalo Ranch, 134–35, 138

morel mushrooms, 19–20, 22–24, 30

Morey's Seafood Markets, 133

Nader, Ralph, 73

Native Harvest, 73–74

Natura Farms, 32

Negret, Vincent, 34

Neumann Farms, 103–4

Neumann, Joyce and Ron, 103–4

North Star Gardens, 32

Northern Waters Smokehaus, 133

Northfield Farmers' Market, 47

Ohlson-Read, Jody, 147

Olsen Fish Company, 116

Organic Agriculture Resources, 159

Organica Seed, 159

Ott, Diane, 158

Park Seed®, 159

Pastures A Plenty Farm & Co., 158

Paulucci, Jeno, 168

Pepin HeightsTM, 100

Phyllis, Sister, 20–21, 45–46

Pickle and Pepper Guys, 48–49

pick-your-own, 30–32, 95

Pint, Lori and Norm, 12–13

Polan, Michael, 155

Polemeier, Matt and Betty, 64

Pompadour, Madame, 11

Prairie Haven Farm, 12–13

Pride of the Prairie, 155

Princeton Farmers' Market, 103

Produce Acres, 9–10

pumpkin patches, 95, 104

Read, Steven, 147

Red Stag Supper Club, 149

Restaurant Alma, 147

Riehle, Joe, 31

root cellars, 107

Russ Kendall's Smokehouse, 133

Rutabaga Festival, 76–77

salad greens, washing and care, 26
Sawyer, Tom, 30
Schmidt, Gary, 13
Schmidt's Meat Market, 12
seed catalogs, 159
Seed Savers Exchange, 157–58
Shannon, Valerie, 134–35
Shepherd's Way Farms, 147
Simple Harvest Farm, 47
Southside Farm and Garden Store, 157
Spring Hill Nurseries, 159
St. Cloud Farmers' Market, 94
St. Joseph Farmers' Market, 9–10, 20–21,
     45–46, 94
St. Paul Farmers' Market, 7, 64–65, 146
Sunrise Bakery, 168
Thousand Hills Cattle Company, 118–20
Three Rivers Wine Trail, 34–35
Tomato Bob's Heirloom Tomatoes, 159
Uncle Joe's Berry Patch, 32
University of Minnesota, 32, 34, 36, 78–79,
     89–91, 95, 132, 159
Wemeier family, 64–65
White Bear Lake Farmers' Market, 61
White Earth Land Recovery Project
     (WELRP), 73–74
wild rice, 72–75, 80–81, 156
Willenbring, Russ, 9–10
Zeman, Kathy, Nick, and Theresa, 47

Recipes
Asparagus Vinaigrette, 14
Beef Stock, 164
Bison Chili, 138–39
Bulgur Pilaf, 17
Butternut Squash with Maple Syrup, 86
Caramel Apple Cheesecake, 169–70
Chantilly Cream, 152
Cheese Fondue, 150
Chicken Stock, 163
Christmas Coleslaw, 127
Clementine Vinaigrette, 81
Crock Pickles, 54
Eggs Lorene, 27–28

Festive Apple Cake, 128–29
Fruit Soup, 143
Gouda Grilled Cheese, 141
Green Beans with Toasted Hazelnuts, 126
Grilled Corn with Lemon and Pepper, 67
Grilled Rainbow Trout with Lemon Pepper
     Butter, 38
Hard Sauce, 129
Heartbreak Cake, 152
Honey Lemonade, 52
Kale and Walnut Sauté, 108
Lake Superior Smoked Whitefish on
     Hardtack, 137
Lena's Rutabaga Malt, 87
Maple Sugar Crème Brulée, 18
Minnesota BLTs, 55
Minnesota Ice, 37
Minnesota Meatloaf, 83
Minted Crown Roast of Lamb, 16
Minted Sugar Snap Peas, 40
Muddled Mint Tea, 43
New Potatoes with Chive Butter, 39
Nick's Devilish Eggs, 53
Oven-Roasted Carrots and Parsnips, 111
Oven-Roasted Tomatoes, 65
Pasta Pomo D'Oro, 151
Pastry, 113
Pears Poached in Isis Wine with Raspberry
     Coulis, 70–71
Pickled Pink Potato Salad, 56
Pinto Beans, 139
Poached Apple Supreme, 100
Porketta Sandwiches, 168
Potato Leek Soup, 162
Potato Rutabaga Soufflé, 125
Raspberry Dressing, 97
Raspberry-Blueberry Cream Cheese
     Shortcakes, 59
Ready Set Rhubarb, 28
Remoulade Sauce, 167
Roast Loin Pork, 109
Roasted Beet Salad with Blue Cheese & Curly
     Endive, 96–97
Roasted Garlic Custard, 123–24

Roasted Garlic Mashed Potatoes, 82
Roasted Pumpkin Pie with Sour Cream and
     Brown Sugar, 113
Roasted Rosemary Chicken, 101
Romanesco Broccoli Sauté, 86
Rosemary Croutons, 150
Sautéed Morels on Buttered Toast Points, 24
Shortcut Cassoulet Exotica, 98–99
Smoked Chicken Salad with Jicama, 68
Sparkling Cider Sauce, 109
Spicy Vietnamese Long Beans, 66
Spring Green Salad with Tarragon
     Vinaigrette, 25
Standing Rib Roast, 121–22
Strawberry-Rhubarb Sunburst Pie, 41–42
Vegetable Stock, 165
Virgin Mary Aspic, 166–67
Wild Rice Dried Cranberry Salad, 80
Yummy Edamame Dip, 63, 160

About the Authors

Shelley Holl was born travelling. As the daughter of a naval aviator, she attended six schools and lived in both England and Morocco before settling in Minnesota for the first time at age twelve. So began an unsettled, but persistent, kinship to the prairie that had attracted her similarly-restless immigrant grandparents. Later she would touch down in half a dozen American states and shape a college degree in journalism and fine art, Photoshop expertise, and a growing facility with paint into a unique platform from which to observe the world—but she always returned to Minnesota.

She is a painter, photographer, gift and fashion-accessory designer, teacher, and former travel columnist for New Orleans' *Times-Picayune* newspaper, where her already-avid interest in food became passion. She is the author/illustrator of *Louisiana Dayride: 52 Short Trips from New Orleans*, published by University Press of Mississippi in 1995 and *Waterbourne Witness: Elegies for My New Orleans*, illustrated essays to accompany her exhibition of fifteen paintings about Hurricane Katrina.

BJ Carpenter is a professionally trained chef, culinary instructor, certified dietary manager, and freelance food writer. Her culinary career began in her family's backyard garden picking beans and strawberries before learning to read or write. An early interest in words compelled her to learn to print her name; she got her first library card at age five.

Her first piece of food writing, a now infamous note penciled in first grade under her mother's name requesting she be allowed to leave school grounds during recess to buy candy with everyone's milk money, garnered acclaim from elders and peers alike. In second grade she held a pro-bono position shelving books in the school library. Her next job, washing dishes and helping in the school kitchen in fourth grade, came with pay: twenty-five cents a day and a free lunch.

In later years, she owned her own restaurant and catering business. *The Minnesota Table*, written with Shelley Holl, is her first book.

Acknowledgements

When you set foot on a farm, you cross the border from greater America and the public world of shopping malls, restaurants, gas stations, libraries, and highways to a tiny country that has rules of its own and a host of reasons to keep the borders closed, leaving you firmly on the other side. That never happened to us.

So, thanks to all the food-making folks who set aside mountains of work, fears of bio-terrorism, or annoyance with our dog to open their doors and let us in.

Thank you to dear friends who took time to help, though their extra moments were begged, bartered, or stolen from more pressing duties: Nan Bailly, Deb Black, Carmen Bonilla, Mary Christenson, Sherry Derus, Maggie DeGennaro, Jerilyn Hanson, Linda Hewett, Elsa Hofmeister, Lynn Rosetto Kasper, Tim Kretzmann, Cheryl Miller, Jude Nutter, Werner Pavolovich, Andrzej Peczalski, Will Powers, Mary Ryan, Mary Louise Ruth, Sally Swift, Elaine Voberil, Marilyn Ziebarth, and, of course, our families.

Special appreciation to editor Kari Cornell, who understood that *The Minnesota Table* was more than a cookbook and strived to preserve our vision.